The Real
Colin Blythe

John Blythe Smart

Published by Blythe Smart Publications in 2009
also reprinted that year

A CIP catalogue record for this book is available from the British Library.

ISBN: 978 - 0 - 9545017 - 5 - 4

Cover, Type: Blythe Smart Publications
Printers: M F K Digital

Note 1 - The facts are correct at the time of printing, but this does not preclude later adjustment in the light of further research.

Note 2 - There are a number of Civil Registration records where the quarter date has been used so, for example, June 1865 covers the period April to June 1865.

Blythe Smart Publications
Kingsbridge - Devon - England

Contents

About the Author

John Smart was born at Farnborough, Kent in 1960 and was educated at Alleyn's in south London and Nottingham University, his main academic interests being historical geography and history of architecture.

In addition his forebears included E.G. Blythe and E.H. Niemann, 19th century artists, and Colin Blythe the famous cricketer leading to a further interest in matters historical. As a result he undertook genealogical study at home and abroad over many years.

Meanwhile, his family supported Millwall from the 1920s and he followed them from 1970 as well as watching cricket matches with his father. Indeed, it was this varied sporting experience which provided the initial inspiration for his writing career.

After visiting numerous football grounds he researched soccer history and produced *The Wow Factor - How Soccer Evolved* with two editions in 2003-05, followed by a fiction book *The Wizards of Wight*. More recently he published a seminal work on the first F.A. president *Arthur Pember's Great Adventures* and a concise version *The Founders of Soccer* in 2008.

A social study regarding Colin Blythe seemed the obvious choice for the next book for some time, thus a similar style of research and writing was applied to his famous relative to produce this volume.

Introduction

Most people have heard of Colin Blythe. This includes both the ardent cricket supporter, the casual follower of the game, and those who do not know their willow from their leather. Even that advocate of the high score, the American sports pundit, claims to be acquainted with the famous Kent and England cricketer of the previous century.

His narrative is one that grows and grows and layer upon layer has been added to the cricketing myth over the decades, ranging from the sober and factual right down to the flamboyant and exaggerated.

During his career there were numerous reports of his exploits in the press some of them profound with sporting wisdom, others full of caricature and largesse, as well as the biographies of his fellow cricketers who talked with considerable admiration about his abilities. From this material his story has been collected and collated then like a game of Chinese whispers passed down to the present generation.

With such diverse sources, some of them based in fact and some of them rather fantastical, it becomes increasingly hard to separate the truth from the more fanciful. Colin Blythe is liable to become a parody, a burlesque, like cartoons in the evening papers depicting his sporting prowess which amused the reader as they journeyed home in the smog.

His ability on the field is without question but the character of the man has been formed, not so much by Blythe himself (from his own lips) or even from more factual accounts, but by those who would purvey a certain image that they wish to formulate to the public.

Some of these images are more designed to meet a particular end in their composition, to put over and impart a partial view of sport, a hidden social agenda, or perhaps a personal interpretation imbued with that idiosyncrasy of cricket - "the gentleman and the player." With regard to this how can one rely upon such a subjective characterisation?

Everyone knows about Colin Blythe. Or so is their ardent claim. One of the most enduring images is of the affable, cocky Cockney, who emerged from the back-streets of Deptford to amaze and awake the nodding crowds with his deft abilities and sleight of hand.

But this interpretation of his background and character is only a partial truth and has some serious flaws. It comes from a stereotype, a convenient mould, placing him in a rigidly defined social structure serving the needs of the journalistic writer and popular opinion. However, there is another story one that comes from the proverbial horse's mouth.

The first myth that should be launched over extra cover is his position in the social order. This has been gleaned by a somewhat limited perspective, one that takes a small piece of history and thereby interprets the whole. It is like questioning one hundred people on a certain topic and stating that this is the opinion of the whole nation!

True, Colin Blythe did emanate from Deptford but this in itself did not define him as a person, since he came from a family who had considerable creative ability and talent like himself. In addition they did not adhere to a certain class and rode the vicissitudes of fortune. Once this fact is known his ability to mix with all types of people on and off the pitch becomes far easier to appreciate and understand.

Within the text a number of established facts are placed under scrutiny and myths regarding the cricketer are finally brought to account. Such a new perspective is made possible by referring to papers that the cricketer collected during his own career, papers which tell the story *he* wanted told, thereby revealing *"The Real Colin Blythe."*

In memory of
**Stanley Blythe Smart
(1915-90)**
Nephew of Colin Blythe

"A noted ball player and
juggler of figures who left his
mark on many scoreboards"
- after making a century for
Alleyn's Old Boys

CHAPTER 1

Family Roots

It has been said that Blythe left very little information regarding his history although this is an incorrect statement since there is a large body of material about his life. This ranges from private details he collected himself to a vast archive regarding his innumerable cricket games.

A person though does not emerge into this world in isolation, thus individual attributes or sporting ability are a product of both family and environment. It is therefore impossible to understand the genius of Blythe or his character without looking first at the circumstances he grew up in. Indeed, he lived in a world of Victorian values and drives which was soon to undergo an exigent metamorphosis.

He was born in the late 19th century into a large family who both lived and worked together. Such a tight-knit lifestyle was honed from desperate financial necessity and a common desire to improve and create something lasting and beneficial, but his talent was not exclusive and sport was just one facet among the abilities of this extraordinary family.

Blythe was certainly a Kentish Man and English through and through yet his antecedents came from the outer limits of the British Isles. During the 7th century the Angles, Saxons, and Jutes indulged in an earlier invasion of the island and brought many permanent settlements to the country as well as their infiltrating language of Germanic origin.

The truncated "Blyth" came from the Old Saxon blithe or blithi and was generally a descriptive term meaning merry or joyous connected to a stream (or perhaps an area). It was most prevalent in the northern climes being associated with several places in the Kingdom of Northumbria which at the time reached from Yorkshire to the Lammermuir Hills south of Edinburgh. Good examples being the coastal settlement of Blyth, Blyth Bridge near to Peebles, and most significantly Blythe in Lauderdale.

Northumbria south of the Tweed was incorporated into England by the 13th century, whereas to the north Lord Lauderdale owned lands including the Barony of Blyth. The borders of Scotland developed important trading patterns and the ancient borough of Roxburgh utilised Berwick as a port for commerce for several hundred years.

However, the former was destroyed by the English in 1460 and Berwick was taken permanently twenty years later, thus many residents then moved northwards to Edinburgh which soon came to prominence.

One of the outcomes was that Blyth was a Scottish name common in the border regions although its origins were basically Anglo-Saxon. During the 16th century surnames were adopted regarding taxation, and it became standard to use cognomens relating to location although others originated from 'distinctive' personal characteristics.

In Scotland the name Blyth was generally from locale thus the "Blythes" are most likely traced to the Scottish borders, and probably moved up to Edinburgh for trading opportunities. There is little doubt that the family of the cricketer emanated from this premier city, although their early history involves a certain degree of speculation - "a best possible fit."

EDINBURGH

The Fort of Eidyn which was later called "Auld Reekie" (rather like the "Great Wen") was developed on a strategic site of a volcanic plug, with the castle at one end and a main trading-street with high tenements and wynds or alleys leading off behind. In the east were Calton Hill and Arthur's Seat two vast rocky outcrops, whereas to the north was a deep valley occupied by the Nor Loch a dubious source of water for the city.

As a centre of trade it became the capital in 1437, whilst a university followed in 1582 bringing enlightenment as "The Athens of the North." However, until the 18th century most buildings were located on the high road leading from the castle, and a long thoroughfare The Walk led past Calton Hill up to the city's port at Leith - a separate settlement.

The whole place was steeped in historical traditions, literature, learning, magnificent buildings, and later on clan history whilst the trading populace found opportunities in the country and throughout the Empire. A number of families named Blyth lived within the city high upon the hill but others were residents of the smaller suburbs just beyond.

The earliest record of the family there comes after the union of the two countries, and John the son of James Blyth and Agnes Brown was baptized at South Leith on 17 April 1670. The original sanctuary was at Restalrig to the east but was replaced by a chapel on Kirkgate during the reformation of the Scottish church, whilst the parish covered an extensive area from Leith down to the present site of Princes Street.

John Blyth married Agnes Glen at South Leith on 30 April 1696 and then worked as a cordwainer (or shoemaker) in the ancient village of Restalrig, this being a significant occupation regarding the latter discourse. Seven children emanated from the marriage and a son Colin Blyth was born on 22 April 1707 then baptized at South Leith a week later.

When the family resided there the new town was but a dream of the planners and architects, and Colin Blyth married Helen Cross at South Leith on 23 March 1732. Like his father he was employed as a cordwainer whilst he moved nearer to the city and lived at St. Ninian's Row, a street situated between the marshes of the Nor Loch and Calton Craig.

This was also known as Beggars' Row and was located in the valley beyond the main streets of Nether Bow and Canongate, with Leith Walk leading away to the northeast. Nearby there was a physic garden, orphan asylum, and the ancient Trinity Church but as a residence it was probably far from healthy due to the bogs and marshlands just beyond.

Colin and Helen Blyth remained at St. Ninian's Row in the shadow of the castle and the father continued as a cordwainer, whilst they had twelve children from 1733-51 although some may have died in infancy. The street was a detached part of the parish of St. Cuthbert's thus the offspring were all baptized at this church situated away to the west.

The father's name was of considerable significance and his brother John was a merchant, whereas his brother Robert was also a shoemaker in the city. In addition to this he was described as a freeman despite being just a humble cordwainer of St. Ninian's Row, although there are few records of the family in trade directories of the time.

The most significant birth was a son named James Blyth born on 8 May 1743 and baptized at St. Cuthbert's, the witnesses being John Blyth senior and James Connors of Calton. The family may have worked with leather as shoemakers, but he was drawn by adventurous opportunities suggested by the tall ships and naval vessels plying their trade from Leith.

Indeed, this was a time of great change during the Georgian period and the Nor Loch which was polluted with sewage was drained in 1759. James Craig son of an Edinburgh merchant then designed a new town in 1766, which was in the form of a grid with housing of classical ideals and Princes Street just to the south. This major thoroughfare facing the castle reached right up to St. Ninian's Row and was partially built across it. [1]

Only a few records of the family survive at this point but John Blyth a brother of James was a merchant at St. Ninian's Row, whereas Colin Blyth was a shoemaker at Walk Side in Leith in the 1770s. It seems likely that James worked with the latter brother who was born three years before him, until making a change that had some significant results.

---

[1] Old Calton burial ground was to the east and with St. Ninian's Row they were bisected when Waterloo Place was built over to Princes Street in 1818. The area was further changed with the addition of Waverley Station and other rail links in the valley in 1846. Today, just a small section of St. Ninian's Row remains.

As stated the port of Leith was full of ocean going vessels and mariners with stories of the Southern Oceans and fortunes to be made, and James Blyth had few prospects at home in Edinburgh thus he went to sea as a merchant seaman at about this time (in his late twenties). This gave him some initial experience and he was then able to improve his position and the future prospects of his whole family.

James Blyth entered the Royal Navy in c.1780 and by this period he was almost certainly based in southern England - in particular at Portsmouth. The records indicate he joined the "Medway" during a ships rendezvous with the "Diligente" at Cowes in the Solent on 10 January 1782, although the muster rolls contain certain discrepancies.

The commander of the ship, Captain Alexander Edgar had risen up the ranks and was recently returned from a brief retirement (he was later a rear admiral). Blyth clearly had a degree of experience and was promoted from able seaman to master of the sheets being supplied with tobacco, slop cloaths (ready made garments), and an annual pay of £15.

Captain Edgar, meanwhile, came on board at the same time with four servants although other captains had considerably more - being entitled to receive pay of £48 annually. The main discrepancy in the musters was that Blyth was said to be aged 24 (or perhaps 29) when he joined the ship and also that he came from "Fifeshire."

However, such inaccuracies were not uncommon and he may have wished to appear younger than he was. True, there were other men called "James Blyth" serving in the Navy one of them a boatswain of Chatham, but the later records support the theory that he joined the "Medway" which plied the waters of the Channel during the next year.

NELSON'S NAVY

From this point the life and times of James Blyth are well chronicled and although the above holds a degree of conjecture, there seems little doubt that the following narrative is completely accurate. In fact, aspects of his place of birth, occupation, children's names, and age at death also suggest that the above discourse is authentic.

The "Medway" then arrived in Plymouth and the crew were paid off on 21 April 1783. Captain Edgar took a new commission almost immediately and was put in charge of the "(Santa) Leocadia" which was captured from the Spanish two years earlier. The vessel was originally constructed at Ferrol with 36 guns in 1777, but became a fifth rate "ship of the line" and had just arrived in the harbour under Captain Charles Hope.

James Blyth of the "St. George" having received the relevant training put in an application to qualify as a Royal Navy gunner on 4 August 1790. This was no mean feat and he was examined for his suitability on 2 September having produced two important testimonials.

The first was a certificate from Captain Alexander Edgar under whom he served on the H.M.S. "Leocadia" which testified to both his diligence and his sobriety. The second was a certificate from the Navy Office confirming that he had served ten years, four months, three weeks, and three days at sea. Having been duly examined by gunners from three Royal Navy ships and Granvil Smith a mathematician, he was certified fitly qualified to be a *Master Gunner* on any ship of war of the third rate.

Within this qualification there was a certain amount of historical interest, since James Blyth had learnt every aspect of trajectory in the air and knew exactly how to deliver a (cannon) ball to the enemy be it the Spanish or the French. Indeed, he could handle every aspect of the delivery with complete precision and knew of any reason for deviation in flight. Such similar ability was accredited to his descendant over a hundred years later.

His passing certificate then stated, "We have examined Mr. James Blyth late master's mate of the H.M.S. Leocadia in all the articles ordered by their Lordships for the examination of a gunner for H.M. sea service, and we confirm the following facts:"

1. He is skilled in vulgar and decimal arithmetic, extraction of square and cube roots, and in practical problems in geometry and plane trigonometry.
2. He is capable of knowing when a cannon is truly bored and not honey combed.
3. He knows how to dispart a cannon, so as to direct it justly to the place aimed.
4. He knows how to tertiate or round the thickness of the metal of a cannon at the touch hole, trunnions (supports), and muzzle.
5. He knows how to adjust a shot to a cannon and a due proportion of powder.
6. He is capable of taking or judging of heights or distances, and more especially when at sea.
7. He is able to find the weight of a cannon and doth know the names and denominations thereof and the names of the parts thereof, and the dimensions of the bore and the shot for them and the weight of the shot.
8. He knows length and fortification of a cannon of each sort and size, and how many persons will be necessary to attend each piece in time of service.
9. He knows when the trunnions of a gun are placed firstly in the carriage, whether the cannon itself be fit, and of a due length for the gun, and whether the tracks are equally high given and return equally quick.
10. He knows how to charge and discharge a piece of ordnance, readily and artist like, and how to sponge the same and to muzzle and secure the same in bad weather.

After a few months languishing in port the purser added 220
50 marines to the ship's payroll. James Blyth had already serv
Captain Edgar thus he joined the vessel at Plymouth on 1 Aug
taking on the more senior position of master's mate (or midshij
lieu of this he received a two month advance of £4 1s and state
was aged 34 and born in "Edinburgh."

At the end of the year the "Leocadia" was moored offshore at
and three of the crew absconded, but Blyth now had a good pos
was present as she sailed into the Channel on 19 May 1784. A mc
the vessel reached St. John's, Newfoundland and spent some time
Bay (renamed Calvert Bay in 1922), however returned to Cadiz
the River Tagus, Lisbon by the October.

Arriving back at Spithead on 3 November she sailed around the
and past Sheerness to Chatham, but by the December was moor
Portsmouth harbour. James Blyth was taken ill soon after the voy
although still on the ship's payroll was admitted to the Haslar Hos
the shores of the Solent at Gosport, on 11 February 1785.

Captain Edgar stayed with the ship another two years but this was
end of this particular story. Meanwhile, Blyth recovered from his
scurvy or yellow fever and shortly took a step forward up the ranks
the "St. George." This was a second rate ship with 90 guns on thre
and a crew or complement of 750 men.

The vessel was fitted out in about 1787 and was stationed at Port:
then came under the command of Sir George Collier - the latter he
relieve Penobscot during the American War and was actually involved
capture of the "Leocadia." He re-entered naval service in 1790.

In terms of size the ship was much like the "Victory" her dimension
long by 50' wide on four levels, whilst the ballast was 160 tons of irc
301 tons of shingle, coal and wood supplies of 365 tons, and provisic
the crew sufficient to last nearly four months.

James Blyth joined the ship soon after his sojourn in hospital and sh
moored off Portsmouth in July 1790 at which time she received new
ballast, and victuals - whereas the rigging was attended to. There w
pension connected to the "lower ranks" thus Blyth decided to apply
warrant that would secure him in an unknown future.

A warrant officer was an important position in the Navy one that
hard to obtain from the ranks, and there was a whole list of such posi:
falling below the gradation of officer including purser, boatswain, gui
carpenter, chaplain, and yard foreman. Much competition existed for t
since they carried a pension not dependent on years of service.

Blyth was in his late forties when he passed this significant qualification which was confirmed in the abstracts for pursers, boatswains, gunners &c. on 30 September. Initially, he failed to find an appointment and remained on the "St. George" which was stationed at Spithead and Portsmouth until the middle of the following year (1791).

Thereafter, she set sail passing St. Helen's and Dunnose, Isle of Wight, then arrived at St. Alban's Head off Swanage and Portland Bill picking up a pilot at The Mewstone, Devon on 23 August. Three days later they were moored at Hamoaze, a stretch of water on the River Tamar off Devonport between the counties of Devon and Cornwall.

There they remained until March 1793 when the vessel sailed back to Portsmouth prior to critical orders from the Admiralty. During the year France had annexed Belgium and set up a revolutionary government thus war was declared and Nelson became commander of the "Agamemnon." In the April the "St. George" was sent to Gibraltar and Cape Trafalgar and patrolled the area near Toulon (until September), but Blyth probably left the vessel before she sailed from Portsmouth.

In fact, his first warrant was granted on 10 August 1793 stating: "James Blyth of good testimony and who has passed an examination for a gunner, to be gunner of the Prince Edward Armed Sloop, the former gunner not appearing at his duty." From that point the whole direction of his life was changed, whilst he was involved in some serious conflicts being aged about fifty at the time - these are best detailed by ship.

"Prince Edward" - The vessel was built as the "Mars" in 1781, but was captured from Batavia and became a 60 gun third rate (or sloop) with 100 crewmen. Blyth first joined the vessel at Deptford on 27 July 1793 his pay £8 17s per quarter and soon after Captain William Browell was placed in command. They promptly saw action and attended Lord Moira's (F.R. Hastings) Army of 7,000 men overseas, the aim - to support the Duke of York and Allies in Flanders. Captain Herbert Browell a brother of the commander was put in charge of troop movements.

After mooring at the Nore near Sheerness in August 1793 she made a return trip to Ostend the next month; then went to Sheerness, Margate, the Downs, and Dover Roads reaching Dunkirk and Ostend by December. A further trip was made from Dover and South Foreland to Ostend and Niewport in April/May 1794, whilst later in the year she was a receiving ship for prisoners at Spithead. Blyth left the vessel at Deptford on 27 November and was then appointed to the "Vesuvius" Bomb an eight gun ship from the West Indies but this warrant was cancelled.

"Princess Augusta" - This was a much older vessel being built in 1710 and became the Royal Yacht from 1773. William Browell was appointed as the commander and she took on victuals at Deptford in late 1794, whilst he wanted the best men and Blyth joined him there on 8 December that year. The complement was not above fifty and the yacht consisted of just eight guns. At the time matrimony was in the air and the vessel was fitted up with the intention of bringing Princess Caroline over to England.

Due to a bad storm the yacht never sailed beyond Sheerness and returned to Gravesend then waited for a larger ship to collect her. Captain Browell made the acquaintance of the Prince of Wales who enjoyed his company during the wait, and the prospective bride arrived but was far less perfect company. The vessel sailed the party up the river on 5 April 1795 with the royal standard and pennant to the fore and fired a salute on the starboard side at Greenwich Reach - a congregation of barges surrounded her and a line of pensioners stood along the shoreline.

Browell was then invited to royal parties at Greenwich Hospital (and was later the hospital's Lieutenant Governor), whilst the marriage took place at St. James's on 8 April but the couple were formally separated the next year. The vessel was then back at Deptford and Blyth who no doubt assisted in "the salute," a significant piece of history, left the ship on 22 June 1795. As a postscript Vice-Admiral Hardy was her commander from 1815-18.

"Dryad" - The latter was a brand new 36 gun fifth rate frigate launched at Deptford on 4 June 1795 her complement 264 men. She was initially commanded by Captain Robert Forbes and Blyth the gunner joined during the final fitting out on 1 July that year.

Forbes died off Norway in October and was replaced by Captain Lord Amelius Beauclerk, 3rd Duke of St. Alban's, and at the end of the year the vessel was at Sheerness but removed to Ireland, having some success with French privateers - the most significant action being on 13 June 1796 when the "Proserpine" was spotted off Cape Clear at 1 a.m.

The enemy ship was alone and attempted to escape but there was a long pursuit and at 8 p.m. the vessels hoisted colours, engaged one another, and several shots were fired. They were both well matched but the enemy went to run again and was thus badly damaged over 45 minutes.

The "Dryad" however suffered just nine casualties and the other vessel was captured with the resultant prize money. The former stayed in Ireland under Commander Beauclerk over the next two years, while she went back to Plymouth in 1797 and remained there permanently the following year. She was later renamed "Amelia" and was a receiving ship in 1832.

During the sojourns back to Plymouth for repairs and victualling there was a significant event most pertinent to this short history. There is little clear evidence of Blyth's religion other than that he was Church of Scotland or Presbyterian. As such he attended the Princes Street Independent Chapel in Devonport whose minister was the prominent Rev. Andrew Kinsman, a coadjutor of George Whitefield the leader of Calvinistic Methodism.

Richard Phillips married Elizabeth Turner in the parish church of Stoke Damerel on 26 September 1771, but they also attended the chapel and had several children baptized there until 1782 including Richard Turner (1775), James Turner (1776), and Margaret baptized on 31 July 1778.

Financially these were hard times with no welfare state and only the poor house or transportation as a viable safety net, thus a pensioned gunner in the Royal Navy was a good match for a poor family with several children. Indeed, James Blyth a gunner of the "Dryad" frigate (age 53) was married by licence to Margaret Phillips (age 18) a spinster at Stoke Damerel on 22 February 1797 before Rev. Thomas M. Hitchins - both parties signed and the witnesses were Mary Horwell and William Roberts.

There was clearly a large age difference but the marriage produced three children who all had remarkable lives, and without whom this story could not have taken place. Meanwhile, James Blyth continued to serve on the "Dryad" until his warrant concluded on 13 April 1798.

"Zealand" - This was a foreign vessel seized by Vice-Admiral Richard Onslow off Plymouth on 4 March 1796, being a third rate ship with 64 guns and a complement of up to 491 men. She came under Captain Parr and the flag of Vice-Admiral Lutwidge from October 1797 whereas James Blyth arrived on board by warrant on 25 April following.

During his time there the vessel was moored at the Nore on the Medway and was generally a guardship. From 1799 she was under Admirals Graeme and Mitchell whilst Blyth who now had a quieter life started a family, and his wife who resided at Frindsbury bore him a daughter Margaret born on 20 May 1800 and baptized there on 8 June. The father then left the vessel the next year on 26 May and she became the "Justicia" in 1812.

"Royal Oak (I)" - This was a large third rate vessel with 64 guns and a complement of nearly 500 men, although she was ordered by the Navy as early as 1765 and was launched at Plymouth dockyard on 13 November 1769. By the turn of the century she was near the end of her active life and became a prison ship in Portsmouth harbour. Blyth was appointed gunner there on 29 May 1801 and the complement was then 84 men.

A son James Turner Blyth was born at Portsea on 20 October 1801 and was baptized at St. Thomas, Portsmouth some six days later, however the father remained there for some time firstly under T. Rowe and then under Lieutenant S. Liddle. The vessel was briefly in ordinary (out of commission) in 1802 whereas Blyth left just after Trafalgar in November 1805, and the ship herself (the "Assistance") was broken up ten years later.

"Royal Oak (II)" - A replacement to the old ship was started at Dudman's Yard in Deptford and James Blyth was appointed a resident gunner (and maybe advisor) from December 1805. The yard operated from about 1783 to 1812 and was situated between Grove Street and the River Thames just north of the Victualling Yard - it had 23 separate slips.

No doubt the family then lived in Deptford which included the old town by the river beside the Green, and a newer locality to the south between Church Street and Butt Lane (High Street) centred on the elegant structure of St. Paul's church. The "Royal Oak" was another 74 gun vessel but Blyth left on 19 September 1807 - although the launch took place two years later on 4 March. In fact, she became the flagship of Rear Admiral Beauclerk in 1812 and sailed to Chesapeake Bay and New Orleans, but was eventually a hospital ship and spent time in Bermuda.

"Asia" - By then James Blyth was aged over sixty and his later positions were basically on land, thus he travelled into Kent and became a gunner at Brindley's Yard, Frindsbury from 20 September 1807. In fact, Josiah and Thomas Brindley were nephews of Lord Nelson and operated 20 slips there from 1794 to 1814. The "Asia" was soon to be built and was laid down two months after his arrival - being launched just before he left.

However, there was shortly a significant event and a son Colin, named after his father in Scotland, was born at Rochester on 8 October 1808 and baptized at the ancient church of St. Nicholas just beside the cathedral on 23 October. James Blyth was now close to retirement and left the "Asia" to take up a final warrant on 11 November 1811, whereas the ship travelled to Cherbourg and Chesapeake Bay, but with the war over she came out of commission in 1816 and three years later was renamed "Alfred."

Just before leaving the vessel he applied for his son James Turner Blyth to be admitted amongst "the charity boys" of Greenwich Hospital School. By this time he lived in Chatham and produced a copy of the baptism, an oath that he was the father, and a brief record of service. The local minister also certified that the son was a real object of charity, whilst Thomas Bishop a gunner of H.M.S. "Haine" at Chatham and Thomas Thomson of Duke

Street, Deal put up a £50 bond for him to be apprenticed as a seaman. This ensured that he did not run away or embezzle the clothes or instruments but this was to be void if he was found unfit. The application and papers were dated November 1811 and James Turner Blyth was admitted amongst the charity boys of the school on 29 February following. [2]

"Belliqueux" - This was a 64 gun third rate vessel that saw considerable service after being built in 1780. She sailed to Cape Colony and Botany Bay in 1799 then went to Madras and Bombay under Captain George Byng in 1805. After stopping at St. Helena on 9 June 1811 she reached the Downs on 8 August but was paid off at Chatham soon afterwards.

From that time she was in ordinary and Blyth was gunner at £11 10s per quarter with a young servant from 12 November 1811, the other crew a boatswain, carpenter, purser, and cook. He was in his sixties at the time and looked to his retirement which officially took place on 30 September 1812 although he remained until 11 March next, whilst the vessel became a hulk two years later and was broken up soon afterwards.

James Blyth gunner of H.M. Navy obtained a certificate of service from the Pay Office on 2 April 1813, which confirmed he had worked for just over nineteen years in a pensioned position.

His pension commenced three days later and was based on his pay as a gunner, which for a third rate ship was £3 10s per month whilst a master's mate received £2 12 s 6d - the salary being paid after various deductions such as the Greenwich chest and the officers widows' fund.

---

[2] The Hospital School attached to Greenwich Hospital beside the Thames had its first boys in 1712, but widened its entry to most of the Navy by 1731. An initial building was erected near to the hospital in 1758 and a larger one for two hundred boys was constructed in 1782-84 with further support from Lloyd's.

Meanwhile, the Royal Naval Asylum was initiated in Paddington in 1798 and George III granted the asylum the use of the Queen's House in 1806. The next year the colonnades and wings were begun and by 1815 there were 800 children residing there as well as being educated.

In January 1821 the two amalgamated as an upper and lower school and the old buildings became the infirmary, whereas the Admiralty took over in 1829. There was a tough naval regime but good scientific attainment and several pupils became admirals or distinguished navigators. The west wing was enlarged and the upper school took 400 boys already educated and nominated by patrons, whilst a similar number attended the lower school (some girls) aged 9-15.

Several buildings were demolished when the R.H.S. moved to Holbrook in 1933, and those remaining became the National Maritime Museum.

The responsibility for paying pensions lay mainly with the Admiralty in the 19th century, although Greenwich Hospital also paid for the inmates and a certain amount of out pensions. Regarding James Blyth his first instalment arrived on 24 June 1813 and covered a period of 81 days thus the amount was calculated at £10 2s 6d.

Thereafter he received his pension on a quarterly basis and this was in the region from £10 14s 9d up to £11 19s 6d - depending on the length of the quarter. His annual income was therefore calculated at £48 allowing for a deduction of £2 6s paid to the widows' abatement. It is interesting to note the amount was similar to that received whilst in service, although at that point he was also supplied with clothing, lodgings, and victuals.

RETIREMENT

At the time of his retirement James Blyth had reached the age of seventy and even with such a pension he had a wife and three young children to support. Initially they lived at 16 Best Street, Chatham which was in an area of poorer housing located on flat land lying between the hill and the River Medway. No doubt their neighbours included some local tradesmen, dock workers, and also mariners or naval personnel.

With such pecuniary problems in mind the father soon sent out an urgent request from his abode at 16 Best Street addressed to T. Baynes Esq. of the Royal Naval Asylum, Greenwich - dated 5 August 1816:

"Sir - Permit me humbly to lay before you that I am an old officer a superannuated gunner from H.M. Naval Service, having no property of my own and having a wife and family to support. I find my pension not adequate to the task. I therefore humbly solicit you will be pleased to take my son Colin Blyth into your Royal Naval Asylum, he is a healthy boy seven years of age the 8th October last - in so doing I shall conceive myself singularly indebted. I remain, Sir, your most obedient humble servant."

J a m e s   B l y t h

In response to this request T. Baynes sent a petition to the father and asked him to return it with other papers. He completed the long document addressed to H.R.H. the Duke of Cumberland and other commissioners of the R.N.A. stating he was a superannuated gunner of the "Belliqueux" and that his son Colin was eight years old. The petition noted the boy would reside there until he was apprenticed in the merchant service or Royal Navy and gave a list of qualifying papers to be included.

James Blyth also supplied a list of the ships he had served on as a gunner and inside he attached an affidavit from George Harker the minister of St. Mary's and two of the churchwardens: "We certify that James Blyth now at Chatham has three children whom he is unable to maintain." This was all sent off on 15 August and the son Colin was accepted into the Asylum on Monday, 16 December that year between 9 and 11 o'clock.

The whole matter had shades of Dickens who was well acquainted with the local rope walks. The latter's father was a clerk in the Navy Pay Office at Portsmouth and when he was a young boy they moved to Chatham in the years 1817-22 and were no doubt neighbours of the Blyths. Indeed, once he was a successful writer depicting scenes quite similar to these, he moved to Gads Hill Place at Higham not far from Chatham.

Perhaps an unfinished work might have contained the following discourse within its pages: "Young Colin a wisp of a boy lounged on the steps of his terraced house in Chatham's winding-streets, and watched trickles of water search for a way through the mud to find the river and escape to the sea. He had little idea of what was soon to befall him as he was wrenched from his family's bosom - leaving his elderly, grieving father behind.

Soon he was engaged on a journey himself although unlike the water he was not ready for escape at so young an age. The carriage jolted westwards through the rutted-mud of a Kentish winter and he was deposited amongst buildings very alien to him. There stood the Naval Asylum in all its splendid grandeur, but he felt very small on entering its portals which were large and cavernous. Standing in awe he was most alone as he entered the dormitory with its musty atmosphere of children and naval aspirations...."

Meanwhile, his brother James was learning all aspects of navigation just across the road in the Hospital School, and his parents and sister continued with their lives in Chatham. As time passed by there was a festive wedding Arthur Martin being married to Margaret Blyth by banns in the village of Frindsbury, just across the Medway, on 25 December 1823. [3]

Soon after the marriage the couple left the Chatham area and a child was born at Poplar in May 1825 (*an infant*) who was baptized at Hale Street Methodist - but they then moved permanently to Deptford. Arthur Martin worked there as a blacksmith and a daughter Drusilla Elizabeth was born in September 1826 being baptized at Mary Ann's Buildings (Wesleyan).

---

[3] Arthur Martin was born at St. Agnes, Truro on 27 August 1798 his parents being John Martin a smith and Parthenia Osborne who married at Kenwyn, Cornwall on 2 September 1786. Parthenia was born in 1761 and was daughter of John Osborne a yeoman farmer, whose family resided at Zennor on the north coast (near to Lands End) from the early 18th century.

James Blyth, the father, moved around the corner to 12 Whitaker Street, Chatham and lived there with his wife Margaret in 1828-29. He continued to receive a quarterly pension of roughly £11 and then moved to New Road but died there on 6 October 1829. He was buried at St. Mary's just beside the river and south of the docks five days later, and significantly the burial register stated that he was aged 86 years (born 1743).

The Navy Pay Books recorded the event and noted a small amount owing to his widow at Chatham, whilst she applied for a widow's pension in the last quarter of the year. This was to be paid at the rate for a gunner of £25 per annum and initially she received £4 3s 4d for two months owing, which was sent to Deptford as she was presumably with her daughter.

Thereafter the sum of £6 5s was paid to her each quarter, and this was received at the Pay Office, Deptford then a bill was collected in person or by a surrogate (on the first occasion by Mr. Goode). However, by July 1831 she had returned to Chatham and remained there until 1834 at which time the records become incomplete. Meanwhile, this was only part of the story, just a taste of the character of the cricketer Colin Blythe.

CHAPTER 2

Relations

The naval man, James Blyth, left just three children and none of them had ordinary lives. In the first instance it is worth considering the eldest siblings in detail, since they show that Blythe the cricketer came from an extended family with roots way beyond Deptford. Although at the same time there is a depiction of home life well juxtaposed with such travels, whilst the later discourse provides further relish in terms of characterisation.

The eponymous James Turner Blyth promptly completed his training at the Hospital School and entered into the merchant navy. Few exact details survive of such service prior to 1835, other than records of ships' lists at certain ports, but in this case there were some very valuable documents namely the ship's diaries of the "England" of London.

This merchant barque was built at Chepstow by the Severn in 1814 and was 425 tons being registered to T. Ward, London at a latter date. She was generally used for trade although the Navy also employed her on alternative duties. The first convict ships travelled to New South Wales in 1787 but the number of journeys increased in the 19th century and the "England" was first used for such purposes in 1826.

The second occasion came six years later when James Blyth junior was the master of the vessel. Thomas B. Wilson was naval surgeon for the voyage and kept a detailed diary of events and of the health of the convicts, being appointed to the "England" whilst fitting-up at Deptford on 28 February 1832. Initially he made a survey of the facilities and advised on the fitting of water closets instead of soil cases which was duly carried out.

On 19 March everything was ready and they left Deptford for Woolwich taking on 50 prisoners from the "Justicia" hulk. They were then anchored in the Medway near Sheerness from 22 March and took on 40 prisoners from the "Retribution," another 80 from "Cumberland" hulk Chatham, and 30 boys from the "Euryalus" hulk all in a miserable and wretched condition. In total the complement of convicts was 200 men and boys and they were soon under sail for Van Diemen's Land (Tasmania).

Before departing James Blyth thought it propitious to make a will and stated that he left all that he owned to his sister Margaret Martin, whilst he appointed his brother-in-law Arthur as executor. This was signed and sealed on 28 March 1832 before James Cromarty and Alex. Mustard and then sent ashore to his family for their safe-keeping.

"ENGLAND" OF LONDON

Wilson, the surgeon, noted he received dispatches from the Lieutenant Governor of Van Diemen's Land and the master received his sailing orders on 3 April thus they were underway the next day. There was some concern about two of the prisoners but the overseer insisted they went, and a female convict vessel the "Hydery" had to be towed due to the low tide. As a result the need to depart became urgent and nothing could be done.

There was a steady breeze through the Downs and once they left home-waters the prisoners were freed from their irons and allowed on deck during the day. They had arrived from all around the country including Scotland and courts martial, many sentenced at the quarter sessions or assizes, and the term was from seven years to 'all of their natural life.'

As one Aussie said he would like to look up the judge's descendants and thank them kindly! However, at the time there was considerable hardship and the surgeon went to great pains to ensure a safe passage. The prisoners were arranged in groups of six and one would feed them whilst others were appointed as boatswain to clean up and preserve order. All of the quarters were scrubbed twice a day and the decks once a fortnight.

Some prisoners suffered with catarrh and intestinal problems so each was given a health remedy twice a day viz. lime juice 1 oz, sugar 1 oz, wine 2 oz, and water 1 lb with more in the tropics. One of the seamen Robert Pike went down with febris (fever) almost immediately followed by two of the prisoners with diarrhoea and catarrhus.

Meanwhile, corporal punishment was used sparingly since this tended to excite unnecessary compassion in other prisoners and thus did not suit its purpose. On 20 April they passed the Tropic of Cancer and two days later were in sight of St. Antonie one of the Cape de Verde Islands. In fact, from that point onwards they saw no more land and the main matter of concern was the two sickly prisoners.

Thomas Briggs was simply a boy but was worn out by intemperance and neglect and died in the April, whereas Richard Tomlin had repeated attacks of hepatitis and succumbed in the May.

Soon after there was some fine weather and they passed the meridian of the Cape of Good Hope on 2 June. One of the corporals then went down with a case of pneumonia and they hit some far more severe weather, but they had arrived at Storm Bay in the east of Van Deimen's Land by the 16 July. The vessel then sailed up the Derwent River estuary and was safely anchored at Hobart Town three days later.

A total of 198 male convicts in a clean and healthy state were put ashore on 27 July 1832, as well as one subaltern and ten rank and file of the 63rd Regiment, one woman, some arms, ammunition, clothing, and baggage. The Lieutenant Governor, George Arthur then signed a document that all was in order (and the prisoners were under control) on 8 August.

Shortly afterwards they set sail again and proceeded to Sydney, New South Wales without their "cargo" arriving there on 18 August. The surgeon then concluded his journal and went ashore as did part of the military guard viz. one subaltern of the 45th Regiment, nineteen rank and file from the 4th Regiment, three women, and two children.

Thereafter, James Blyth and the crew of the "England" picked up a new cargo and sailed homewards in the October, however this was to be an eventful voyage since the health of the convicts and sailors had remained paramount - but what of the captain himself? In fact, he fell ill on reaching Cape Town and made a new will on 19 January 1833, but died soon after hence the vessel returned home under a new commander. [1]

The final chapter in this story was when Arthur Martin tried to prove the will of James Blyth in London. Initially, he took the original will along and was granted its administration on 3 April, then the new document came to light and the former was revoked by interlocutory decree.

He presented the second will which no doubt arrived on the ship and this was proved on 28 June that year. There were some significant differences to the will which was made whilst the vessel was moored at Table Bay in the Cape of Good Hope. Firstly, he left £25 to both his mother Margaret of Chatham and his brother Colin, whilst to John Humphries chief officer of the "England" he left his sextant and charts.

The rest and residue of his estate was left to his sister Margaret Martin of Deptford, not subject to any husband's debt, and he then made Alexander Mustard ship's husband to the said barque and Arthur Martin his executors. In addition, he stated that the president/members of the Orphan Chamber of the Colony were to have no powers within his will. [2]

---

[1] The "England" made a third and final trip from Portsmouth to New South Wales with 230 convicts in 1835, but no record of the ship exists after 1846.

[2] The Orphan Chamber was established under the V.O.C. in 1673 and continued under the High Court. Its original role was to protect orphans' interests but after an epidemic in 1713 it examined all wills of those who died in the Colony or off its shores. It had powers to take all of the funds and decide their destination, unless there was a clause excluding them from any interference.

THE OLD BAILEY

The association with South Africa pointed the direction for the family's next 'adventure' thus we return to a discussion of the Martins of Deptford. The father worked there as a blacksmith and they initially resided at Giffin Street, and a son Cyrus James was born in 1828. However, they then moved to Church Street one of the main thoroughfares and had two more children Octavia Margaret (1830) and Josiah Blyth (1832) *an infant*.

With their naval connections in mind they moved to Nelson Street (now Vanguard Street) which was part of Deptford New Town just to the south of their previous home. A daughter Parthenia Mary was born there in 1835 who was to have a significant role in this history, and a son Arthur Samuel was born in 1837, whereas their sister Drusilla died two years later in 1839 at the age of just twelve years.

By the latter date they had moved back to Church Street and the father then made an unscheduled appearance at the Old Bailey. William J.A. Ive was a shipbuilder and wood merchant at Deptford Green in the late 1830s and employed Arthur Martin as a blacksmith on his premises.

Another of the employees Thomas Wolledge was charged with stealing 80 pieces of wood value 5 shillings with a customer James P. Whitewood on 7 July 1840, and they all appeared at the Old Bailey on 17 August. Ive had told Wolledge who worked for him for two years "to trust nobody" and not to give anyone credit without his specific permission.

On the day in question Wolledge was asked if all his transactions were on the slate and he replied in the affirmative, thus the slate read "three feet of board 16s 3d." However, he was found to have a sum of money in his possession which was irregular, and Ive stated that he had never known him to have such an amount. Each foot of board consisted of about 80 pieces of wood regarding that type of frame and cart.

Arthur Martin was then called to the stand with a vital testimony: "I am the prosecutor's foreman of the blacksmiths. In consequence of something I told Mr. Ive, he told me to watch the proceedings of Wolledge - on the 7th July Whitewood's cart came into the yard - I watched and saw Wolledge put four feet of wood in the cart. Whitewood had seen four feet of wood measured before he went off to the grindstone, and Wolledge put them in the cart. A foot of wood signifies a pile of pieces 18 inches long and these are piled in a frame 6 feet wide and 6 feet deep. I should suppose that eighty pieces of wood would make one foot. Mr. Ive asked Wolledge if he had trusted Whitewood any wood, and his answer was no."

A second employee William Miller was then cross-examined and stated he helped load the cart and that there were four feet of wood. He had asked Wolledge about the matter, and was told that three feet were paid for but "Jemmy" had said he would stand him a drop of beer and pay for the other foot that evening. Wolledge needed some money to send his parents down to Sheerness urgently or else they would pawn his watch, and he told him to tell Ive that just three feet of wood was in the cart.

A police constable Joseph Wyatt had accosted Wolledge three days later and found 11s in the card case, which the latter kept for payments in his counting house at Ive's premises. It was unclear from the evidence if Wolledge had meant to steal the money or even to deceive his employer and both were found not guilty.

However, everyone had to remain in the court since there was a second indictment against the two parties, regarding the theft of 18 pieces of wood value 5 shillings, but on 10 July 1840. Wolledge was first employed at Ive's wood-merchants as a lad and was initially paid some 5 shillings a week, yet behaved so well that the amount was soon raised to 10 shillings.

Despite this Ive became suspicious of him and thus directed Martin and Miller to watch his dealings. The employer was called to the stand but was soon flustered by the proceedings and his answers became confused. He had asked Wolledge for all his money on the day in question and received back £4 5s which he said included the wood sold to Whitewood.

Being suspicious he called the cart-driver back and made some banter asking him how much wood he had? The latter answered he had taken five feet, but the conversation soon became hard to understand and it appeared he had six feet, five feet already paid for and another foot on credit. This was most unusual since he never took less than three feet on credit and the maximum was six feet (or a quarter).

Ive then became more perturbed and told the cross-examiner that he was bothering him about the true nature of the conversations! He had stood by the counting house making it hard to hear exactly what Whitewood said, or the words of the other two witnesses. He disputed he ever wrote down what Martin and he were to give as evidence and said that he went straight to the "station house." In the past he extended some credit to Whitewood but recently had trouble receiving payment.

Arthur Martin then came to the stand again and stated, "I am a blacksmith and live in Church Street, Deptford. On the 10th July I was at Mr. Ive's and took notice of what was doing by Wolledge and Whitewood - I saw the latter's cart come into the yard, and draw up to a quarter of a frame of wood. Whitewood was with the cart and they began to load it and took the whole of the wood that was within the frame. Whitewood hove it into the cart and Wolledge stowed it - this division is a quarter of a frame (pointing to a model) and is called six feet. I did not observe any money pass between the two, but Mr. Ive spoke to Whitewood and he said distinctly 'five feet' and he reiterated 'no more?' but the answer was indistinct. I sent Miller to tell what I had seen and I had no conversation with Ive or Wolledge, and afterwards Wolledge replaced one foot of wood in the frame."

Martin was then cross-examined as to why he had not told the magistrate before that one foot was put back in the frame. He did not know why this was, but said that this made it appear five feet were taken and he added, "I consider it my duty to state all that I know." Further to this he did not recollect Mr. Ive reading from a paper while under examination, nor being handed one by him, and swore to this fact saying that if it were the case he must have forgotten it somehow.

On further examination he declared that he heard Ive and Whitewood talk in the yard, and that the latter was unable to pay a debt since times were hard. He appeared to say that "five feet" were in the cart. Regarding any papers, the only paper he ever saw was the deposition by Ive which was in the counting house, and Ive asked him to read it through and gave it to him. A man whom he did not know asked him for the deposition outside court but he said he would only give it to Ive, whilst he read it through once or twice before appearing in the court.

He was then asked, "Have you got that paper in court with you now?" and replied, "I have, and it is in my pocket. It is the only paper I have ever had regarding this and it was written by Mr. Ive. It may be five days since I first had it. I kept it to be able to give an answer to the magistrate since I could not trust to my memory, and I did not have it at the police office."

Miller then came to the stand and explained that he saw six feet put in the cart; whilst soon after two local policemen also gave evidence. John Turner took Whitewood into custody at King Street for having too much wood in his cart, but said he was of good character and intended to pay for the other foot. He had money on him which was for another debt. The other officer Joseph Wyatt took in Wolledge who said he had done wrong to trust him for a foot when his master had said not to. He had no money on him but there was 11 shillings in the card case at the counting house.

With so much conflicting evidence regarding the amount of wood taken whether it was five or six feet, combined with a lack of clear accounting at Ive's premises, and evidence that Ive had reason to dislike Whitewood and his dealings, the two were again found not guilty. Indeed, Martin may have been compromised by his involvement and soon left the country.

CAPE COLONY

Arthur Martin a journeyman blacksmith resided on the east side of Church Street just behind St. Paul's in 1841. The house was adjacent to some large almshouses and situated between Bridge Street and Copperas Lane whereas the premises included his wife Margaret, children Cyrus, Octavia, Parthenia, and Arthur and his mother-in-law Margaret Blyth aged 61.

There were soon some major changes since the wife Margaret Martin died at Church Street on 12 February 1842 and was buried at St. Paul's. There was only a short period of grieving and Arthur Martin married Elizabeth daughter of John Kennedy at the church on 16 October that year, and it was not long after that they immigrated to Cape Town, South Africa.

This was originally colonised by the Dutch East India Company (V.O.C.) as a staging post for their ships, but was occupied by the British in 1806 with regard to the Napoleonic Wars. Such a change resulted in the Great Trek north by the Boers in the 1830s-40s, whilst the British way of life was imposed through both colonisation and the abolition of slavery.

Arthur Martin arrived with his wife and three children in Cape Town in the 1840s and was an iron founder in the central district just below Table Mountain. He was quite successful with significant connections and made a will in 1856, whereas Octavia was governess to Rev. R. Birt of the L.M.S. at Peelton near King William's Town but died there in 1866.

Meanwhile, George Pocock a surveyor lived in Shoreditch but son John Thomas (1814) travelled to the Cape and Swan River producing a diary of his travels in 1826-30. He started a successful pharmacy business in Cape Town and married Grace Vernon Buzacott in 1841, whilst the following year his brother Lewis joined him there from London.

The business was run by James H. Collard and William F.H. Pocock the son of Lewis (and Ann E. Agard), whilst John T. settled at Rondebosch and had one daughter Gracey. He was a witness on Arthur Martin's will and his wife ran a school for girls with Parthenia Martin as assistant, thus the latter accompanied the family back to England in the late 1860s.

However, there was a crisis in the business and John Thomas returned to Cape Town. His family were to follow but his wife Grace died at 7 Lowless Terrace, Harder's Road, Peckham on 22 November 1868 - the witness her nephew Rev. Aaron Buzacott of Lime Villas, Harder's Road. The latter was a minister at Asylum Road Congregational Chapel and was born in Tahiti since his father was a missionary there and in Rarotonga, whereas his villa was not far from the Blythe family in Lewisham.

Parthenia returned to Claremont, Cape Town with the daughter Gracey who then married John Paterson a land surveyor of Uitenhage to the east. Meanwhile, the former formed an association with the father and when he went to England in 1873 they were engaged. By that time he was very ill and his sister had him committed, but Rev. Buzacott secured his discharge and sent an urgent message to Cape Town asking for Parthenia.

In fact, John Thomas Pocock wholesale druggist married Parthenia Martin at the Congregational Chapel, Maple Road, Surbiton, on 6 June 1874. He was living at 2 Claremont Road and she was residing at the Southampton Hotel whilst he made his will at Lime Street, London a week later.

The couple returned to Cape Town but he died at Mowbray in 1876, and Parthenia inherited £3,000 and 'adopted' his nephew William whom she insisted was trained as a qualified pharmacist in England. As a result the business was extremely successful and a mortgage was taken out on land at Rondebosch-Worcester in 1884, whereas William was mayor of the former and St. James reputedly living in a large house near Cecil Rhodes.

The Pococks and Parthenia later resided at Kimbolton Road in Bedford although she died at Prince Street, Oranjezicht near Cape Town in 1908, whilst the family were to have an illustrious academic future. [3]

Arthur Martin, her father, had a house and shop at 1-4 Loop Street in the central district and died there in 1883 leaving £800 in property and £1,800 in cash, whilst his wife Elizabeth died at Long Street in 1899. His son Cyrus James became a successful bookseller who traded at Sir Lowry Road and Adderley Street, and one wonders if the family knew of their connection to the cricketer when he played in the colony.

At this time their relative William Pocock was a photographer and took pictures of Elizabeth A. Martin (d. 1900) and a Mrs. Spolander at their house in Long Street. Her husband Cyrus died at 70 Sir Lowry Road in 1915 and his extensive affairs were settled from 1918-30.

They had five children Emily M., Cyrus Blyth, Horace G., Alfred E., and Octavius J., and the oldest son married Sarah Alice Miller in Simonstown and resided at "Heathside," Lansdowne Road, Claremont but died there in 1934. In fact, his three children received the name "Blyth Martin" using the original spelling taken from his grandmother.

---

[3] William Pocock married Elizabeth L. Dacomb of Natal and had several children including Mary Agard Pocock a botanist of Cambridge and Rhodes University. Her brother Lewis Greville was a classical scholar at University College but went to Canterbury Univ., Christchurch, New Zealand in 1927. His son J.G.A. Pocock became a famous historian and professor who later went to Baltimore.

THE ADDIS FAMILY

With regard to the previous discourse it is apparent that the Blythe family, in perpetuity, were of solid character with some patriotic tendencies and prepared to fight for their country at some risk to themselves. Although at the same time they had an urge to look beyond the bounds.

They had a large degree of learning and a considerable determination in their personal affairs, all of these being attributes that were passed down and then added to the personality of the cricketer.

But, this was clearly not the entire story. Another facet pertained to the family one that brought to his character an intense, artistic side without which his talent could not have been moulded. In fact, this other strand was the complete antithesis of the Scottish clan, being its exact compliment, a counterpart that when discovered revealed his true nature.

The Addis family had no connection to the northern regions and in some ways supported the theorem that the cricketer was a Cockney. Indeed, they lived and worked in the alleys of Bermondsey south of Southwark from an early date and Joseph Addis a weaver resided at Marigold Alley, Swan Alley, and Long Lane near to St. Mary Magdalen in the early 18th century.

He married Mary Wilson there on 7 June 1704 and had several children including a son Benjamin also a weaver. One can imagine that they lived in houses with workshops on the upper floors, with windows open to the sky which allowed copious amounts of light to illuminate their looms.

Benjamin and Elizabeth Addis had several children in 1733-46 and a son Thomas (Junin) Addis was born at Court Yard, Bermondsey on 8 March 1744/45 - the calendar began on Lady Day, 25 March until 1752. In the fashion of the Blyths he became a cordwainer and began a trend when he married Sarah Bayton daughter of Samuel at the nearby church of St. Giles, Camberwell on 19 August 1766 (he died in 1812).

Initially they went and lived near to St. Olave's, Southwark but then had a series of addresses located around Bermondsey Square viz. Marigold St., Bermondsey St., Star Corner, Grange Rd., Long Walk, and Coach Yard. A number of children were born the most significant being Samuel Bayton (or Bacon) Addis at Long Lane on 2 June 1768.

The latter was impatient to get on with life and married Sarah Howell at St. Giles on his twenty-first birthday, 2 June 1789. He then moved away from his parents and established himself as a black/whitesmith at Church Street in Deptford. This was the start of a very successful business operation and in the 1790s he described himself as an edge tool maker.

He soon had his hand in several pies and was also listed as a salesman or tradesman, whilst he had three children but the only one to survive was Joseph James Addis baptized at St. Paul's, Deptford on 8 April 1792. The latter followed his father's lead and married Margaret Elizabeth Barrell, who came from Blackfriars Road, at St. Giles on 4 November 1810.

The son brought new impetus and worked hand-in-hand to establish their business, and was initially a victualler at Butt Lane and Church Street. By the 1820s he described himself as an edge or carvers tool maker at the latter address but had a pub the "Lion and Lamb" on the Green. His father also had the "King's Arms," Church Street and was an auctioneer, however the main line of work was within the tool trade and by the end of the decade there were also premises at New Cross.

Both Samuel and Joseph Addis appeared regularly in the Deptford rate books for Church Street and owned more than one property, while the son was entitled to vote from the late 1830s. His father died in February 1832 being buried at St. Paul's, whilst he had an extensive will leaving his watch and dial to his grandson Samuel (more of later). He then placed his property in trust for the benefit of 'the children of Joseph' while the residue of his estate was left solely to his son.

Despite just one child the Addis family became quite extensive and one could say profligate, thus the nine children of Joseph and Margaret born in 1811-29 had numerous offspring themselves - the most significant siblings Samuel Joseph (1811), Elizabeth Margaret (1813), Ann Rebecca (1821), and James Bacon (1829).

There was a full household at Church Street and the Addis family lived on the east side near to the Martins. The father Joseph continued to work as a carvers' tool maker and was clearly well known in the area, remaining there up until his decease on 23 December 1858. Indeed, he established a sound base for the family and was buried at Nunhead Cemetery.

Regarding his offspring his daughter Elizabeth married John Shirt at St. Giles in 1836, and they went to live at 3 Sidney Street, Mile End (of siege fame). However, the most significant factor was the new dimension that this marriage brought to the family. John Shirt was in fact a musician either a teacher or performer although sons John Joseph, Nathaniel George, and James were all tool makers in the East End.

This strange mixture continued since John Hadsley Addis (1815) was a blacksmith in Newington, and his brother William Francis (1825) started as a tool maker but became a teacher of music as did his son Oscar. Indeed, the cricketer kept a receipt from G.A. Shirt, 49 Plashet Lane, Upton Park grinding mills and saw works dated 26 April 1902.

This referred to George Arthur Shirt born in Deptford in 1871 the son of Nathaniel, and it is believed that the receipt was for the making of or repairs to Blythe's bat. At the same time it should not be missed that the family were musical - a talent that was in no way alien to the cricketer.

Joseph James Addis left no will and his son Samuel Joseph of Gravel Lane in Southwark took out letters of administration in June 1859, but the effects came to just £20. His widow Margaret Elizabeth briefly resided with the Shirt family but died at Sidney Street on 8 March 1862.

HIGH DRAMA

The chronicle or narrative of the family then took on a dimension that went way beyond fiction and was a case where fact became evidence! The main protagonist in this story was Samuel Joseph Addis (the eldest son) who had joined his father in the tool trade, then married Sarah Wallis a daughter of the local postman at St. Giles on 10 July 1831.

This was to be a difficult marriage and they had just two daughters namely Elizabeth Sarah born at New Cross in August 1831, and Harriet Jane born at 1-4 Giffin Street in April 1833. However, the father was a highly skilled and sought after artisan who made high quality woodcarving tools.

Initially, he worked with his father and grandfather in Church Street, but by the 1840s became established at 6-7 Lower Fore Street in Lambeth. This was situated beside the Thames just below the Palace and parallel to both Lambeth High Street and Walk (now Albert Embankment). Indeed, Samuel had a double life and took his family on a merry walk himself.

He then resided at Union Court, Southwark by 1851 however he was not at home although his wife and two teenage daughters were present. At first glance the reason for this was not apparent but some interesting facts soon came to light. Meanwhile, his business was based just around the corner at 20 Gravel Lane and from there he fine-tuned his skills.

His brother James Bacon Addis married Jane Evans at St. Saviour's (the Cathedral) on 1 December 1847, and also became a carvers' tool maker who was initially based in Deptford. However, by 1851 he was working near his brother at Little Charlotte Street which was a short thoroughfare running down from Blackfriars Road to Gravel Lane.

The Great Exhibition was opened in Hyde Park on 1 May 1851, and each brother exhibited in the tool section located on the north gallery, upper floor (west side). There was considerable competition and Samuel stated that he received honourable mention for his designs, but James also of 29 Lucas Street, Deptford won a medal in the class of edge tools (XXI).

The Exhibition may have been the reason why Samuel was absent but there was a less obvious explanation. Richard Pheasant had various jobs as a box maker, clerk, tailor, and shopkeeper and resided at 8 Old Fish Street Hill near St. Ann, Blackfriars in an area of alleys by St. Paul's. His daughter Emma Frances was born at Farmars Place, Waterloo Road in 1830 and in her late teens formed an association with Addis.

The outcome was that coterminous with his significant business success five illicit children were born from 1850-64, all of them given the name of Addis Pheasant. Most of the baptisms took place away from either of their homes at St. Andrew's, Holborn and various addresses were given such as Shoemaker Row, Water Lane, and Old Fish Street. Indeed, the father was recorded as Samuel Joseph Pheasant, whilst Emma once gave her maiden name as Condie (which was actually her brother-in-law).

Her brother John Farnell Pheasant was a tailor of 32 Water Lane and then 8 Ireland Yard, Blackfriars and possibly there was a business connection. In fact, this was a long term relationship which had severe consequences in the future. Meanwhile, there were two marriages at St. George the Martyr in Southwark and the daughter Elizabeth Addis married Henry Shaw in 1852 while Harriet married Thomas Herring in 1853.

Both the girls gave their address as Suffolk Street which was at the east end of Gravel Lane, whilst their husbands were an iron founder and edge tool maker each of whom had come down from Sheffield.

Samuel Joseph Addis an edge tool maker was residing at 2 Gravel Lane in 1861 with his wife Sarah, members of the Herring-Shaw families, and his nephew (Nathaniel) George Shirt an edge tool grinder, whereas his brother James was at 3 Lambeth Place with his wife and three children. However, the census hid the fact that all was not well.

The level of business rivalry, not to mention domestic, was clearly intense and from the mid-1850s this became apparent in the trade business adverts. Samuel regularly stated that he was an edge tool manufacturer at 2 and 20 Gravel Lane and that he was "sole inventor" of the improved carvers' tool exhibited at the Great Exhibition. Meanwhile, his brother James recorded that he had received the "only" medal for that class of tools.

In fact the whole situation was untenable and became so at the start of the next decade. The City was apparently a place of great subterfuge at the time and George Bayton a publican, self-styled gentleman, and possible relative of Bristol married Mary Margaret Sealey of St. Osyth, Essex at St. Andrew, Undershaft (near Lloyd's) on 4 December 1860. He was proprietor of the "Bull's Head" at 80 Leadenhall Street and a son George Henry was born the next year, whilst he also had a servant-girl called Elizabeth White.

One might ask "what was the mystery in all this?" and well they might, but the more significant question was how did Samuel Joseph know them? The small family then moved to Chrisp Street in Poplar and George Bayton now a plumber died there on 1 March 1863. This left his wife who was twenty-three on her own with a young child to support.

There was then another development incredible in the extreme, one that stretched credibility both to the limits and beyond. George White described as an engineer married Mary Margaret Bayton (father a gent) at All Saints, Poplar on East India Dock Road on 15 September 1863.

At the same time Samuel Joseph Addis left his wife and moved lock, stock, and barrel to 49-50 Worship Street, a road between Finsbury Square and Norton Folgate. He continued to advertise at this address and stated again that he was sole inventor of the improved carvers' tool exhibited at both the 1851 and 1862 Great Exhibitions. Adding it was the only one which received honourable mention there being "no" medal awarded.

Sarah Addis presented a petition for judicial separation on 10 June 1864 stating Samuel was of the *London Mechanical Tool Works*, 49-50 Worship Street. They had lived as man and wife at Giffin Street, Deptford Green, Fore Street, and 2 Gravel Lane and had one surviving daughter.

On divers occasions between 1853 and May 1862 the said Samuel had committed adultery with Emma (Sophia) Pheasant at 4 Gravel Lane; the same also occurring from May 1862 up until June 1864 at 49-50 Worship Street. The petitioner asked that he pay money and other relief as seemed fit, but there was inaccuracy in the second charge, and Samuel appeared at the court in July thus the matter (apparently) went no further.

However, there was then an amazing occurrence. Samuel Joseph Addis White the son of George and Mary Margaret an engineer was born at 50 Worship Street on 20 January 1865. The next year the business moved down the road to Nos. 68-70 and five more children were born there up until 1871 - all of them baptized at St. James's, Curtain Road.

The baptism and birth records provide a whole array of details stating the father George White was a 2nd engineer R.N. on H.M.S. "Tunsin," or an edge tool maker at 70 Worship Street. Indeed, by 1869 the pretence was dropped and the father was given as Samuel Joseph Addis in the baptisms but the name Addis White was given in the birth records.

There seems little doubt that "George White" was an alias to conceal the fact he was already married, and that the shaky signature at Poplar in 1863 was almost certainly his. Indeed, a ship called the "Tunsin" was built by the Union Steam Navigation Co. for trade in Shanghai that year and was later converted to a pontoon landing stage at Swatow (Shantou)!

Pseudonyms apart, business was still going well and he won a prize medal at the Paris Universal Exhibition in 1867, his work remaining of a superior quality and in great demand.

Meanwhile, the truth of the matter was clear to see - Samuel J. Addis a tool manufacturer lived at 68 Worship Street, Shoreditch in 1871 with his wife Margaret (of St. Osyth) and children Emma, Margaret, and Elizabeth (Pheasant) and Samuel J., Edwin, Harriet, and James B. (White).

He made his will on 29 May 1871 and left 12 shillings per week to his wife Sarah then £10 to his daughter Elizabeth Shaw, whereas the residue of his estate was divided between Mary Margaret White, Samuel, Edwin, Harriet, and James Bayton Addis White, George Henry Bayton, Emma Frances, Margaret, and Elizabeth Addis Pheasant.

Samuel Joseph Addis died at 70 Worship Street of stomach haemorrhage on 3 June 1871 and the will was proved by William Keeler of 34 Clifton Street a horse collar maker. The effects were not insubstantial at £1,500 but after his decease the whole matter soon unravelled.

His real wife Sarah Addis died at 5 Ashburnham Road, Greenwich on 1 March 1877, whereas Emma Pheasant was found in the City of London Workhouse at Homerton, but with so many names Mary Margaret remained elusive. Of the children, Margaret and Elizabeth Pheasant and Edwin and Joseph Addis (White) were admitted to the Brentwood Separate School, an industrial institution, from the Shoreditch parish, while their sister Emma married Joseph Clements a bookseller in Willesden.

Despite such financial family problems there was an interesting postscript regarding the brother James Bacon Addis. During the year 1863 he became bankrupt and approached Ward & Payne in Sheffield for work. They were keen to employ him as his work was superior thus he went north in 1864 however the local unions refused him admittance.

As a result he went back to London, but Ward & Payne were not to be denied and established him as a subcontractor at Rockingham Street near their works. Soon after he was assaulted in a public house just opposite his home, and it transpired the miscreants were union men (who carried out many other bad acts) although they acted independently.

The whole matter went to court and was also reported on during a Trades Union Commission in 1867. Ward & Payne, tired of the whole affair and interruption to trade, installed machinery the next year and Addis went into business for himself and resided at Court 16, Rockingham Street - whereas he traded at 127 Portobello in the early 1870s. By then he had become most successful being under the patronage of H.R.H. the Prince of Wales and other notables such as Lord Lichfield.

He continued to advertise the quality of his tools being keen to note that he was 'brother' of the late S.J. Addis and the only maker of carvers' tools in the name of Addis in the country. To add a twist to the story Ward & Payne purchased the trademark "S.J. Addis London" with its square and compasses in 1875, which had been in use for some twenty years.

James Bacon Addis resided at 46 Newcastle Street, Sheffield in 1881 and traded at the Arctic Works, Rockingham Street just west of the centre but died in March 1890 aged 60. His family continued to work there until the next century, whilst the tools made by Samuel Joseph Addis at Gravel Lane became important collectable examples of this type of work. [4]

There seems little doubt that the Addis connection added a dimension to the Blythe family, one that was no hyperbole but an artistic temperament essential to any finely tuned talent. Indeed, this extra dimension was clearly apparent in the next generation and beyond.

---

[4] Gravel Lane was parallel to Blackfriars Road and ran down to Great Suffolk Street, which went east to the Queen's Bench Prison (replaced the Marshalsea). In 1863 the new London, Chatham, & Dover Railway was built by Peto, Betts, and Crampton with its terminus at Blackfriars and Holborn Viaduct. This ran right past Gravel Lane and may have affected No. 2 which was at the southern end. Gravel Lane itself was eventually part of Great Suffolk Street.

CHAPTER 3

Discovered

The third of the three siblings, the namesake Colin Blyth senior, attended the Royal Naval Asylum from about 1816-23 and may have spent some time at sea. However, there is also a suggestion that his father taught him the rudiments of shoemaking - which was the family business.

Further to this he lived in Church Street, Deptford and was acquainted with the Addis family, thus he "married" Ann Rebecca Addis the sister of Samuel Joseph in about 1840 when she was just nineteen years old.

There may have been a certain degree of disaffection from his family at this "reputed" match, thus they initially moved to Southwark and lived right near to her brother. Colin (now surnamed Blythe) a boot-maker and his wife Ann resided at Gray Street, just west of Blackfriars Road, in 1841 and a son James William was born there soon afterwards.

Continuing in this line of work he returned to Church Street where a second son Edward Gibbon was born in 1844. However, he had greater aspirations than leather and became a dealer in silk handkerchiefs living at 3 Friendly Place on Loampit Hill in Lewisham by 1850.

This was an area of new housing beyond the confines of Deptford suitable for local merchants and those who worked in the City, whereas he was a commercial traveller in the silk trade at 1/6 Arundel Place soon after. The latter was a row of houses on the north side of Loampit Vale by Lewisham Station with open fields behind and brick fields just to the south.

His mother Margaret Blyth(e) died at Hales Street, Deptford off Church Street on 10 September 1850 and was buried at St. Paul's, whilst her son the informant then made a claim to the Navy Board for pension outstanding to the value of £6 5s. A number of papers were sent to support the claim and this was admitted in the December.

Meanwhile, his new home was in a semi-rural environment and provided evidence the Blythes had raised their social position. A year later the family had moved to 1 Brockley Cottages on Common Lane (now Upper Brockley Road) one of two properties situated on the west side.

During this time the couple had several daughters and a son Walter Blythe was born there on 17 May 1854, the father being a handkerchief printer and a dealer in silk goods. Up to this point he may have been an employee but he was then listed as a warehouseman for silk goods at 3 Honey Lane, Cheapside in the City from 1858-60.

In addition he moved across the road to 18 Common Lane (or St. David's Terrace) a three-storey property at the end of a terrace, with only some market gardens and Manor Farm beyond. This was a respectable well-to-do situation and in 1861 he was described as a merchant for silks etc.

The household included his wife Ann, sons James and Edward merchant's clerks and their other children Emily M., Ann H., Mary, Margaret, Walter, Emma, Florence and a servant-girl Sarah A. Shirt a niece.

Business was clearly going well and the next year he moved to substantial new offices as a shirt, brace, and tie manufacturer at 38 Gresham Street. He remained in these premises for some years which were situated on the north side at the corner with Aldermanbury Street, and just beyond were four similar buildings, Church Passage, and the basilica of St. Lawrence Jewry. Today, the site is the forecourt of the Guildhall Library and is beside an attractive bucolic pond in front of the church.

However, back in the 19th century this was a scene of much activity and all five properties embraced a multiplicity of offices whereas No. 38 housed "Colin Blythe," Robert Strong manufacturer's agent, and Wells & Haverson the latter being a stationery company.

"SILLEY" POINT

Blythe raised his family in the social scale but his fine silk handkerchief was soon crumpled. This was the time when Addis co-habited with his reputed wife at Shoreditch receiving a judicial separation, and it seemed unlikely any more scandal could visit the family but that was exactly what happened. Everything about the Blythes bespoke Victorian correctness but there was a clanking skeleton creeping about somewhere in the shirt closet!

Colin Blythe then moved to 8 Ffinch Terrace a substantial house down Brockley Lane in 1865, and the next year to a detached villa on the north side of Blackheath Hill - the latter was near to Trinity Church (and school) just below the common opposite to Dartmouth Hill. None of his children were yet married and there were probably one or more servants, however there were soon some unexpected developments.

Indeed, Henry Silley son of a publican was born at Marylebone in 1815 and married Eliza Young at St. Pancras church in 1838. He followed his father's profession and was proprietor of the "Hare" at 16 Heath Place on the northwest corner of Cambridge Heath and Hackney Roads in Bethnal Green from 1861-62 - just below the Regent's Canal. Three years later he moved to the "White Hart," 35 Hoxton Old Town at the southern end of Hoxton Street although his wife died at this time.

There is often little indication of 'how people meet' in historical records and at best the answer can only be surmised, but in this case it was probably through S.J. Addis Esq. who lived a short distance down Curtain Road at Worship Street - and may have known Silley and introduced him.

This all seems a bit vague until the following information is divulged. In fact, Henry Silley a publican of Bloomsbury married Ann Rebecca Addis a "spinster" of Lewisham at St. Mary's, Lewisham on 30 November 1867. The marriage took place by licence and the witnesses were Mary Flude and Thomas William Greenaway (husband of her sister Eliza).

Clearly there were strained relations on Blackheath Hill but this move was unprecedented and right in the face. The implication was that Colin Blythe had never actually married her and all that had gone before was for polite company. Unlike in the case of Samuel J. Addis there was no evidence of a divorce, or otherwise, and no doubt such a break-up had a severe effect especially on the son Walter who was just thirteen at the time.

The outcome was that the father moved to 3 Clyde Villas recently built in a new development at East Down Park. The area to the west, part of the parish of Lee was already developed, however across a small stream in the environs of Lewisham there were still fields. This new section was just off Lee High Road and is now East Down Park and Wisteria Road.

He then made a will which was provisionally dated 17 November 1867 (before the marriage), but a later affidavit stated it was actually signed on 29 February 1868. Everything was left to five daughters, whilst he appointed William Marks of 8 Trump Street executor and asked him to close up his business and invest the money in freehold or the Indian Government, or lend J.W. Selvus of Constitution Hill, Birmingham the sum of £500 and use the interest for the support of these daughters. Once the youngest Emma had reached twenty-one all the money was to be divided amongst them viz. Emily M., Ann H., Mary, Margaret O., and Emma H. (or their children) and £20 was to be paid for the benefit of his son Walter.

He also added two codicils on the 5/8 March 1868 stating that his son James William Blythe was to share equally with his sisters in the will, and that the said son was permitted to carry on the business at Gresham Street provided there was no loss. Significantly, his son Edward who adopted an unusual profession was not included, nor was his 'daughter' Florence who was born four years after her other siblings.

Colin Blythe senior died at 3 Clyde Villas of anasarca a dropsical affection on 22 March 1868 and has a memorial in Nunhead Cemetery. His will was proved soon after in the April and his effects came to under £3,000, whilst his family were left with an uncertain future.

In general they went off in a number of directions. Henry Silley was a publican at "The Corner Pin," 1 Poplar Place, Crayford in 1871 living with his wife Ann and step-daughters Emma and Flora, and at the "William the Fourth" at Kensal Green in 1876. James Blythe, warehouseman employing three, was married with two children and lived in Greenwich, while Edward was an artist lodging at 31 Alderminster Road, Bermondsey.

The eldest daughter Emily Margaret was initially a barmaid at Farringdon Metro but married John Crago of the shirt and tie trade, whilst Ann Harriet married George Langford a barman, potato dealer, and commission agent and both lived in the Camberwell area. Indeed, the latter resided at 51 St. James's Street in 1871 with Mary and Margaret Blythe.

James William Blythe ran his father's business in the name "Colin Blythe" at Gresham Street until 1873, and married again to Jane Yeldham a widow and his landlady in 1881. He lived in Clapham and Brixton and started his own business as a silk agent at 114 Cheapside in 1889, but the next year moved to 13 Gutter Lane and 'manufactured' handkerchiefs and ties.

Everything went smoothly for a while but then like Martin before him he found himself at the Old Bailey. Blythe explained that the house was let off in portions to various warehousemen and that each had a separate door. He left the premises on Saturday 22 December 1894 just before three and did not come back there until Monday at 10.30 a.m.

On arriving at the door, the entrance to his section on the third floor, he found the panel broken and boxes strewn about whereas the cash box was empty and many items were missing. The price of the ties was 9s and the handkerchiefs were 24s a dozen making the missing amount £20.

It later transpired that David De Roode went to visit Raphael Coster at Wentworth Street, Spitalfields the same day and offered him ties at 8s and handkerchiefs at 12s a dozen. £8 was then paid and most were sold outside Coster's shop. After some enquiries an officer visited the latter, whilst De Roode said he bought them off a stranger in Oxford Street.

Two witnesses went to De Roode's house near Mansell Street and Royal Mint Square and observed he had some ready cash, thus he was taken to Cloak Lane Station and remanded at Mansion House - being sentenced to eight months hard labour. James W. Blythe continued to work at Gutter Lane but died in 1900 and is also commemorated at Nunhead.

His brother Edward Gibbon Blythe was an aspiring artist who had some success, and lived at Deptford with his wife Anne and daughter Nellie in 1881. Ten years later he was based in Hastings as an artist and at the turn of the century resided near Brixton. He was then a picture and bric-a-brac dealer at 42 Old Town, Clapham and died in 1930 at the age of 86.

There is little record of his work but there was a knock-on effect of some significance. His youngest sister Emma Harriet was introduced to his artist friends and married Edmund Henry Niemann at St. Andrew's, Stockwell on 29 November 1879 - her brother being one of the witnesses.

The latter was a landscape painter of some distinction, whereas his father Edmund John Niemann did similar subjects and exhibited at the Royal Academy from 1844-72. Initially they lived at Coldharbour Lane, Brixton and then Richmond but eventually returned to Stockwell.

Nearly all of the family married in the 1870s and Margaret Blythe was no exception. Her husband Alexander Ritchie came from Aberdeen and was a grocer or commission agent and they lived in Camberwell.

Meanwhile, Henry and Ann Silley resided with the Cragos at Rotherhithe in 1881; but Ann died at the "Milford Arms," London Road, Spring Grove (near Brentford) on 25 July 1887 and her daughter Emma of 8 Marlboro Villas, Richmond was the informant.

WALTER BLYTHE

The youngest son had an unpromising start in life after the death of his father and just £20 sitting in his pocket. Unlike the rest of his family he is absent from the 1871 census and there is a suggestion that he went to sea. The evidence for this being his occupation as an engineer since one way of obtaining such skills was through a marine apprenticeship.

This was "the age of steam" and in subsequent years he described his occupation as engineer fitter or even steam engine maker. In the 1870s he returned to live and work in Deptford in the vicinity of Evelyn Street, and was later employed at the Woolwich Arsenal about four miles away. His initial life in Deptford was quite hard as revealed by the records and no doubt this had an obdurate impact on his famous son.

Regarding the fledgling cricketer his character was almost complete but there was one vital ingredient missing. From the Blythes he had received a steadfastness and patriotic streak whilst from the Addis family he inherited passion, great dexterity, artistic and musical ability. These alone may have made a good cricketer, a plodder who scored the runs and took wickets, but they did not quite account for the genius of Blythe.

The final component in the mix to take him above the average was some beguiling Irish magic that came with a fiddle and a jig! The cricketer has always been pronounced to be a great English patriot but he was far more cosmopolitan than that, with antecedents of varied British extraction which explained his inherent ability to mix with a variety of peoples.

Maurice Dready was born in Co. Cork in 1791 and came to England in his twenties, although it is believed this caused a rift with his family in Ireland. He was one of the poorer Catholic brethren and took labouring work in the large and frenetic H.M. Victualling Yard, which was situated beyond the Royal Dockyards to the north of Deptford.

A local man William Burke married Mary Murther at St. Paul's, Deptford on 24 December 1815 and resided at New Row, but the former died in August 1819. This asymmetric line of terraced cottages was built in the 18th century between Lower Road (Evelyn Street) and the old town at New King Street. The name was clearly apt at the time and they were situated on the south side (now demolished) later forming part of Prince Street.

In fact, Maurice Dready married Mary Burke a widow at St. Nicholas's on 29 September 1822. There were few Catholic churches nearby and five children were baptized at Our Lady of the Star, Croom's Hill, Greenwich from 1823-32 although at least two died in infancy. The family home was Sayes Court, Lower Road just off New Row and a child "Josephus son of Maurice Dready et Maria (Murtock)" was born on 14 January 1832.

Two more children followed soon after: Maurice in 1835 and Mary in 1839 and they took up residence at 35 New Row. Initially the father was described as a labourer and the two sons were cooper's apprentices whereas the mother Mary Dready died there in 1850. By that time her husband was recorded as a foreman in H.M. Victualling Yard.

Their next door neighbours at No. 36 were Thomas and Mary Ann Cox a shoemaker from Dorset who had one daughter. Indeed, Joseph Thomas Dready a cooper married Jane Cox at St. Margaret's, Westminster on 24 September 1854. The exact reason for this illustrious choice of church is unknown although they may have had relatives in the district, whereas the couple had four children at 36/31 Prince Street: Elizabeth (11 July 1855), Joseph (1857), Harry (1860), and Alice Jane (1861).

The father Maurice Dready enjoyed a responsible position as "leading man of stores" in the Victualling Yard and received a civil pension, thus he retired to 18 Victory Street in Deptford New Town near to the bridge but died there on 5 June 1861. In his will he left all his effects to his daughter Mary Dready an assistant of "ladies devoted to charity" at Nazareth House, Hammersmith but failed to put a date on the will.

As a result his friend and neighbour Haddock Thomas Hughesdon of 38 New Row made an affidavit at Chancery Lane stating the will was made a few days after the 7 July 1852. He knew this to be correct since during that month there was an election to appoint an M.P. for Greenwich and he and Dready were on the committee returning Admiral Stewart.

A few days later the testator was taken ill and for that reason he made his will. With this out the way his daughter the residuary legatee was sworn, no executor being named, and the effects were under £100.

His son a cooper resided at 31 New Row in 1861 with his wife Jane and three children, Alice being born there later that year - however there was soon a considerable change of circumstances. A cooper in general made wooden-staved vessels including cask, barrels, and buckets for storage of victuals but whether there was any inherent danger is unclear.

Some professions such as hatter used chemicals that could lead to a later deterioration and this may have been a factor, thus Joseph Thomas Dready was admitted to Barming County Asylum in the late 1860s. The Victorians unkindly referred to these forgotten people simply as "lunatics" although at a future date Dready was stated to have dementia.

There was clearly an undiagnosed problem that in the modern era might have been attended to since he stayed there the rest of his life. What made the situation worse was that his sister Mary was also admitted, whereas his brother Maurice was eventually an inmate at Caterham Asylum.

However, the next generation continued with their lives and Jane Dready a needlewoman lived at 31 Prince Street with her four children and a lodger in 1871. The next year a son Alfred "Dready" was born but the father is unknown and possibly a previous connection came into play.

John James Payn a baker married Rhoda Cooper at St. Paul's, Deptford in 1856, but then moved away initially to Woolwich and was at 22 George Street, Hammersmith in 1871 with his wife and four children. Rhoda Payn died there in 1874 and this was followed by an unexpected marriage, one that paralleled the arrival of Blythe in the neighbourhood.

A precedent had already been set thus John James Payn, a baker and a widower, married Jane Dready "widow" at St. Bartholomew by Smithfield on 4 August 1878. However, her husband was still alive in Barming.

Clearly there was no chance of his recovery or return and this was the only way forward but it was still a rather shocking revelation. Whilst all this was taking place Walter Blythe had come to live and work in Deptford and it is not inconceivable that he lodged with the family or was a colleague. In fact, the brothers Joseph and Harry Dready were in the same profession and worked locally as a boiler maker and engine smith.

The outcome seemed obvious and Walter Blythe an engineer (the son of Colin a carrier) married Elizabeth Dready at St. Clement's, Treadgold Street near to Shepherd's Bush on 25 December 1878. They gave their address as 70 Latimer Road which is now partly covered by the M40 (flyover), whilst the two witnesses were John and Jane Payn.

The parents stayed there and lived at 48 Overstone Road, Hammersmith with sons (Edmund) William and Alfred, the first being from the baker's first marriage. However, the rest of the family remained in Deptford and it is from there that the story of the cricketer really begins. [1]

EARLY DAYS

Colin Blythe the first child of Walter and Elizabeth was born at 78 Evelyn Street, Deptford on 30 May 1879. The house was part of a terrace on the west side between Wotton Road and Rolt Street, just opposite Prince Street, and at the front was a shop Mrs. Mary Jane Hogg haberdasher. At one time this was called "Prospect Place" and nearby there were other shops such as coffee rooms, a wheelwright, furniture broker, grocer, and cooper.

Indeed, the first son had good prospects of his own but was born into an environment where personal privacy was at a premium. A sister Jessie was born just eighteen months later on 2 January 1881 and the extended family then resided at 206 Evelyn Street.

This second property was across the road just south of Prince Street and nearby were "The Globe," a printer, shoemaker, tailor, and chemist. In fact, the numbering went up the west side to Blackhorse Bridge and Surrey Canal, then down the east side to Creek Road and the High Street.

Walter Blythe an engine fitter was head of the household and lived there with his wife and two children, Joseph Dready boiler maker, Harry Dready engine smith, Alice Dready needlewoman, one lodger, and Harriet Payn a young servant (and a relative). Two other families occupied adjacent rooms within the same property which was clearly overcrowded.

Colin and his sister Jessie were baptized together at St. Luke's further up Evelyn Street on 30 January 1881, whilst daughters Florence and May were born soon after and they lived at 63 Rolt Street in 1885 - a year later they moved a short distance north to a more permanent residence.

As a result the next two children Walter and Alice (known as 'Lal' by her siblings) were born at 39 Gosterwood Street. By then education had been made available to all and Colin attended Duke Street Infants School, which was situated with a primary school on the southeast corner of Rolt Street and Duke Street. Indeed, he was admitted to the primary school with some fifty other local children on 18 April 1887.

---

[1] Joseph Dready formerly a cooper of Deptford died at Barming in 1893 whereas his "wife" Jane Payn died at Merton Road, Wimbledon in 1896. In fact she was still married to John Payn (the baker), and her son Alfred Dready a watchmaker lived at 20 Tennyson Road, Wimbledon until 1911.

There are few details of his time there other than the fact he was in the ordinary standard, had a public elementary education, and was not exempt from R.E. A brother Charles was born in late 1889 and the family remained at 39 Gosterwood Street on the next census, the father being a steam engine fitter or maker. By this stage the Dreadys had left although Alfred "Payn" a clock-maker 'jobber' was a boarder with them.

The next year they moved southwards again to 26 Wotton Road, thus the children after Colin probably attended Clyde Street School which was just behind. The young cricketer left Duke Street (Alverton St.) School with his brief education completed on 9 April 1892, and was soon apprenticed as a fitter and turner with his father at the Woolwich Arsenal.

There was a short four mile trip to the works by tram or possibly train from Deptford - clearly a daunting experience for a young lad of fourteen. At the time the works extended from Warren Lane just beyond Powis Street as far as Griffin Manor Way, Plumstead (site of Arsenal's Manor Ground), although by the First War they had become considerably larger.

Certainly it was a most historic site and Colin Blythe would have entered through the Beresford Gate (main entrance) at the end of Powis Street, and seen in front of him the Royal Brass Foundry and Dial Square Workshops. It was a hive of activity being laid out in "New York" fashion with Street No. 1 leading down to the ordnance depots, wharves, and river.

There was a proliferation of workshops, machinery shops, and forges near to the main entrance, whilst the armaments were made and stored in safer bunkers to the east (away from the town). Avenue A ran along the shore by the Thames whereas Avenue H was near the main gate and a cacophony of noise emanated from the burgeoning industrious works. [2]

Deptford was an overcrowded area with industrial backdrop but then as now there was an outlet through sport. Indeed, Blythe played both cricket and soccer at boys clubs in Blackheath from the age of eleven.

---

[2] Woolwich Warren was established as an ordnance depot in 1671 and the Royal Brass Foundry was added in 1717 - sixty years later it had extended to over one hundred acres and a large boundary wall was erected using convict labour. Like other such sites it was extremely politically sensitive and was left as a blank space on O.S. Maps of the time. It became the Royal Arsenal in 1805 and the Military Academy moved to Woolwich Common the next year, whilst it was a renowned centre for engineering with a vital role during the Crimean War. A football club was formed and named after the Dial Square workshop in 1886 then moved to the Manor Ground two years later and became the Woolwich Arsenal in 1891. Today the brass foundry, founder's house, Dial Square, and old R.M.A. building are still present beyond the Beresford Gate.

It soon became apparent that he had an inherent talent regarding cricket aided by his lithesome figure and a degree of dexterity inherited from his family. However, he was rather shy about his ability and remained reticent when friends suggested he went for a trial. Thus it was by chance, but a chance that was inevitable, that he entered into the game of cricket.

In fact his talent took a considerable time to blossom and in the meantime an even larger family was growing around him. Four more children were born at 26 Wotton Road, Deptford in the 1890s namely Alexander, John Henry (Jack), Edwin (*an infant*), and Sidney.

Meanwhile, there are a number of descriptions of Blythe's emergence into first class cricket, detailing how he wandered up to Blackheath one day and was spotted by a scout as he reluctantly bowled a few balls into the nets. Some of these have developed a mythical quality however a description by the cricketer himself is perhaps the most reliable version.

His contemporary Sir Pelham Warner furnished a vital account of what was to prove a rather significant event in 'his book of cricket,' and this is probably the closest we will come to the truth. In fact, the latter was most complimentary about Blythe's abilities (see next chapter) and discussed the episode with some considerable aplomb.

At the age of eighteen he decided to walk up to Rectory Field which was beyond Blackheath on the road to Charlton, a considerable distance from his home. It was a leafy venue, a home to rugby football since 1858 and at the entrance were the ancient "Poplar Cottages" beside an avenue of trees. This was the first time he had watched Kent play professional cricket and the match was against Somerset on 15-17 July 1897.

The game itself was quite high scoring and Frank Marchant captained Alec Hearne and Jack Mason of Kent against Sammy Woods and his colleagues. Meanwhile, Walter Wright a professional had come from Nottingham to Kent (and the Mote Park Club) and was present that day.

Blythe spent some of his time in the nets when the action waned and recounted events in a rather understated way: "I don't think there were many more spectators than players, but Walter Wright came out to practice and asked me to bowl him down a few. Captain McCanlis happened to be present and then took my name and address."

Kent won the game by a good margin of 213 runs, but no doubt once the bails were lifted Blythe journeyed home and pondered the outcome of this happening, if any. Maybe he thought nothing would come of it. Yet in this one incident the whole course of his life was changed and soon afterwards he had a successful trial at Charlton. The rest as they say is history and he then helped Kent to become the top side in the country.

TONBRIDGE NURSERY

At the same time the club showed great foresight establishing the first ever training facility at the Angel Ground in Tonbridge. Promising youngsters from within the county were skilfully coached in the nets and practice shed thereby negating the need to bring in players from outside.

The Tonbridge Nursery became the premier institution of its kind and with the River Medway, water meadows, and castle ruins nearby it was an idyllic location in which to study "the art of cricket."

George Webb and Captain McCanlis both appeared for Kent and were instrumental in creating a successful side. The former, an athletic outfitter, coached Hutchings at the local school and had a major role in developing Blythe as a premier bowler. The Nursery's significance was considerable and trainees Fairservice, Fielder, Hardinge, Hubble, Humphreys, Seymour, and Woolley were some of the greatest players of the day. [3]

One of the first to go there was Blythe who over the next two years spent his time between Deptford and Tonbridge, and with some crucial training in place he made an appearance for the Kent Second XI at the County Ground, Hove on 20-21 July 1898.

This was one of several enticing cricket locations being on Eaton Road with the sea end providing some healthy winds, and Blythe sent down just 14.3 overs with eight other bowlers. His only wicket was the tail-ender Walter Humphreys for 7 runs, whilst he put on 8 himself in the second innings - although the game was eventually lost by eight wickets.

The official County Championship was inaugurated in 1890 and the eight initial members might be given the encomium "The Founder Members of County Cricket" viz. Gloucester, Kent, Lancashire, Middlesex, Nottingham, Surrey, Sussex, and Yorkshire. However, the numbers soon expanded and Somerset joined the next year whilst Derby, Essex, Hampshire, Leicester, and Warwickshire joined in 1895.

The number was taken to fifteen members with the arrival of Worcester in 1899 however this did not mean that each team played twenty-eight games per season. Generally, the tally came to a smaller figure for calendar reasons, and this no doubt affected the championship since on occasions the top two teams did not play one another at all.

---

[3] Frank Woolley later established an indoor training school on Stocks Green Road near to Hildenborough just north of Tonbridge. This had a long low building for practice in poor weather and a level playing field outside.

Up to this point the contest was dominated by Surrey and Yorkshire although Lancashire were also the winners in 1897. Meanwhile, Kent had a less auspicious start and generally lost more games than they won from 1890-98 thereby finishing quite low down in the table.

However, this was all to change with the arrival of several new players who had trained at the Nursery. In addition, there was a new captain in the form of J.R. Mason in 1898 and at the same time Tom Pawley (another 'old boy') was appointed as the first club manager. The latter also helped to train players at the Nursery and under his guidance Kent had a proficient set up resulting in a polished, professional outfit.

During the 1899 season the anomaly of five balls per over still persisted but the most significant factor for Kent was the arrival of Colin Blythe on the scene. The main bowlers up until then had been Martin, Wright, and Alec Hearne but there was room for improvement and as stated by Dudley Moore in his Kent history "relief was on the way."

Blythe continued to make rapid progress at the Nursery during 1899 and bowled eighteen overs for the Kent Second XI at Hove in July, taking just one wicket in a game that was lost. However, the coaches George Webb and Captain McCanlis decided he was ready to take the step up and he made his first class debut at the age of twenty years.

A strong Yorkshire side led by Lord Hawke arrived at the Angel Ground in Tonbridge on 21 August, and maintained very good form with every chance of winning the county championship. During the game things were going well for them and test player Frank Mitchell came in at No. 4, and promptly trounced the Kent bowlers Mason, Bradley, and Alec Hearne all over the ground to reach 55 runs.

Blythe was then introduced and had a most auspicious start in first class cricket since with his first delivery he clean bowled Mitchell, although he went on to bowl just four overs in the innings for 25 runs. No doubt there was a ripple of applause in the crowd and a sense they had witnessed the dawn of something quite propitious for the club.

Yorkshire were then all out for 164 and Kent made a grand total of 369 with C.J. Burnup scoring 171, although Blythe was out for 0. There was a concerted comeback and the opponents reached 325 with the best batting from E. Wainwright (100) and Lord Hawke (81), however Blythe bowled a further fourteen overs taking the tail-ender D. Hunter for 5 and Kent won the match by eight wickets.

This was a significant game for three reasons as reported in the press at the time. Firstly it saw the arrival of a new talent in the bowling arena, secondly the spectators witnessed one of the largest run totals ever scored by "Pinky" Burnup, and thirdly the victory had the effect of transferring the championship from Yorkshire to their rivals Surrey.

During the rest of the season Blythe played in only three other games, however these were all of some note as he began to pit his skills against some of the best batsmen of the day. The condition of the pitch was no anathema to him and he often produced his best results on a poorer wicket although at first it was unclear how well he would do.

His second game took place against Warwick at the Private Banks Sports Ground, Catford on 24-26 August and the Kent side won by ten wickets. The game was notable since this was the last time that the teams played for fourteen years, and Kent laid out their stall by scoring 420 runs with J.R. Mason (119) and W. Rashleigh (120).

Warwick only reached 120 runs and they were forced to follow on but could not make the total, whereas Blythe took the batsman Devey for 10 runs in each of the innings - clean bowled and lbw. Other players in the opposing side were Lilley and Quaife who feature later on. [4]

Clearly Blythe enjoyed his home turf and he was even more successful in his third game against Surrey, back at Rectory Field, on 28-30 August. The game ended as a draw however he bowled with Bradley and Mason and took three in each innings for a total of 39 runs. This was the first in a long line of wicket-taking which remained constant throughout his career.

His final game of the season was against Sussex at the County Ground, Hove on 31 August. Kent made 230 in the first innings and Sussex had to follow on after achieving just 110, whilst Blythe took three wickets and Jack Mason four. During the innings C.B. Fry reached 7,500 runs and in the second led the attack, however Blythe bowled him for 82 (caught Alec Hearne) and Sussex collapsed all out on 167 runs.

The Kent side had won a third victory with the help of Blythe but during the season only won six games in total, although they were poised to climb up the table. He was like the final piece in the jigsaw with several talented batsmen, the fast bowler Walter Bradley who took three hat tricks in two seasons, and the more-than-able wicket keeper Fred Huish.

But despite a fairly reasonable start the bowlers figures didn't indicate or suggest what was to come in the following years. He had taken just fourteen wickets at a cost of 310 runs, whereas his best was three for 15 and he had failed to reach that hallowed target of five wickets in an innings. This was not championship form but as they say "from small acorns…."

---

[4] John H.G. Devey was also a good soccer player for Birmingham St. George's and Aston Villa, scoring the winning goal in the 1895 Cup Final.

1900-01 (SEASONS)

The uncertain promise of that first season was soon fulfilled and by the end of 1900 Kent had reached third place in the county championship. Their bowlers may have been assisted by the introduction of the six-ball over and enjoyed eight victories and four defeats in their twenty-two games.

A number of players contributed to this progress and Alec Hearne was noted for both his batting and bowling, whilst Burnup was to be in fine form yet again. Blythe himself became established in the side and played in every game notching up 114 wickets at an average of 18.47 runs - the century then being his trademark in almost every season.

The bowling trio of Blythe, Bradley, and Hearne were unable to stop Yorkshire in the first game at Catford in May losing by 131 runs, and there was a draw at Old Trafford at the start of June. However, the latter game was of some significance since Cuthbert Burnup scored 200 this being the first double century for Kent - and reached a total of 5,000 runs.

During the game Blythe achieved four wickets for 86 in the first innings including Archie MacLaren caught Huish on 23 runs. Such an achievement may have brought him to the attention of the former, who had captained England in Australia in 1897-98 and was soon to arrange a tour himself. In fact, the Lancashire side also included J.T. Tyldesley (see later), whilst other captains of England were Lords Harris, Hawke, and W.G. Grace.

Blythe was now mixing with the best and Kent took on Middlesex at the Angel Ground on 21-23 June. Winning the toss the home side put on 180 runs mainly due to H.C. Stewart and the captain Mason, whereas in reply the visitors only managed 110 runs. The tally was gradually increasing as the bowler took five for 46 including the openers Warner and Hayman, while Kent declared on 202 and won the game by 152 runs.

Such progress soon continued and against Notts at Rectory Field at the end of June he reached fifty wickets in first class cricket. The side then travelled up to Headingley but did not play on the second day and the game ended in a draw. Yorkshire fielded G.H. Hirst, Lord Hawke, and the fine bowler Rhodes but only managed 132 against Kent's 230, whereas Blythe achieved five wickets for 41 runs.

There was then a significant game at the County Ground, Leyton on 26-28 July which saw the debut of the fast bowler Arthur Fielder. He was the second of the new generation although in this instance he made little impact on events. Essex notched up a record tally against Kent of 551 runs and the wickets were eventually taken by Bradley and Mason.

However during a third wicket stand Perrin and McGahey of Essex added 323 runs in just 255 minutes, and together they launched thirty-six 4's over the distant boundary! Kent then replied with just 161 and 104 but went away with a lucky draw due to rain on the second afternoon.

Despite such a setback Kent were clearly in the ascendancy and Blythe continually broke his previous bowling records. During Canterbury Week the side played Lancashire at the St. Lawrence Ground on 6-8 August, and in the first innings he took six wickets for just 40 runs including Tyldesley and the other three openers. In the second he took five for 32 including MacLaren, but there was no victory since the advent of rain on the first day stopped Kent although they were well ahead.

Thus Blythe's first full season ended with Kent in third place. However, during the winter he was taken ill, one of several health problems that were at times to blight his career, and the Kent Committee sent him down to the coast for a fortnight's rest in March 1901. With this problem in mind he joined up with team-mates Huish and Humphreys for a months coaching under Fred Martin and Walter Hearne.

During the next season he played in all but one of the twenty-one games but was not so successful due to very dry conditions. In fact, Kent also went backwards winning seven and losing seven of their matches, whilst Blythe failed to reach the century taking 93 for his lowest average of 23.12 runs. It was a testament to him that every season thereafter he reached the target of one hundred wickets in a season.

Up until then he had played in run-of-the-mill county games but he was then introduced to the next level, as Kent took on what became an annual season-opener against the M.C.C. at Lord's on 20-22 May.

They were off to a good start in the fixture their captain Jack Mason leading the way on 141, whilst Burnup reached 49 and the final total was 321 runs. Warner and the M.C.C. then put on 212 and Blythe bowled with Bradley to take his three wickets, including J.T. Hearne brother of Walter (see later) who he bowled for 25 runs. In the second innings Kent put on a further 331 the main scorers being Burnup (84) and F.D. Browne (53) and ultimately they won by a margin of 205 runs.

Blythe then took part in the first of many 'international fixtures' as Kent took on the touring South Africans at Foxgrove Road in Beckenham (now covered by housing). The game took place on 23-24 May and the visitors batted for a total of 225 the wickets falling to bowlers Blythe, Mason, and Hearne. Burnup and Edward Humphreys then made a century opening for Kent, whereas Blythe recorded his best-to-date of 20 before being caught and the side notched up 227 runs.

In the second innings there was some of the best bowling yet to be seen as Blythe and Bradley each took three wickets in four balls, their respective figures being six for 53 and three for 43.

But that was not all. Amongst the tourists Tancred, Bisset, Halliwell, Rowe, and Graham were clean bowled by Blythe as he spun the ball up the crease with some deceptive ease. As a result the game was poised when the South Africans were dismissed for 139. Kent then won the game by seven wickets after putting on an identical score, Burnup making 70 runs, but it was the sterling bowling that had sealed the victory.

The wickets and the best tally to date continued to be notched up as Kent beat Surrey at the Oval on 1-3 July. The visitors won the toss and Burnup and Hearne added 111 runs to reach a total of 189. Surrey replied with 131 however Blythe took seven wickets for 64 runs in just 19.4 overs including Bobby Abel, Hayes, Hayward, and the captain Leveson-Gower.

Without doubt Kent were the bogey team for Surrey who always seemed to come unstuck (and get rather jittery) upon the arrival of the Men from Kent. In the second innings Kent added another good total and thus won the game by 110 runs - with Blythe taking a further four for 57.

There was another first during the season with the inaugural game at the attractive Nevill Ground in Tunbridge Wells. A local club Bluemantle C.C. established the venue in a leafy suburb among affluent Victorian housing, with natural banking at the southern end, in 1862. But without doubt it was a good decision by Kent to take their matches to this location.

Lancashire were the first visitors on 15-17 July and there was a tight game which the opponents won by 67 runs. Blythe's success continued as he took another six wickets for 70 runs in the first innings the other bowlers being Bradley, Mason, and Alec Hearne - in fact the latter reached a total of 950 career wickets during the game. Thus the 1901 season ended with Kent in a dip but Blythe in the ascendancy.

CHAPTER 4

Australia 1901-02

Colin Blythe clearly had a prodigious talent that improved season by season, however his style was not of the aggressive or perfunctory variety but was more in the realm of the dexterous and perfectionist.

His run up to the crease began with a kind of shuffle of the feet, then there was a small hop but thereafter he adopted a more regular approach, whilst the most significant factor was the distance the left arm was swung behind the back. The ball was finally released side-on and the batsman rarely had sight of the delivery until just before it occurred.

A great variety of pace was used (mainly slow) and he made the ball break back with finger spin on the orthodox leg side, but also utilised an arm action to produce a break from the off. The batsman was further perturbed by his repeated accuracy of bowling towards the wicket, and his tendency to pitch the ball up numerous times to encourage an off drive. With the opponent lulled into security he delivered a deceptive corker!

This was a talent that required a great deal of practice to perfect the right line and flight and Blythe was an accomplished exponent. He would stand almost upright as he released the ball and had a smooth, elegant delivery, being almost unplayable on wickets that were affected by rain or that had crumbled to some extent. Warner, the England captain, later gave glowing accolades to a bowler whom he faced on numerous occasions:

"Colin Blythe of Kent was the very model of what a slow left-hand bowler should be. No finer bowler of his kind has ever appeared. Peel, Briggs, Peate, Rhodes, and J.J. Ferris were in their day great bowlers, but he would be a rash man who would aver that even Peel, for instance, was a greater bowler than Blythe. On a sticky wicket Blythe did exactly what he liked with the ball, and on wickets which favoured the batsman I have seen him keep runs down and get men out as well."

One of his most significant attributes was his ability to vary the pace of the ball, and Warner pronounced that every slow left hander had of necessity to cultivate such 'flight.' Blythe discussed this attribute himself and thus provided a small insight into his success:

"Bowling an occasional ball from a yard or two behind the crease is a very good plan to adopt, and by bowling to a quick-footed batsman a slow left hander will learn that he will have to bowl slightly faster to some batsmen than to others."

However, in 1901 Blythe's talent was in its infancy and Warner suggested seven rules for the embryo Blythe to remember. Rules that would put him in good stead during his later career:

1. Obtain a through command of length, as it is no good varying pace and flight without a good length.
2. Try not to be put off if you are hit.
3. Perseverance and patience are essential.
4. Never be annoyed if catches are missed, as they will be caught in the end.
5. Don't worry too much about breaking the ball, as this happens naturally with a left hander. Bowl the ball that comes with the arm every now and then, twice in three or four overs - Blythe bowled a distinct swerver with the new ball, and it was then more frequent.
6. Keep your arm as high as possible.
7. No two batsmen play exactly alike, so alter your field to suit his style.

This was sound advice and the young player had come to the attention of some 'big names' within the game and soon went on a trip. Meanwhile, at the start of the 1901 season Blythe still lived with his family at 26 Wotton Road, Deptford - a thoroughfare of terraced houses which ran down from the junction of Evelyn and Prince Streets then south-westwards to Edward Street (once called Loving Edward's Lane).

It seems that at this stage he was unsure of his new career, since like his father he described himself as an "engineer fitter" and not a professional cricketer. Indeed, he maintained such work on a permanent basis during the closed season, and continued to live with his family other than when he was boarding-out during the cricket season.

By all accounts the Blythes were well known in the locality for their lively behaviour, and Colin lived there with his parents and ten siblings including Jessie a telephone operator, Florrie a cashier, and his brother Walter who was a general labourer, whilst his last two sisters Mabel Constance (Connie) and Nellie were born at this time. No doubt the level of excitement was raised with some news during the autumn of that year.

At this point it helps to consider the basic history of test cricket. There were numerous gentlemen's tours but the first test is regarded to have been Australia v England in Melbourne in 1877, followed by several reciprocal matches. Some of these were arranged and captained by gentlemen and were only raised to test status at a future date.

Lord Harris the founding father of Kent was captain of England during games in Melbourne in 1878-79 and at the Kennington Oval in 1880. In fact the promotion of the game was carried out by Charles Alcock secretary of Surrey (and founder of the F.A. Cup), and it was he who presided over the first Ashes contest played there in 1882.

W.G. Grace then featured as captain of England on various tours and as stated MacLaren was captain in Australia in 1897-98. This was followed by a tour to South Africa under Lord Hawke in 1898-99 whereas Grace and MacLaren captained England at home against Australia in 1899. With such international cricket well under way Blythe was presented with a fortuitous circumstance at the start of the new century.

THE MACLAREN TOUR

The Melbourne Cricket Club invited the M.C.C. to send a team however they declined, thus Archie MacLaren of Lancashire organised what was to be the last private tour of Australia. And what a tour it was to be. However, in some quarters there was dissent regarding his selection procedures and this affected the cricket - but not the social aspect.

In particular, Yorkshire believed that he had a weakened side and refused to allow their players to participate thereby ruling out George Hirst one of the greatest all-rounders, Wilfred Rhodes the left-arm bowler, and Stanley Jackson an associate of Churchill at Harrow and another all-rounder. Fry and Ranjitsinhji of Sussex were also unavailable.

This presented MacLaren with a problem most particularly in the bowling department thus he called Blythe up for the tour, which was certainly an unexpected baptism on the international stage. Although Blythe had done well, he was presented with an opportunity both sporting and social that he could only have dreamed of two years earlier.

Up to that stage he had made his mark in Kent and on the county scene, but it was this tour that brought him to prominence in the eyes of the press and the public. There seems little doubt he considered it a great privilege to play for England, likewise to travel to the other side of the world and indulge in numerous new experiences.

During the early 20th century an engine fitter had little chance of raising the funds for such travel, and the bowler was almost certainly overcome with great excitement at the prospect. In addition, he was to meet all kinds of new people from both different cultures and classes mixing with them to a considerable degree.

He did not take such an opportunity lightly and took in every detail of his first overseas experience savouring the travel, the cricket, the people, and the natural wonders he witnessed on the way.

Perhaps for some of his team-mates (who were more privileged) it was less of a revelation, but it appears that the whole team had a greatly enjoyable time and were like celebrities arriving in a foreign land.

So, what of the cricket? There has been considerable debate about Blythe's fitness for international cricket and test matches. Some state that he was ill and was thus left out of games, whilst others speculate that he found the pressure was too much for him due to a highly sensitive temperament.

Such a discussion appears to have the cart before the horse, since it would be correct to say that international sport is of itself highly demanding and many have succumbed under the pressure. This is true of cricket and of most other sports, and those who maintain complete success at the highest level (over a long period) are often in the minority.

Certainly where international leather on willow is concerned there have been many factors that determine selection. Any player is simply one of a team and selected regarding ability, fitness, and place within the squad or even on a personal whim of the selectors. It seems true of most tours that there are conflicting opinions as to who is best for the job.

In terms of bowling a number of players would seem an obvious choice and some decision had to be made as regarding selection. After all there were just eleven or so places, and there were a number of good bowlers in the country all with their own vagaries in terms of ability.

However, regarding Blythe the figures speak for themselves as he took part in nineteen test matches during his career. There are many who would aspire to such a record but there is another factor not to be missed. In the games where Blythe was able to perform England invariably won the match and with a considerable degree of panache.

The latter point clearly needs to emphasised, namely that when Blythe performed England won. This alone highlights his exceptional talent and makes it a complete non sequitur to suggest he failed in any way on the world stage. The match statistics dispute any negative assertions showing that he out-bowled many of his contemporaries.

Thus Blythe joined the MacLaren XI to Australia in late 1901 and took his place in a team of some considerable talent. In the absence of any other options he appeared in all five of the test matches, his team-mates coming from most of the counties around the country:

S.F. Barnes, H.G. Garnett, and J.T. Tyldesley all played as colleagues of MacLaren at Lancashire, J.R. Gunn and A.O. Jones were from Nottingham, and A.F.A. Lilley and W.G. Quaife came from Warwickshire. The others being C.P. McGahey (Essex), G.L. Jessop (Gloucester), C. Robson (Hants), L.C. Braund (Somerset), and T.W. Hayward (Surrey).

Without doubt the main omission was Wilfred Rhodes who had taken 261 wickets in 1900 and 251 in 1901, however MacLaren was vindicated in his choice through the selection of Sydney Barnes - prior to the tour the latter bowler appeared in just a handful of games for Lancashire but proved to be both a revelation and a great success.

MacLaren & Co. sailed on the noble R.M.S. "Omrah" (1899) from Tilbury on 29 September under T.H. Ruthven with 550 passengers. The route was via the Suez Canal and Blythe went cabin class, whilst victuals were taken on board from Mount Lavinia Hotel during a stop-over in Colombo.

Several diversions were arranged to pass the time and there was a grand sports day in the Indian Ocean on 30 October, the meeting of the O.A.C. being held on the "Omrah U(E)psom Downs" for all passengers. There were no prizes or gambling but the international was a benefit for Lawford (to have his hair cut) under the auspices of the clerk of the weather! Events included cockfighting, tug of war, quarter mile race, prehistoric tournament, a grand-national, and a wheelbarrow race.

No doubt Blythe and his colleagues entered into the spirit of things and were well relaxed upon their arrival. After a brief stop at Fremantle they sailed into Largs Bay and up the Port River to Adelaide in early November, whereas Mr. J. Creswell and members of the Australian Association and Melbourne C.C. came out in a launch to meet them.

Once the yellow flag was hauled down confirming a clean bill of health, the party boarded, and with hearty handshakes welcomed the Englishmen to Australia. The vessel then docked at the pier and the team later reached the South Australian Hotel where a formal welcome was extended.

AN INTERVIEW

At this point they got down to some serious cricket issues and MacLaren tried to clarify certain salient points. In particular he talked of the band of cricketers under his control and the eager reporters asked him to elucidate matters - "You had some difficulty in getting your side together?"

"Yes," responded MacLaren, "but I have succeeded in getting a very good combination, though there were not a few who were sorry to see me meet with so much success, and many were the attempts made to discount our chances of making a respectable show against Australia. The Yorkshire county committee threw a big obstacle in the way when they commanded Rhodes and Hirst to decline my invitation. I do not think Rhodes would have been difficult on your Australian wickets, but Hirst is a bowler who has vastly improved on his form in 1897."

This matter dealt with the reporters asked another pressing point, "The team is claimed by several English writers as being a non-representative one?" MacLaren put forward a firm rebuttal stating that seven of the side had played in the last game against Australia, whilst even Stoddart did not improve on such a record back in 1896.

Every professional he invited accepted the invitation the only exceptions being Hirst and Rhodes whilst of the amateurs Fry, Ranjitsinhji, and Foster would have certainly strengthened the batting. Unfortunately, all three of them were only stopped from coming by unforeseen engagements. There was then a most pertinent question regarding bowling, "Do you consider you have a side together suitable for Australian wickets?"

"In selecting the men," stated MacLaren, "I took full advantage of my experience gained during two Australian tours. I have not brought a bowler of the remarkable accuracy and length of J.T. Hearne, for the simple reason that a dodgy bowler, one who will try experiments, would prove of much greater service. As a bowling side it is certainly the best available, and I think the best possible."

Regarding the field he added, "If they show the form they did last year, you will say that they comprise the finest fielding combination that has ever visited Australia. They may miss catches, but I do not think they will, at any rate not after they get used to the Australian light, for there is a good deal of difference between your light and what we are used to in England."

The questions came at full tilt like a fast delivery down the crease and the Australians tried to draw MacLaren out, stating, "You have a lot of variety in batting and bowling?" His answer was then one of the most revealing regarding the team with a detailed assessment of their strengths:

"In batting we have an extraordinary hitter in Jessop, a great punisher and at the same time a brilliant batsman. We have Tyldesley, whose style is most attractive; Garnett who will no doubt remind the Australians of their William Bruce, a crisp and wristy left-hander; McGahey, who can play both a brisk and defensive game as the occasion demands; while there are Hayward and the rest down to the stonewaller Quaife to steady the team. One of the drawbacks of the previous England Eleven was the want of a hitter like Jessop, the want of an absolute defensive man like Quaife, and the want of a good variety of bowlers. We possess all three qualifications. In my opinion, the Australian public will be particularly pleased with our cricket."

He further believed that due to a dry home season the players were well prepared for the Australian climate and wickets, whereas he concluded by answering another outstanding and yet to be answered criticism, namely, "Some surprise was caused over the inclusion of Barnes?"

"Barnes," said MacLaren, "impressed me very much indeed as a bowler. He is a bit fast, and I shall be very much surprised if he doesn't perform well, though I don't expect any of our bowlers to get a better average than 20 runs per wicket, which is very good in Australia. Blythe is a good steady bowler. Braund mixes them a lot, and so do Gunn, Jones, and McGahey. During the season just closed in England the bowlers went in a good deal for the leg theory; that is bowling wide on the leg and having the majority of the fieldsmen posted on the leg side. Our bowlers are not so pronounced as that. They mostly stick at a spot between the legs and the leg stump."

Meanwhile, another paper announced, "Bowler Blythe of MacLaren's team promises to be the merest passenger, as far as their batting is concerned. The tenth man in most All-England elevens has rarely given the Australians any trouble, but Blythe is a phenomenal duffer. During the past English season when big scores were the rule rather than the exception, Blythe made an average of six (although the statistics state seven)."

MacLaren had tried to put a good spin on the prospects of his team and their abilities in the face of considerable criticism at home, indeed he may have been confident in his assessment. However, the Australians (as ever) had several different ideas on the matter and the tour was not the success that MacLaren had clearly hoped for.

One issue regarding this might have been the number of games. Whilst the Australians focussed in on the important test matches the English played numerous back to back games around the country.

They arrived in town after town with much fanfare and indulged in a cricketing fest combined with a large degree of entertaining and socialising. It seems certain that in the modern era these activities would have been frowned upon, and as the test matches fell to the Australians the press at home would have engaged in a writing apoplexy on the matter.

COUNTRY CRICKET

Naturally the first game of the tour was played against South Australia at the Adelaide Oval on 9-12 November. However, it was not a good start and MacLaren's XI lost by 233 runs although Blythe managed to take five for 45 runs in the second as well as a catch. In fact, Jessop made the highest score of 38 and in the second innings the total was just 86.

There was an improvement in fortunes against Victoria at the Melbourne Cricket Ground on 15-19 November, when Blythe took three for 37 and the visitors won by 118 runs. On the second day there was a dinner for the players given by the Melbourne Club at Scott's Hotel.

Regrettably, neither of these games furnished any real information as to the capabilities of the team thus they entered into their third engagement as an unknown quantity. They were not alone in this respect and with the exception of Clem Hill none of the South Australians or Victorian players had shown good form. The problem was exacerbated by the fact that up to this point the wickets did not reach the required standard.

Blythe took some time out during his stay in Melbourne and travelled out to Caulfield, one of the city's premier race tracks. Whilst there he watched the fifth running of the Futurity Stakes which was a seven furlong weight-for-age thoroughbred race. Indeed, the first horse he backed in Australia was "Sir Foote" at odds of 40 to 10 and it won at a fine gallop.

At this time the weather had improved leaving every prospect of a good wicket for the next encounter in Sydney. The players sailed north on the "Omrah" which docked at Circular Quay, and were invited to a luncheon on board by the local manager of the Orient Pacific line and the ship's commander on Thursday, 21 November.

Soon afterwards they paid a visit to the Sydney Cricket Ground and were well impressed by the pitch, majestic pavilion, fine grandstands, and several other modern facilities. An inspection was also made of the wicket and it was noted that the light was better than for the previous games.

With these factors in mind MacLaren was confident that his team would show their strengths in terms of batting and fielding, but as often he had little to say about their bowling. A fine game was certainly in prospect and there was no doubt some degree of disappointment since Blythe, Garnett, and Robson were omitted from the team.

By all accounts the match against New South Wales at Sydney on 22-27 November was a splendidly fought contest. MacLaren was on fine form and made 145 runs in the first innings, whilst it looked like the home side would lose in the second innings but there was a rally from the likes of Noble (74) and Poidevin (151) to save the day.

The match began on a Friday and by the second day the attendance had reached 30,000, whereas W. Howell clean bowled Barnes with the last ball of the game in front of 8,000. As a result the New South Wales team won the contest by a small margin of just 53 runs.

The newspapers were pleased to observe that MacLaren had regained his health and fitness, but were concerned regarding the form of England with respect to the forthcoming test matches. In addition they speculated that their own players Monty Noble, Clem Hill, and Hugh Trumble were likely to select the Australian team for the first test, although Joe Darling would probably have to replace Hill in the side.

During this initial sojourn the visiting players were accorded with a large degree of hospitality thus Blythe received an honorary membership card for the Tattersalls Club, a racing, sporting, and social club found in the centre of the city since the mid-19th century.

However, the English side then disappeared into the hinterland at the end of the month for a long series of exhibition games against local opposition, but it may be questioned whether this was the best preparation.

The first game was against a Northern District 18 (Albion C.C.) at West Maitland just north of Sydney on 29-30 November. The players stayed at the Exchange Hotel and some 3,000 spectators turned up to see the home side put on a large score resulting in a draw. Tyldesley, Barnes, and Lilley stood out although Blythe and Quaife took most of the wickets.

Good weather prevailed and the team headed north to the newly built Imperial Hotel, Glen Innes near the border with Queensland. Blythe again took part in the match which started on 2 December and brought a large number of spectators from the surrounding locality.

The home side who were another district 18 batted first making a total of 141 runs - however, shortly after the England XI came in to bat there was "a hurricane of a storm" which suspended play.

In the evening the side were invited to "A Grand Smoke Concert" in the town hall which included a lengthy programme of comic song, recitation, and banjo. After such merriment the team had to arise the next morning and take to the crease again, but were undeterred and finished at 309 runs for seven wickets. The initial bowling was done by Blythe and Quaife with ten and seven wickets apiece and there was an innings victory.

The next contest was at the Moran Oval, Armidale just to the south and the players stayed at the historic Tattersalls Hotel in the town. Meanwhile, a flyer announced that it was "The Event of the Season."

Old England were to take on a New England side on 4-5 December with several local district players against a team which included amongst its number: "Jessop the greatest hitter in the World, Hayward and Tyldesley two of England's finest batsmen, Lilley the premier wicket keeper of the day, A.O. Jones, and other famous players."

Special trains were arranged from Tamworth and Guyra and play was to start at 11 a.m. each day. Despite a draw, the crowd weren't disappointed since Gunn scored 119 and Blythe took four for 4 runs, whilst the next morning the players had an invitation from Crompton & Co. Ltd. to join a driving party to the Gara Falls and Hillgrove Mines.

The falls consisted of a series of cascades with spectacular views, although the company purchased rights in 1900 and were developing a hydro-electric system to supply Armidale fifteen miles away. No doubt Blythe enjoyed the trip to this stunning scenery with a luncheon at Gara and in the afternoon went to the mines - Hillgrove being a gold mine from 1880-1920.

The extensive tour finished on the coast against a Newcastle 15 at the No. 1 Sports Ground on 7-9 December (13 to field). During the sojourn they stayed at the opulent Centennial Hotel which was established in 1888 and reputedly had the largest dining room north of Sydney.

This gave the footsore players a brief respite whereas MacLaren who was suffering from rheumatism, Hayward who was lame, and Blythe were left out of the team. In their two innings England put on over 500 runs and Newcastle a further 300 runs but the match ended in a draw.

Despite so many games there was time to spare and they travelled to the Carrington Hotel in Katoomba west of Sydney. The next day they visited the Jenolan Caves in the Blue Mountains a limestone-stalactite formation of exceptional beauty discovered in 1838, although new caves were found soon after their visit. They stayed at the eponymous J.C. hotel which included the N.S.W. "railway refreshment rooms" and left in some awe.

MacLaren's players had managed to avoid defeat against lesser opponents and prepared themselves for the greater challenge, thus they continued by train to Redfern Station, Sydney and were greeted by a large crowd. In fact it appeared the preparations were a success.

HIS FIRST TESTS

Geology was not necessarily the most apt groundwork for an important match, although no doubt the healthy country air had helped. Meanwhile, the first test took place at Sydney Cricket Ground on 13-16 December with Blythe in the side and the visitors won the toss.

On a good batting wicket they established a formidable score of 464 runs with MacLaren (116), Hayward (69), and Lilley (84) - the former two players reaching 1,000 test-runs during the innings. Blythe himself came in at the end and scored a best of 20 runs in just 40 minutes.

In reply Australia only managed 168 runs and Blythe took three for 26 although it was Barnes who took centre stage with five for 65. In the follow on the home side scored just 172 all out and Blythe improved taking four wickets for 30 runs. It was a convincing victory by an innings and 124 runs but needed to be savoured regarding later results.

This was a promising start for Blythe concerning his test career and in total he secured seven Australian wickets for just 56 runs, whilst he bowled both Trumper and Noble (caught by Lilley) in the second innings.

There were then two games near Sydney not involving Blythe. The first against a Goulburn 22 was won by six wickets and they stayed at the Royal Hotel. In the second they had a draw with a Bendigo United C.C. 18 at the Upper Reserve, and sojourned at the nearby Hotel Shamrock (built 1854) with its grand Victorian façade just across from Roseland Park.

The games took place at the end of December and the side went into the New Year in high spirits. At this stage Blythe headed the England bowling figures with 43 wickets for an average of just 9.9 runs.

The second test was at Melbourne on 1-4 January and the tourists stayed at the Oriental Hotel on Collins Street but were soon brought down to earth. In the first innings Australia put on 112 whereas England were all out for a dismal 61 runs. In the second innings the Australian tail-enders produced an amazing performance and Clem Hill scored 99, whereas the last two R.A. Duff and W.W. Armstrong added 104 and 45 runs apiece.

During this remarkable stand by the two young Australians there was a complaint from Jack Blackham that smoke from the nearby railway line was affecting their sight. One reporter suggested the railwaymen were doing it on purpose since they had placed a bet on the Englishmen to win.

Another asked why they might have done this? The reporter explained that during the carnival he was taking a walk in the Fitzroy Gardens and espied Blythe sitting there reading a book amongst the leafy greenery. No doubt the park reminded him of home and his facial expression suggested he was one of the nicest fellows in the English team.

Indeed, "At all events, looking at him there, so immersed in the pages of his book, one would have said, 'One thing is certain, the coming test match is not worrying Blythe.'" Perhaps on this basis the locals were lulled into thinking that the English were imbued with supreme confidence, however Australia eventually added 353 runs to their total and England were all out for 175, thus the game was lost by 299 runs.

Blythe managed to take five wickets but the real talking point regarding the game was "the over-use of Barnes." He was most prolific with six for 42 and seven for 121, but MacLaren misjudged his stamina and he was quite exhausted after bowling sixteen then sixty-four overs. In the next test he managed just seven overs and retired hurt in the second innings.

The side continued to do well against local opposition and initially won a game at Central Park, Stawell situated inland from Melbourne. There was then a second contest against a Ballarat side and they were met by officers of the club at the Western Railway Station at 12.50 p.m.

A game was played at the Eastern Oval involving eighteen players whilst "the attendance was large and among those present were Harry Smith and

'Syers' who had taken part in the match played by Ballarat against H.H. Stephenson's team in 1862." Hayward and MacLaren made fine centuries whilst Blythe bowled but did not bat and it finished in a draw.

Soon afterwards they returned to the Adelaide Oval for the third test on 17-23 January. On this occasion Blythe only managed one wicket although he did put on 10 runs, but the side slumped and lost by four wickets while the continental climate gave little chance of "rain stopped play."

This was followed with three more local games against a Country XI in Melbourne, New South Wales in Sydney, and a Bathurst (W. District) 18 when the side stayed at the historic Royal Hotel built during the 1840s. Blythe was rested during all of these three matches whereas each of them resulted in good victories for the tourists.

This should have prepared them for the fourth test in Sydney on 14-18 February, but again Blythe took just two wickets during the game and there was a seven wicket defeat. England scored 317 in their first innings and Australia matched this with 299 runs, whereas England collapsed totally in the second innings and were all out for just 99.

Blythe had more success in a game against Victoria back at Melbourne on 22-26 February and took five wickets in all, the Englishmen winning the game by eight wickets. During the match there was some good scoring and MacLaren made a century with Quaife and Tyldesley on 45 apiece.

Matters improved to a degree in the final test at Melbourne on 1-5 March and Australia began with 144. Blythe was back on form and clean bowled the opener V.T. Trumper for 27 runs after 34 minutes. England, however, did not press home the advantage and made 189 allowing Australia to put on the pressure with a second innings of 255 runs.

The run chase was on and as the wickets fell it looked increasingly unlikely that MacLaren's side would make their target. Blythe came in at the end and reached 5 not out in twelve minutes, but the other ten were gone and the total was just 178 - some 32 runs short of victory. The last five put on an extra 50 and Monty Noble of Australia took six for 98 runs.

Blythe consoled himself with an interest in horse racing and made a trip to Flemington Park with its tiled terrace and carriage paddock. "Revenue" had won the Melbourne Cup there just before the team's arrival, and looked like a good bet for a small and leafy flutter.

The autumn meeting witnessed another premier race the Australian Cup which was started as early as 1863. There was a big field and "Revenue" was clear favourite at odds of 5 to 4 on, but Blythe chose to back "Blue Metal" an outsider at 60 to 3 which eventually (and naturally) won the race by a short head - the favourite, meanwhile, finished way down the field.

The tour was wound down with a trip to Broken Hill and the players were greeted - then retired to the Freemasons and Grand Hotels. A reception at the town hall was cancelled due to the length of the journey and the game was against a Barrier Ranges side at the McCulloch Park (Oval). There was some disappointment since MacLaren and Hayward did not appear but the weather was warm and breezy and significantly free of any dust.

The crowd was some 1,000 in number and Robson the captain of England decided to bat. The main feature of the match was the batting by the home captain Caust who scored 99 not out and the game ended in a draw. There was also a victory against South Australia at Adelaide on 14-19 March but the next day the "Omrah" began the long trip back to England.

THE ASSOCIATION GAME

It was assumed that this was the end to competitive affairs, but during a stop at Fremantle (the harbour for Perth) there was an unusual invitation to play a local team although this was not regarding cricket.

The Western Australia Association was formed in 1896 and it was Aleck Peters who organised games against an English cricket-side in 1902 (and 1904). Fremantle Wanderers were the premier team at the time winning the local league on four occasions, however they declined to take part in the game and this had a definite effect on the outcome.

The English side were superior to the home team all round and included Jessop in goal, Lilley and McGahey as the backs, Tyldesley Quaife (captain) and Garnett as half-backs, and Jones Blythe Braund Gunn and Hayward as forwards. The Western Australia team were led by G. Hatton and the game was played out at the local 'oval.'

Several hundred spectators turned up for the contest and the performance of Quaife was good enough for an England v Scotland fixture. Indeed, the combined effort produced some of the best moves seen in the state, whilst a lack of collective effort by the opponents produced their downfall.

The England cricketers won by a 4-0 score line and Quaife was only too pleased to help develop local soccer talents - in particular by giving some instruction in the benefits of the passing game. Clearly they did not miss the help of C.B. Fry who was busy with Southampton F.C. at the time. [1]

---

[1] Charles Burgess Fry (1872-1956) played soccer at Repton and Oxford and joined the Corinthians amateurs in 1894. He then played for Southampton v Tottenham in 1900, and also in all eight of their Cup games during 1901-02. This included the Cup Final replay at the Crystal Palace which was lost to Sheffield United however he was clearly most famous as a cricketer.

The English team were then accompanied by their opponents to the mail steamer and given a hearty send-off which terminated with a rendition of "Auld Lang Syne." Afterwards they had some time to rest whilst the press used this brief interlude to sharpen their caustic pens. It was clearly a blow to MacLaren's pride and all his fine rhetoric of six months earlier that the headline stated, *"A Voyage in Vain."*

The general opinion of the tour was that they would have made a better show but for the regrettable break-down of Barnes in the third test. There was every hope that his knee would recover on returning to Manchester so that he was ready to bowl for Lancashire, and in fact whilst undergoing "the hot-air treatment" he had lost a stone in weight!

In general, MacLaren was considered a good manager, although he was in error in working Barnes to a standstill in the second test. Most agreed that Braund was the top all-rounder and with MacLaren and Jones in the slips the fielding was certainly the best in the world.

Jessop, Quaife, and Tyldesley backed them up well in the outfield and in all they were the best fielding side to visit Australia. Lilley had established himself as the premier wicket keeper within the game, especially with the departure of the Australian J.M. Blackham from the arena.

MacLaren had not been successful during the English season, but was almost unstoppable on Australian soil and was by far the best of the English batsmen scoring five centuries in total.

In fact, a century was expected from him every time he played at Sydney and in terms of runs he finished 20 per innings ahead of Tom Hayward. Despite this the batting was not as expected and both Jones and Tyldesley disappointed, whilst the famous Jessop did not score above 35 in his nine innings nor did he reach three figures in the minor matches.

Possibly the altered conditions of both wicket and light went against his reputation, and many who came to see him left disappointed as a result. Despite this he made some admirable strokes (but some not) and Trumble described his batting as "north, south, east, and west."

Such a story of the English batting was true for most of the side although Lilley showed a degree of pluck, whilst Garnett arrived with the reputation of the best left-hander in England. However, Blythe had a better batting average in all matches than Garnett did in all of his first class games!

Whatever the considerations and disputations the final results were there for all to see. MacLaren's England had won their first test with the help of Blythe but then succumbed to the Aussie wave with three bad defeats and a narrow reverse at the end. The series was lost four to one and no drubbing on the soccer field could put matters right.

When MacLaren arrived he stated any weakness might be in the bowling department, but this proved to be wrong and it was the batting that failed. In terms of the bowling Blythe and Gunn did well but it was Braund who had done the bulk of the work bowling 3,815 balls in the main games. In terms of the averages Barnes was top with 41 wickets at 16.80 runs followed by Blythe with 34 wickets at 20.91 runs.

In particular it was hard to explain the collapse that took place on their favourite Sydney ground in the fourth test. That being said the tour was undoubtedly a great social success and the Australians wished them well as they journeyed home to prepare for the summer season, and, "A renewal of the struggle for the time-honoured 'Ashes' of cricket."

CHAPTER 5

The New World

Having arrived back in England in April 1902 there was little time for Blythe to settle down from his adventures, although he may have spent some time relating his travels to his family. It was an English springtime, the bails were on, and the cricket season was about to begin.

During the next two years Blythe and Kent continued to improve thus cementing their niche position within county cricket, as the bowler steadily notched up some impressive figures. In fact, during 1902 he played in all of Kent's twenty-two county games and took 127 wickets whilst the team won eight and lost the same number. Cuthbert Burnup also remained in form and scored 1,000 runs for the fourth season running.

There were a number of good cricket games during the season, a season when Yorkshire did the treble winning their third championship in a row. However, Kent batted off to a sticky start playing some difficult games in May at Lord's, Leyton, Old Trafford, Park Avenue, and the Oval without securing one single victory.

They then had their annual game against the M.C.C. at Lord's on 29-31 May with a Kent side that included Maurice Bonham-Carter. Blythe was off to a good start on what became one of his most prominent grounds, and took four wickets for 61 runs then an impressive five wickets for 27 runs, although Kent lost the fixture by one wicket.

He then took part in his first varsity match when the Kent side travelled down to Oxford on 5-7 June to play a game at University Parks. The home side included Cloudesley Marsham who was shortly to become captain of Kent, and also Bonham-Carter who was related to the Norman family of Bromley within that county (also Kent players).

The game itself was undistinguished and the weather resulted in a draw, since there was no play on day two and only thirty minutes on the third. Blythe no doubt spent his time indulging in the dreaming spires and courts of the various Oxford colleges, ambling around at his hotel, or socialising in the pavilion between rain showers.

However, there was one piece of action recorded in the score book which considering the nature of Blythe's bowling was surprising, and indicates he could inject a degree of pace into his disguised ball. Kent went in first and made a creditable 275, whereas Oxford began their reply with the openers Marsham and E.W. Dillon (another Kent captain).

The latter led the Oxford attack and had made 42 runs when a long ball from Blythe turned as it caught the ground, ran up his bat, and hit him full in the face. This was in the days before helmets and chin guards thus Dillon retired from the game hurt, and Oxford had reached just 78 runs when the impending rain eventually stopped play.

Success finally came at the County Ground, Worcester on 9-11 June when Kent put on a total of 218 runs the main batsmen being Burnup, Seymour, Mason, and Marsham. The bowlers then contributed well and Worcester were all out for 112 runs with Blythe taking a good six wickets for just 43. Kent only managed 138 in the second, but they had the measure of their opponents and finally won the game by 98 runs.

Next there came a series of home fixtures in June and during Tonbridge Week they beat Gloucester at the Angel Ground by an innings and 23 runs. During the match Blythe took his tally to 300 wickets in first class cricket and also scored a creditable 23 runs before he was caught. His batting was clearly improving and in the return game at Ashley Down, Bristol, at the month's end - he managed an identical batting score.

Tunbridge Wells Week followed in July and there was a mixed bag of results, although Blythe greatly enjoyed himself with the ball at the Nevill Ground. The first game against Hampshire was won by an innings and 195 runs with Blythe taking five for 50 followed by three for 48, the other two bowlers being Bradley and Mason.

The Kent side then lost the game to Sussex on 17-19 July by one wicket although Blythe took three for 48 and six for 45 runs. The visitors included the idiosyncratic polymorph Fry and the regal Ranjitsinhji, whereas a duel was developing which brought some harsh words at a latter date.

In fact, Blythe delivered a deceptive ball on the leg side but Fry came too far forward and was promptly stumped by Huish on 27 runs. In the second innings there was a repetition of events and Fry was caught and bowled by Blythe on 24 runs - no doubt to his considerable chagrin. Meanwhile the bowler also took Ranjitsinhji the captain of Sussex for nought.

Another good performance followed against Somerset at Mote Park on 28-29 July when Kent won by an innings and 102 runs. Burnup, Marsham and Humphreys took the total to 299, whilst the visitors only managed 100 even though their side included Len Braund and Sammy Woods.

During the first innings Blythe took three wickets for 43 runs, but the honours went to his team mate Alec Hearne (of the Catford School) who notched up seven wickets for just 34 runs - including his 1,000th wicket. However, it was Blythe who shone in the second innings follow on as he took a record of eight for 42 runs in just 12.4 overs.

Blythe was clearly entering a purple patch and Somerset were all out for 97 runs whilst the game was concluded in just two days. For most bowlers this might have been the apex of the season, but in Blythe's case there was still more ammunition in the spin clip and a week later he took part in a game that literally stunned the spectators.

CANTERBURY WEEK

August had arrived with all its promise of fine weather and good wickets and Canterbury Week was well under way. There was a carnival atmosphere in the Augustine city and the Old Stagers brushed down their costumes for the evening's performance, in the distance there was the faint murmur of a violin, but the sweetest music was definitely on the pitch.

St. Lawrence was decked out in all its glory with tents, pavilions, and other regalia of the time whereas Edwardian spectators arrived in their modern attire as a new age dawned. An expectant atmosphere rent the air with no hint of a memorial, no inkling of conflict (except of leather on willow), and a reassuring oak to stop any unforeseen scoring by the opponents.

There was a draw in the first game against Essex as the spectators enjoyed a batting bonanza, with the two teams recording 600 runs between them in the first innings. Burnup and Marsham were in fine form for Kent putting on 100 runs, whereas the stockbroker A.P. Lucas and Fane, Perrin, and McGahey did well for Essex. Rain prevented play on two occasions but Blythe took his career wicket tally up to 350 wickets.

However, the real sensation occurred during the match against Surrey on 7-9 August, when Kent produced an unparalleled performance which was presumably within that locality - "the shape of things to come."

Kent won the toss and their batsmen were soon free-scoring with some fine personal totals viz. Marsham (92), Hearne (73), Burnup (60), and the captain Mason (45). Blythe came in at the end and put on just 8 before he was run out but the total was by then an admirable 389 runs.

Surrey, who continued to stutter against their rivals Kent, came to the crease and made just 139 in their reply - the wickets falling to Blythe (4-69) and Mason and Humphreys who took three apiece. Naturally there was a follow on and matters did not look good for Surrey although there was no inkling of the humiliation that was soon to come.

T.W. Hayward and E.G. Hayes led the batting for Surrey and took the score up to 55 runs for one wicket. However, to the astonishment of the spectators Blythe then took five wickets for 3 runs and Mason four wickets for 1 run, a tally that included six disappointing ducks.

Indeed, the Surrey side were all out for 59 runs which was one of the worst collapses in county cricket during the championship's history. Blythe eventually recorded five for 32 although Mason's record was better, while Kent naturally won by an innings and 191 runs - no doubt celebrating in some style at the end of the carnival week.

Similar form continued and Kent also beat Worcester by nine wickets at the Angel Ground on 18-20 August, Blythe taking an impressive five for 60 and six for 61 which was clearly a one man job.

The bowler then renewed his acquaintance with old friends from Australia as the Kent side took on the Aussies at the St. Lawrence Ground on 21-23 August. They did well against a national team which included players such as Monty Noble and V.T. Trumper although they lost by 89 runs, whereas Blythe took six wickets during the two innings. Kent's season ended with a defeat against Yorkshire at Catford and a draw with Sussex at Hove.

Blythe did not receive a call up for England against Australia in the test matches that summer, despite the fact the captain was his former boss and promoter Archie MacLaren. It is of some interest that although the side now included the batsmen Fry, Ranjitsinhji, and Stanley Jackson (and the bowler Rhodes) the outcome was not much better.

England only managed a victory in the last game at the Oval and lost the series. In fact, much was made of selection problems during the previous tour to the Antipodes and MacLaren's personal choices, but even with the missing players the performances were basically the same.

Meanwhile, Burnup was on fine form and secured a place in Lord Hawke's side which toured New Zealand, with some games in Australia, in 1902-03. Warner was appointed captain but the games were not of test status.

THE 1903 SEASON

The next year Blythe stepped forward and (again) played in all twenty-two county matches for Kent, taking his wicket tally to 142 for the season. The side produced a similar kind of display and won seven of their games but lost six, thereby establishing themselves further in the championship.

With such analysis the pinnacle was yet to be reached but certainly most believed it was just a matter of time and application. Meanwhile, Fielder the fast bowler had made just two appearances against Essex and the M.C.C. in the last three seasons, but now replaced Mr. Bradley in the team.

It was a particularly wet summer and this favoured the approach of Blythe who could apply himself on both the awkward and the good wicket, whilst Burnup took over as captain for just a single season.

The first game was against Nottinghamshire at the Private Banks Sports Ground in Catford on 21-23 May however Kent lost by four wickets. In fact, the opponents included his old team-mates A.O. Jones and J.R. Gunn from the MacLaren tour of Australia.

There was then an interesting fixture against the M.C.C. at Lord's on 28-29 May, which again revealed the new circles in which Blythe had the privilege of moving (the ball). The M.C.C. went in to bat and that heroic cricketing figure W.G. Grace scored 11, whilst Sir Arthur Conan Doyle made just 3 taking the total up to 177 runs. On this occasion Blythe took 0-36 in ten overs and the wickets fell to both Fairservice and Fielder.

Clearly the omens were looking good for Kent after the introduction of players into the team with such highly suitable cognomens! The visitors then replied with 147 runs, whereas Blythe added a useful 11 before being bowled down by J.T. (Jack) Hearne and caught by W.G. Grace.

These were certainly names to conjure with in terms of ball juggling since Jack Hearne was the master of the off break and almost unplayable on a bowling wicket (career total 3,061 wickets), whereas W.G. Grace was one of the most successful all-round amateurs from 1865-1908 (career total 2,809 wickets). Such figures provided suitable aspirations for Blythe and without the intervention of war he may well have overtaken them.

In the second innings the M.C.C. made 145 runs including Grace with 31 and Conan Doyle on 16, however Kent soon chased down the requisite total of 176 runs and won the game by three wickets.

Many records were to follow but there was a disappointing draw at the Angel Ground on 18-20 June. Kent won the toss and went in to bat and made a useful 148 whereas the opponents Gloucester were dismissed for a dismal score of 31 runs. Blythe took two wickets for 12 however the hero was Alec Hearne whose tally came to eight wickets for just 15, whilst matters could have been worse but for four extras.

Kent added another 60 runs in the second innings, but Gloucester were then saved from a complete humiliation by the weather with no play being possible on the third and final day.

Soon afterwards some visitors from the New World brought a distraction from the pressures of county cricket. In America cricket never really caught on, but there was a marked exception in Philadelphia where the first class game was played from 1878 up until the First War.

Four main clubs contested regional games namely Germantown (1854), Philadelphia (1854), Merion (1865), and Belmont (1874), whilst there were other smaller clubs and college teams. However, the level of competition was quite poor thus a number of reciprocal tours were arranged.

The Philadelphian side had its first trip to England in 1897 although this was somewhat of a disappointment followed by a second visit in 1903. On the latter occasion fifteen first class games were organised in total which included fixtures against Oxford and Cambridge Universities, the M.C.C., a Plum Warner XI, and numerous county matches.

The most successful and well-known character within the team was John Barton King. Unlike his contemporaries he was not a gentleman of leisure, but his talents were so much in demand that his colleagues secured him "a paying position" allowing him more time to pursue the game.

He began his career with a local side Tioga in 1888, but joined the more senior Belmont team in 1896 then went on all three of the Philadelphian tours over to England. His most successful visit was in fact during 1903 and in the game when his team beat Lancashire he took five wickets for 7 runs in a spell of only three overs (his total nine for 62).

Often referred to as "the Bob Hope of cricket" he gave a lengthy after-dinner speech during the final tour in 1908, continually punctuated with laughter and merriment. His batting achievements were exceptional but he was best known for the introduction of swing bowling or "the angler," a talent which he learnt when pitching up a baseball.

Consequently, the Gentlemen of Philadelphia descended on the Foxgrove Road Ground in Beckenham on 25-27 June 1903. They were certainly not to be taken lightly since ten years earlier they beat a full strength Australian side which stopped off to see them after a visit to England.

During the latter the Philadelphians set a staggering total of 525 on the small ground at Belmont, where the grass was somewhat long and the ball skidded away. King used his swinger to good effect and took five for 78 to secure a good victory by an innings and 68 runs, whereas the Australian captain wryly remarked - "They class with England's best."

Such class was still in evidence at Foxgrove Road and Philadelphia put on 311 runs with Bart King on 47 and J.A. Lester on 70. Blythe managed only one wicket for 82 although Fielder fast bowled four for 51.

Kent then replied with a total of 176 runs on the second day and in the second innings they restricted the Philadelphians to just 116. During the innings Blythe took two for 31, and his delight was no doubt intense when he caught and bowled Bart King on only 7 runs.

The tourists were all out near the end of the second day thus the night watchmen were Blythe and Fairservice who added 10 runs. Next morning the former managed to reach 20 before he was caught by Jordan off one of King's swingers - Kent lost the game by 62 runs however friendships were cemented producing some beneficial results.

James Blyth - was born in Edinburgh, but was a gunner on "a ship of the line" from 1793-1813

Chatham, Kent

His residence from c.1807 - A view showing the town, with the River Medway and dockyards beyond

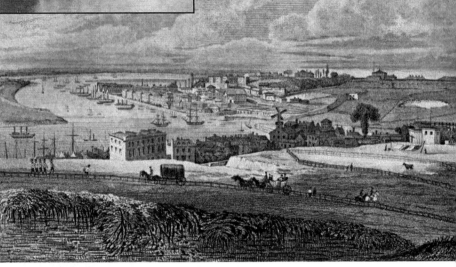

Royal Naval Asylum, Greenwich

Colin Blyth was a pupil from 1816

The school was on the left side, but was enlarged and later housed the National Maritime Museum

5-8 Ffinch Terrace, Brockley Lane
(Upper Brockley Road)

Colin Blyth(e) made his money in silk and lived in the far-end house in the mid-1860s

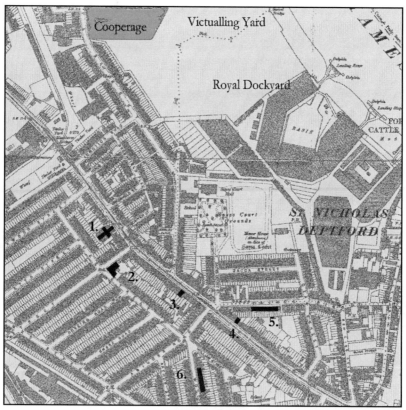

Deptford (1890s)

1 - St. Luke's below Gosterwood Street   **2** - Duke Street School on Rolt Street
3 - 78 Evelyn Street - birthplace of C. Blythe   **4** - 206 Evelyn Street (1881)
5 - New Row (later Prince Street)   **6** - Wotton Road (1892-1904)

New Row built in the 18th century

Home of Maurice Dready "leading man of stores" in the Victualling Yard, and of son Joseph Dready a cooper there

Evelyn Street, Deptford

A view from the corner of Prince Street up to the Blythes' home at No. 206

REGISTRATION DISTRICT				Greenwich					
1879 BIRTH in the Sub-district of St Paul Deptford				in the Counties of Kent and Surrey					
Columns:-	1	2	3	4	5	6	7	8	9	10

No	When and where born	Name, if any	Sex	Name and surname of father	Name, surname and maiden surname of mother	Occupation of father	Signature, description and residence of informant	When registered	Signature of registrar	Name entered after registration
95	Twelfth May 1879 206 Evelyn Street	Colin	Boy	Walter Blythe	Elizabeth Blythe formerly Dready	Engine fitter	E. Blythe mother 206 Evelyn Street Deptford	Eighth July 1879	My Hough Registrar	

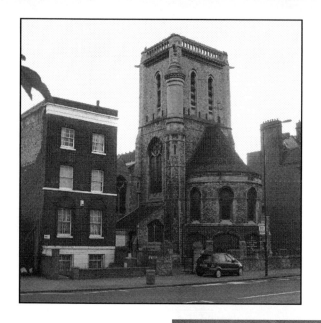

St. Luke's, Evelyn Street (built 1872)

Blythe was baptized there with his sister Jessie in 1881

Woolwich Arsenal

The brass foundry by Beresford Gate was built in 1716-17

Beyond were Dial Square, the works, and Street No. 1 to the Thames

Rectory Field, Blackheath

Rugby in 1858 and Kent C.C.C. from 1887-1971

Blythe was "discovered" there in July 1897

Back: Tyldesley, Braund, Garnett, Maj. Wardill (sec.), Robson, Barnes, Blythe, Gunn, Quaife **Front:** Jessop, Hayward, MacLaren (capt.), Jones, McGahey, Lilley

Note Blythe's distinctive dress which was also apparent during other tours

Sydney Cricket Ground, November 1901

The game against N.S.W. was lost by 53 runs, but there was an innings victory in the first test and Blythe made 20 runs with seven wickets

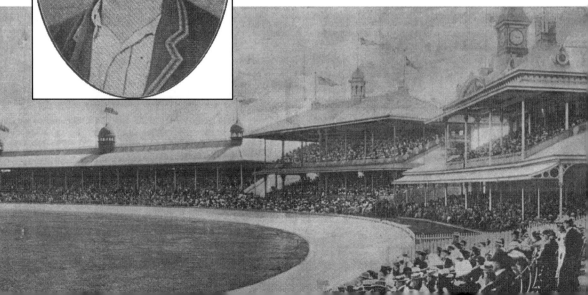

Above: Adelaide and Sydney Tests

Coming off with S. Barnes and some pensive
moments watching Lilley and Jones - both
games were lost in Jan-Feb 1902

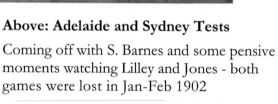

Below: Perth - the soccer team won 4-0

Studies of Colin Blythe

Returning home on the "Omrah" in March 1902 and a picture in his
Australian tour blazer

**Kent C.C.C. American
Tour of 1903**

They played Philadelphia,
the Colts, and New York
from the September

Blythe took part in all four
matches, and in the two
first class fixtures he took
ten wickets with a best
of five for 30

The **"Celtic"** - travelling from New York to Liverpool in October 1903

Left: A photograph of C. Blythe with Fred Huish and James Seymour taken by the actor and playwright Seymour Hicks   **Right:** Only the captain Burnup did not sign

The St. Lawrence Ground - during Canterbury Week in August 1905
Blythe recorded thirteen "ten wicket matches" at the ground

374 New Cross Road

Blythe's home from 1904
up until his marriage
three years later
(four-storey left)

**M.C.C. South African
Tour 1905-06 (5th Test)**

Back: J. Phillips (umpire), Blythe, Lees, Relf, Moon, Denton, Board, F. Hearne (umpire)
Front: Crawford, Fane, Warner (captain), Hartley, Haigh
Also on the tour I. Difford (man.), Capt. Wynyard, Leveson-Gower, and Hayes

The "Kinfauns Castle" - Southampton to Cape Town in November 1905

Life on board ship - a little card school with the Warners, time out for a team photo, and one of many deck entertainments

August of 1903 was to be a good month and the side enjoyed considerable success during Canterbury Week. Essex were their first opponents at the start of the month and won the toss but only managed 121 runs in their innings. Such a restriction was solely due to Blythe's effort since he took a record of nine wickets for 67 runs in just 28 overs.

His victims included England players F.L. Fane on 22 and C.P. McGahey caught and bowled on 0. Kent then accrued 324 runs and after Essex made only 248, Dillon and Burnup cleaned up to win by ten wickets. Whilst to the great delight of the local revellers Kent also defeated Worcester by 196 runs in the second game of the Week.

There were then further pertinent contests and they beat Surrey at the Oval by 292 runs on 17-18 August, Blythe taking seven for 41 and five for 26 the others to A. Hearne; whereas they played Yorkshire, the three times champions, at the St. Lawrence Ground on 20-22 August.

The visitors chose to bat but this was probably a mistake and the openers Brown and Tunnicliffe went out to Blythe scoring 16, and he eventually secured six wickets for only 35 runs. With his first dismissal he notched up 500 wickets in first class cricket to ripples of applause, but the Yorkshire attack was in tatters as they all succumbed on just 79 runs.

A famous victory was in the offing however rain stopped play on the second day thus Kent came in to bat on the third morning. They declared on reaching 181 runs the wickets falling to G.H. Hirst and Wilfred Rhodes but time did not favour the home team's cause.

Despite this there was great anticipation among the local spectators, as Blythe put on a dazzling display clean bowling Lord Hawke on 4 runs and reaching a figure of seven wickets for 26 runs. However, the game was stopped due to poor light with Yorkshire on 51 for eight and the match was pronounced a very disappointing "draw."

Of the champion's total 12 runs were extras and H. Wilkinson made the highest of 17 the rest being out for under 10. It was the victory that didn't happen and the bowler took thirteen wickets for just 61 added.

Such success continued during the next game against Hampshire at Dean Park on 27-28 August. The home side put on 154 runs and Blythe took six wickets for 80, whereas Kent scored 245 runs including a record score to date for Blythe of 28. In the second innings he took another four wickets and Hampshire only managed 74 runs leading to an innings defeat.

It had been an interesting season and at the end Middlesex needed just a draw from their remaining fixtures with Sussex at Lord's and Surrey at the Oval. Indeed they won their first championship - not because they had come up to Yorkshire but because the latter had gone back.

Both newspapers and public alike noted this fact, while in the game at Canterbury Hirst and Rhodes failed which did not bode well for England. In fact, there was considerable amazement when Yorkshire were all out for only 79 and Kent passed them without losing a single man.

The wicket at the St. Lawrence Ground began well but became worse and this was normally the kind of wicket on which the Tykes bowlers had most success. But they did not - and if it were a dry summer in England (!) they would be no better than others, while regarding Australia the rubber could only be won if a (Tom) "Richardson" were present as before.

AMERICAN TOUR

Kent, meanwhile, remained in the ascendancy with a number of talented players in the side who displayed considerable camaraderie and attractive, alluring social empathy. Consequently it was no surprise that they were the first county-side to be invited on a tour of North America, the day at Foxgrove Road providing the catalyst for this invitation.

With the season finished the team travelled up to Liverpool and joined the grand "Oceanic" on 9 September 1903. Just a few months earlier this had been the largest vessel in the world and was built for the White Star Line by Harland & Wolff of Belfast.

It had been a long season and they no doubt hoped for some relaxation during the voyage to New York (although this was not to be). Meanwhile, like the changing room at Lord's there was a division by notation and the amateurs went first class and the players travelled second.

Such a fact was revealed in the ship's manifest which had Seymour, Blythe, Huish, and A. Hearne down as professional cricketers; E.W. Dillon had no job description; William M. Bradley was a clerk and Weigall, Stewart, Baker, Hutchings, J.R. Mason, and Burnup were down as stockbrokers. The party were completed with Thomas E. Pawley cricket manager and their passage was paid by the "Associated C.C. of Philadelphia."

In addition the group included Sir Arthur A. Priestley M.P. for Grantham (1900-18) who had previously been on two tours to the West Indies - in particular with Bosanquet and Ranjitsinhji to North America in 1899-1901. As a result he had a particular interest although he only ever played a single first class match in England viz. for the M.C.C. in 1895.

Unfortunately it was a terrible and wretched trip across the pond and only three of the cricketers avoided seasickness, whilst there was a hurricane the day before they arrived in port! This was not the best of preparations but once on dry land they laughed away their trials and tribulations.

The vessel reached New York on the evening of 16 September and the entourage promptly took a train down to Philadelphia. Arriving late, they went straight to their rooms at the Aldine Hotel, Chestnut Street above 19th in the centre of the city for a chance to recover. [1]

A division of labour was employed the following morning since most of the party had never been to the United States before. As a result some hurried off to have a look around the city and see the sights, whereas the others including the captain Burnup remained behind at the hotel.

This provided the opportunity for an interview and a local reporter headed up his article "*Kent Cricketers are Athletes.*" In the first instance he noted that there were thirteen athletic Englishmen who were easily distinguished from the other hotel guests as being both bronzed and brawny. Indeed, it was clearly apparent they had spent their lives in athletics!

The correspondent then sat down with C.J. Burnup who was only too happy to talk to him. The leader of the side was smaller than most of his team-mates but displayed a nervous energy and clear, keen eye befitting his status. He explained that they were delighted to be there and since British teams always received a most cordial welcome, it was never difficult to make up an eleven provided that business did not interfere.

But was it propitious to play the first game against the Colts? In his opinion it was a good thing and encouraged the young players to improve for selection, whilst they could learn more from the older players in one game than in a whole year's coaching! He also broached a problem which had come to light during MacLaren's Australian tour.

"I think, however," mused Burnup, "that better results are obtained by not placing more than sixteen players in the field. While we were touring New Zealand last winter we kept the opposing fielders down to that number and it afforded far better practice for the bowlers and others."

Regarding the American's visit he said, "Their playing was a great surprise to most people and we all hope the day is not far distant when Philadelphia will play matches against All-England, the same as Australia does. English cricket would be a decided gainer if several of the Americans were to live there, particularly in the persons of Messrs. King, Lester and Clark."

---

[1] The Aldine Hotel was originally a private mansion built by Dr. James Rush, the son of Dr. Benjamin Rush a signatory on the Declaration of Independence, in 1850. With his wife the doctor entertained such notables as President Van Buren, Charles Dickens, George Bancroft, and Fenimore Cooper. The building passed to the publisher Joshua B. Lippincott but was expanded and converted into a hotel in 1877 becoming popular with theatrical stars such as Dame Ellen Terry, judges during the local sessions, and some famous baseball players.

The largest man in the party was J.R. Mason who stood at over six feet tall and almost hid Mr. Burnup, and was indeed one of the best players in England. Meanwhile, it was noted with some interest that, "One of the most valuable members is Blythe, the bowler, and he is expected to work havoc with the Philadelphian' wickets. During the past season in England, Blythe, who is a professional, captured 143 wickets at an average of 13 runs apiece and stood well up towards the top of the bowlers." [2]

During the morning there was a heavy downpour of rain, but this didn't stop the Englishmen getting out their long cricket bags after lunch and heading out to Germantown C.C. at Manheim, just northwest of the city. Certainly, this provided a good diversion for the locals:

"It was about noon when the party came out of the hotel and the sight caused many people to turn around and gaze at them. With their trousers turned up and smoking pipes they seemed impervious to rain and walked to Broad Street Station to catch their train."

The reporter concluded by noting that Mr. A.A. Priestley accompanied the team this being for two reasons. Firstly he had been over there before, and secondly he had invited the Philadelphians to play a game at his estate at Hungerton in Lincolnshire during their previous visit.

Priestley did not intend to play but was a well-known figure and a typical English sportsman. Indeed he was glad to be back amongst old friends and added, "I know the cricket end of the tour will interest me, for your players showed us that their calibre is good enough to tackle any of our county teams." This was especially true due to the disadvantages they had in terms of finding adequate local opposition.

THE COLTS

As it turned out the trip to Manheim was a waste of time due to the poor weather, and the only practice took place on the day of the match. In fact, the rain was so heavy that a new wicket had to be prepared and the ground in general remained very soft. Despite such problems it was decided to start the contest at 12 o'clock on the Friday (18 September).

Some two thousand spectators made their way to the pretty ground of the Germantown C.C. whilst the Colts won the toss and chose to bat. White and Morris opened their innings against the bowling of Blythe and Alec Hearne although the ball turned very slowly on the soft wicket.

---

[2] Only Walter Mead of Essex had a better average that season of 13.67 with 131 wickets, Blythe's figure being 13.75. Others in the top ten included George Hirst and Wilfred Rhodes of Yorkshire, and of course J.B. King of Philadelphia.

However, Blythe managed to make the ball jump rather awkwardly and soon began to take some wickets - "He appeared to terrorise the batsmen and they played very gingerly at him." Initially they went out quickly and only Keenan made any kind of stand although he scored just 11 runs, then after some limited success Mason was brought on in place of Hearne which was a good decision since he took two more wickets.

Christman came to the crease and only stopped the treble by a slight edge, whereas Bradley came on for Blythe and sent the middle stump flying with his first ball. Thereafter there was a continual procession to the pavilion and the nineteen Colts were all out for 79. At the end of the day Kent had scored 47 for two with Hearne finely caught on the last ball.

Play resumed the next morning (Saturday) and Mason and Seymour hit out however both their wickets fell within nine balls. The pitch had dried during the night but in general remained bad and runs were hard to come by with seventeen men in the field.

Dillon made some beautiful strokes and departed with the total on 143, whereas Blythe arrived at the crease at the end and produced one or two good returns "including (of course) his favourite pull."

Kent were all out for 169 runs and looked like winning, whilst White and Morris took to the crease but the latter was out for nought and the players retired for luncheon. Upon resuming play the wickets fell quickly. White was by far the best batsman and put on a few runs, although he was rather fortunate to survive a catch at the wicket which was called in his favour. As it happened he went on to reach 35 before being bowled by Blythe and the side were eventually out for 114 runs.

Burnup and Hutchings started the second innings at five o'clock and the former was caught with just 4 runs on the board. Three wickets were then lost however Dillon made the winning hit at 5.30 and the Kent side of twelve had won by eight wickets.

The crowd for such a contest was a staggering 5,000 on the second day and they witnessed several good catches by the Colts - the best bowling by D. Graham who took seven for 32 runs. Blythe took six for 29 runs on the first day but on the second had to retire queer in the afternoon. After an hour's rest he came out again and pluckily resumed bowling, but he was clearly not at all himself (taking a further four for 48 runs).

In general the Kent players were suffering from the terrible voyage over and hoped to be fit for the "test match" at New York the following week. The reporter added that this was how the game was styled in America. An attempt to fill the gap with a contest in Toronto fell through but eventually there was an additional game against Philadelphia.

By this time the players had met up with most of their opponents from the previous summer in England, nine of them scheduled to play in the forthcoming contests. Some doubt existed about the fitness of King who suffered a peculiar accident a few days earlier. Whilst making a run he ran forward past the bowler, but caught his finger in the man's pocket breaking a bone in his left hand - despite this he was still fit to play!

PHILADELPHIA (GAME 1)

The players then had a few days on their hands and thus indulged in a fair degree of sightseeing. Their first trip was to Atlantic City on the Sunday when Mr. F.C. Perot with the help of Mr. Seymour showed them the sights. On the Monday morning they practiced at Wissahickon Heights the home of their opponents near to Chestnut Hill (St. Martin's), and then attended a baseball match between two of the best teams in America.

The local side Athletics took on Detroit and the match was so enjoyable that several watched the return game the next day. With such distances to travel it was common to play back to back fixtures or even three games.

Manager Mack of the Athletics side was most courteous to the Kent team and after both games took them on a tour of the grounds, the stands, and the dressing rooms. No doubt they viewed the facilities with interest and compared the idiosyncrasies of baseball to the game of cricket. Perhaps Blythe studied the technique of the pitcher whilst the batsmen considered the differences in tactics regarding the "run-getting." [3]

Not content with horse-racing and baseball the side finished practice on the Wednesday and went to Swarthmore to watch American football at the University of Pennsylvania. Afterwards there was a consensus that despite having several soccer players in the Kent side, it was preferable to watch from the stands than to become vulnerable on the pitch!

However, the game was full of interest and to the English eye the uniform of the players seemed most curious, whilst the college participants entered into the spirit of things with a considerable degree of pluck.

On the Thursday there was a further practice at Wissahickon and despite some cordial invitations to enjoy golf and racquettes, the players were just itching to play some cricket - the game to take place over three days at the above location starting on Friday, 25 September.

---

[3] Philadelphia Athletics played in the American League (rather than the National League) from 1901-54. Columbia Park the home ground was a limited venue with capacity of 9,000, whereas Connie Mack led the team from the start until 1950. In the games against the Detroit Tigers in 1903 they won 6-4 and lost 4-7.

The Gentlemen of Philadelphia turned up with seven of the players who went to England the new members being Jones (a left-handed batsman), Walker (who came from Derbyshire and recently qualified), Goodman (who had a high batting average), and O'Neill (a slow left hand bowler). In terms of injury Alec Hearne remained unwell and declined to play though Blythe who was also unwell was included in the team.

Kent lost the toss and the sides took to the field punctually at 12 o'clock in front of 1,000 spectators. Bart King and A.W. Jones led the attack although Bradley who bowled at a terrific pace took the first five wickets. Goodman and Clark then took the total on from 85 to 106, when Blythe finally got one past the latter. In fact, the tail-enders found the batting very hard and Blythe bowled Jordan to end the innings on 128 runs.

Burnup and Stewart opened for the visitors but they soon went out whilst Dillon and Seymour improved matters taking the total to 55 runs. Only an hour of play was possible for the Kent side and Dillon was given out lbw then the stumps were drawn for the day. The game resumed on Saturday morning with Hutchings arriving at the crease.

At once Seymour proceeded to hit out brilliantly and eventually made 42 runs, whereas Huish (No. 8) joined him on 94 and the crowd began to get rather excited. Seymour continued to play well however when trying to pull a King delivery he was caught and bowled.

Mason "arrived late" and came in after him due to the fact he dislocated a thumb when making a catch on the Friday. Despite this he made a good effort but the side were all out for 132 finishing just 4 runs ahead. Blythe took three wickets during the innings but was caught for a duck by Jordan off one of King's deliveries when batting.

Morris and Jones then batted briefly before lunch, but the former was caught with the first ball down and Jones went three runs later. After lunch the attendance had reached 5,000 and when King came to the crease with Lester the total went from 32 to 96 runs, but not without a degree of luck on the part of King. However, it was Lester who made the best stand and finished on 93 runs not out the total reaching 194.

There was some heavy rain during the Sunday break which took a lot of fire from the wicket, however a considerable wind on the Monday increased the chances of making the total. Not only did the wicket dry out but there was a fine day for the 1,000 spectators who turned up.

Despite this the task remained quite difficult. Stewart, Seymour, and Dillon were lost to King and Goodman with the total on 95, but this saw the arrival of Mason to join Burnup at the crease. Mason kept going bravely although he was clearly in some considerable difficulty.

Meanwhile, Burnup produced a fine display of cricket over some four hours never giving up a chance and made eight 4's, eight 3's, and nine 2's. The winning total of 192 was thus reached at 4.45 with Burnup on 94 runs and Mason on 46 runs.

It was a truly great victory thoroughly enjoyed by the English contingent among the spectators, and set the side up well for the forthcoming game against New York at Staten Island. The prizes for batting went to Burnup and Mason, whilst Bradley bowled with some great pace throughout taking nine wickets in total.

Regarding the Gentlemen of Philadelphia there was some surprise that the captain J.A. Lester started slowly, but he then stayed in for three and a half hours and scored thirteen 4's - unfortunately no one stayed with him so he could reach his century. King's bowling was commended as he took seven for 39 runs in the first innings (his best tally against them).

After this fine success at Chestnut Hill the Kent team took the train to New York on the Tuesday and reached the Fifth Avenue Hotel at midday. They then went sightseeing and took in the Fuller Building (the Flat Iron), Park Row (Press) Building, and the Statue of Liberty.

A NEW YORK XI

The next encounter began the following day on 30 September and although not first class was billed as a "test match," whereas most of the opposition had British connections and a number of the spectators were Scottish! The opponents were a selected New York XI, but the wicket was terrible with pot holes and bare patches and it was a wonder no one ended up seriously hurt. It was simply a case of having to adapt to the conditions.

The Kent party took the ferry across to Staten Island and a few hundred spectators were present when they arrived at Livingston Field (Walker Park) at 11.15, although this had risen to 1,000 when play commenced.

Burnup won the toss and in some glorious sunshine the openers Hearne and Hutchings went in to bat against the bowling of Kelly and Poyer. Due to the conditions the ball moved in a most awkward manner and within no time at all both the players had received painful knocks.

Hearne made a fine hit on the leg side but just after this was caught in the slips. Seymour and Stewart followed him to the pavilion and before they knew it they were four wickets down with 26 runs. Mason and Baker came to the rescue in an unpromising situation and took the score to 117 before Mason was stumped, whereas Burnup arrived to an enthusiastic reception due to his earlier bold exploits.

The total had been pushed on to 156 when Bradley joined him after the ninth wicket. Immediately both of the players hit out to the considerable delight of the spectators, until Kelly clean bowled Burnup to leave a quite respectable score of 202 runs.

There was only an hour and a half's batting left in the day and Adam and Poyer did well, thus the home side made 83 runs for three wickets at the close of play. The game resumed at 11.30 with a fair number of spectators and Poyer began with a four off Burnup but was then caught at the wicket. Soon after the wickets fell quickly mainly to Baker and Burnup and the side were all out for 100 - the last seven wickets adding just 17 runs.

Kent then returned to bat and with no runs scored Hutchings was caught at mid off, whilst Seymour was caught with a beautiful running catch in the long field - the team total on 4 runs. However, Hearne proceeded to hit out gracefully and with Stewart the score went up to 74 at lunchtime.

After the break the latter was out to a marvellous catch at point and three runs later Baker was bowled, thus on 77 runs the team declared. It never looked like the opponents could make the total in the few hours available and they were all out for just 54. Kent won by 125 runs and their batsmen adapted well in particular Baker, Burnup, Mason, and Stewart.

The first two also bowled with good judgement throughout the game and always had the New Yorkers at their mercy. Indeed, Baker was a very useful player for the county in terms of bowling and fielding whilst his off drives and leg strokes were all well timed. Blythe had a quieter game with just a single run and three wickets during the two innings.

PHILADELPHIA (GAME 2)

With another resounding success the side returned to Philadelphia on the Thursday evening and arrived at their hotel at 11 p.m. There was just one game to play and they hoped to preserve their unbeaten record.

On the Friday morning the sun was shining as they travelled out to the Merion C.C. ground at Haverford, which was the venue for the second of the official "test matches." The Gentlemen reconstructed their team in the hope of matching the Kent side and introduced Wood, Graves, and H.P. Baily as well as F.S. White who had done well for the Colts.

The introduction of Baily was of considerable interest at home since he formed part of the 1897 combination, whereas for Kent Hearne came in to replace Weigall. The wicket was hard and dry and looked better than any they had played on, although it had a degree of fire which made the ball jump quite dangerously at times.

The batsmen Graves and White started cautiously and after White made an off drive for four, Blythe sent down a fast swerver which pitched on the off side and passed his defences to bowl him at leg.

Bradley was in excellent form and his fast balls difficult to handle thus Graves, Lester, and King went out in quick succession. The two bowlers were much applauded and the last wicket fell after lunch with the score on 66 runs, Blythe taking five for 30 and Bradley four for 32. The total was clearly far less than was hoped for or indeed was expected.

During the Kent innings Stewart and Burnup were soon out followed by Seymour with the score on 42; however Dillon and Mason made a stand and added another 72 runs the former making some strong leg drives. At the close of play Kent reached 132 runs for the loss of six wickets

Play recommenced at 11.30 on the Saturday with Baker and Hutchings batting although the runs came rather slowly. Hutchings made two fine hits at the on side before he fell to an unlucky rising ball, while Huish came in and hit King for four to go a hundred ahead. Bradley was then bowled leaving Blythe on just 5 and they were all out for 180 runs.

A large and fashionable crowd watched the game and there was some animation during the second innings. The home side had 106 but Morris and Clark made a good stand to add 58 for the wicket and they were all out for 177 runs. Bradley again bowled well and Blythe took two for 54.

Burnup and Stewart started for the visitors and Burnup was unlucky to go out to a full pitch from Bart King. The latter joined with Seymour and took the total to 46 at the close of play on the Saturday, and Kent won the game by seven wickets on the Monday morning (5 October).

Before the conclusion of the match there was a dinner/dance at the club house on the Saturday evening in honour of the Kent team and their visit. Indeed the whole trip was most successful and the Americans were rightly pleased with the competition that it had provided.

After the dinner the chairman Mr. Cassatt proposed a toast to the visitors' health, declaring his hope that Mr. Burnup would return the next year to give them a chance to wipe out the victories. The latter responded to great applause and complimented the Americans on their sportsmanship, then proposed a further toast to Mr. Lester. [4]

---

[4] Alexander J. Cassatt (1839-1906) became a superintendent of the Pennsylvania Railroad, and built a large mansion "Cheswold" at Haverford in 1873 which led down to the railway. He was mainly noted for his involvement in horse racing and had a prominent role in local affairs, whilst he became president of the P.R.R. in 1899 and promoted the classical monolith of Penn Station, New York. A bronze tablet was erected to his memory at Merion C.C. in 1910.

Mr. Pawley the manager also spoke of the courtesy and help that had been extended, and read out a letter from Lord Harris containing greetings to both cricketers and old friends. In an atmosphere of warm admiration there was much disappointment that Lord Harris was not there. Mr. Priestley was the last speaker, his humorous patriotic speech making a great impression whilst the company danced till the early hours of the morning.

The side departed from New York on the "Celtic" on Friday, 9 October and had an improved crossing which allowed for some socialising. During the trip Blythe and his colleagues made the acquaintance of Seymour Hicks the actor and playwright which was clearly one of the benefits of celebrity! Meanwhile, they arrived at Liverpool on Saturday, 17 October and the next morning made straight for Euston and their homes. [5]

[5] Seymour Hicks (1871-1949) was born in Jersey and was determined to become an actor in London. He went on his first American tour in 1889 and married the actress Ellaline Terriss in 1893. Together they wrote, produced, and acted and formed a partnership with the American producer Charles Frohman. The couple starred in the successful "Quality Street" (by J.M. Barrie) in 1902 and moved to a house at Merstham, Surrey at the same time.

CHAPTER 6

A Gold Medal

Colin Blythe was not chosen for the test series in Australia in the winter of 1903-04, but then neither were most of his Kent team-mates even though they were improving at the time. However, the first tour under the auspices of the M.C.C. provided an interesting look into the character of Blythe, his relationship with cricket, and his dramatic swing in fortune.

Meanwhile, some things never changed. Newspapers talked of a hearty send-off for the side travelling to Australia but also noted that the M.C.C. had been greatly criticised regarding the composition of the team. It was a similar criticism to the one levelled at MacLaren two years earlier.

In this instance there was no Barnes to provide a degree of mystery, no Blythe with his reliable spin, and no Jessop with his promise of runs. The side were led by Plum Warner and the other thirteen included several who went on the previous tour viz. Tyldesley, Hayward, Braund, and Lilley. To these were added Hirst and A.E. Knight who had the best batting averages for the season and a selection of bowlers including Rhodes, E.G. Arnold, Fielder (of Kent), and Bosanquet.

A considerable degree of fanfare surrounded the departure which took place in late October - whilst the Kent team were in America. Indeed, as if there weren't enough passengers on the platform at St. Pancras for the boat train, most of the cricketing elite turned out to see them off.

Leading the pack was Lord Alverstone president of the M.C.C. and Surrey who arrived too late to see the train leave - due to his duties with the Alaska Boundary Commission, however he had already personally extended his kind good wishes to Mr. Warner.

Amongst those chatting on the platform were Lord Hawke, MacGregor the captain of Middlesex, Sammy Woods the popular skipper of Somerset, and Captain McCanlis of Kent. In fact, the party of dignitaries was fifty strong and represented a large number of county teams.

Six of the professionals namely Hayward, Tyldesley, Lilley, Arnold, Hirst, and Rhodes had gone ahead to Tilbury the previous day, whilst Bosanquet intended to travel overland and join them all in Marseilles.

Warner's party arrived dressed in blazers and ties sporting colours rather reminiscent of I Zingari, and as a result were greeted with much admiration by the crowd at the station. Not long after, they left the Midland terminus and some hearty cheers rent the air as they departed.

The weather was good for the somewhat tedious journey down to Tilbury where they boarded the mighty "Orontes" - the pick of the fleet. Moored nearby was the new P & O boat the "Moldavia" which was under steam and about to depart on its maiden voyage for Bombay. Without doubt the cricketers had chosen an opportune vessel for the long journey since it was certainly "a perfect palace of comfort."

Before departing there was a function on the upper deck and Mr. F. Green president of the company greeted Warner and his party. He alluded in the most happy of terms to the recent engagement of Mr. P. Warner to Miss Agnes Blyth (who was unrelated to the bowler) and complimented her on her great ability in the hunting field. Then turning to cricket he noted that the side was much stronger than some had suggested.

Many hard things had been said about the M.C.C. and the team but it was clear that Mr. Warner had collected the most resilient side possible in the circumstances, and, whatever the outcome, they were undoubtedly a team of tryers! A telegram arrived from Lord Harris wishing them all the best and the "Orontes" departed at about 2.00, although a further thirty minutes had passed by when they finally cleared the dock-gates.

There was much talk about their chances and in terms of batting the side were equal to that of MacLaren's party, whilst they were considered much stronger regarding their bowling. Warner had every confidence his choice of players would offset all the criticisms made against the M.C.C.

With such hopes and dreams the "Orontes" headed out into the Channel on 4 October being scheduled to stop at Plymouth, Marseilles, and Naples en route. She was to arrive in Adelaide all being well on 2 November this being five days before the first game with South Australia.

However, debate about the team's chances was never very far behind thus C.B. Fry sent a personal letter to the papers, "If left, please forward, P.F. Warner Esq., 'S.S. Orontes,' Plymouth." He began by wishing them all the best, noted that any party politics had now been sunk into patriotism, and added that it was a powerful and "representative" team.

He then asked his friend Warner, "Suppose for a moment that this M.C.C. team of yours was an Australian side just landed on our shores. Should we esteem it lightly and fancy we had it beaten from the start?" The answer was definitely in the contrary - since there would be much difficulty in making runs off Hirst, Rhodes, Arnold, Relf, and Braund especially if the first two bowled as they did for Yorkshire.

Then regarding the batting there were Tyldesley, Hayward, Warner and the rest. Yet, there was a different climate in Australia and the fast pitches and bright light might trouble both the bowlers and the batsmen.

Fry concluded with an assessment of the chances of individual players and his main concern was with the bowling due to what he termed "Australian pavements." He was unsure about the inclusion of Fielder (of Kent) since this was based on a single success against Middlesex at Tunbridge playing on a fiery wicket. Several others might have done just as well however he was keen and young - so you could never tell? [1]

The situation compared closely to the previous tour and Fry noted with a degree of retraction, "When Blythe went to Australia with Archie MacLaren I thought he would get more runs than wickets out there. But he proved a pronounced success. So may it be with Fielder."

Meanwhile, this was also a time of innovation and Bernard Bosanquet of the Middlesex-side was perfecting a new bowling style. Being interested in the concepts of spinning the ball he developed what became known as the googly from about 1900. As a leg break bowler he bent the wrist and thus made the ball spin back towards the batsman from the off side, the result a definite element of surprise - although it was a difficult skill.

In respect of this Fry glibly noted, "You must persuade that Bosanquet of yours to practice, practice, practice those funny 'googlies' of his till he is automatically certain of his length. That leg break of his which breaks from the off might win a test match." [2]

The exuberant Fry concluded his epistle to Pelham with a farewell for a season, adding that he would think about him whilst digging with his niblick for a smaller ball in the furze. No doubt with these difficulties in mind he wished that he was out there playing with his colleagues!

Indeed, he was not the only one since Blythe clearly yearned to be on the trip with his friend Fielder and as a result collected details of the departure, a number of pictures, and several match summaries. He clearly felt part of the national team and wanted to be there with them doing his bit.

This was more than a passing interest and revealed his love of cricket and a respect for his colleagues, whilst in one sense he followed the test games and the team's progress just like an enthusiastic supporter.

---

[1] Arthur Fielder had played only one full season for Kent in 1903, and during the Middlesex first innings took four for 66 runs including Warner clean bowled - the game was a draw but Blythe and Bosanquet took more wickets during the match. Fielder took 70 wickets at an average of 18.41 runs (best 7-45) during that season although Blythe took 142 wickets at 13.75 runs (best 9-67).

[2] The googly was also known as the "Bosey" after its inventor and the Australians termed it the "wrong 'un." B.J.T. Bosanquet (1877-1936) played for Middlesex in 1898-1919 and England in 1903-05 - his son Reginald was a newsreader.

As it turned out he had every good reason to support the team. Plum Warner pitted his eleven against Monty Noble and his men and won both games in Sydney and the first in Melbourne, thus he returned home totally vindicated with a good series win and some improbable scores.

Hayward, Tyldesley, Warner, Hirst, and Braund all recorded totals of over 200 runs, whereas R.E. Foster the right-hander from Worcester played nine innings with an average of 60.75. For Australia Trumper and Noble headed the batting, whilst in terms of bowling Wilfred Rhodes bowled over 1,000 balls and took 31 wickets - his average 15.81. In this respect he was backed up by Bosanquet, Arnold, Braund, and Hirst.

The test matches were again played in Adelaide, Melbourne, and Sydney with a trip to Tasmania, but it was all over by the middle of March 1904 and the players headed home to more familiar pastures.

THE 1904 SEASON

Blythe had now played four full seasons watching the records tumble, had a good test match tour to Australia seeing places he had barely dreamed of, and enjoyed a sojourn to New York and Philadelphia seeing some amazing sights. The cricket, meanwhile, was not bad either.

On top of that he had been an avid follower of the team to Australia in 1903-04 and no doubt had aspirations of returning to the national side. He had tasted such success with its camaraderie and travel and clearly hoped for more similar experiences. Cricket, however, would do the talking, but first there was the more "mundane" matter of the regular county game, the bread and butter of the test player.

A re-organisation occurred at Kent and despite Burnup's able leadership a new captain was appointed for the 1904 season. It was a decision that was most propitious and one which reaped considerable dividends.

Cloudesley H.B. Marsham the son of a vicar was the same age as Blythe and was born at Bicester, Oxford in 1879 but his life couldn't have been more different. He was a born cricketer, a right hand batsman, who played with both Lubbock and Robarts at Eton (of the famous banking families) and with Bosanquet at Oxford.

Initially he made few appearances for Kent and played just one or two games in 1900/01 with most matches being for the university (including the one against the county). However, he had a more permanent place in July 1902 but the next year played only a handful of games. Despite this he was made captain at the age of just twenty-five in 1904 and it is possible that some family connections came into play.

Without doubt he had some excellent credentials being the third cousin of Charles Marsham (the 4th Earl of Romney) and the nephew of George Marsham (who was an uncle on his mother's side). Both these gentlemen had important connections within the county and were in fact presidents of Kent C.C.C. in 1880 and 1886 respectively. In addition to this George his uncle had also appeared for the county side in 1876-77. [3]

Marsham proved himself to be a good captain and leader with his trusty pipe and moustache and under him some real progress was made, but at first it seemed his appointment was a disastrous mistake.

The season began against Nottingham at Gravesend on 12-13 May but the side lost by three wickets, although Blythe took three and four wickets in each innings. A tighter game followed at Lord's three days later against the M.C.C. whose team included that famous "sleuth" Conan Doyle. Kent put on a better performance but lost by 33 runs.

They then managed a draw against Essex at Leyton however there was a disastrous innings defeat against Lancashire at Old Trafford on 26-28 May. Johnny Tyldesley returned fresh from his Australian success and put on 146 runs in only three hours, including twenty thumping 4's, before Blythe finally outwitted him and he was caught by Baker.

Kent were given a challenge far too daunting of 292 runs by the home side - being all out for 121 prompting the follow on. Marsham should have led the way to save their honour but was out for a duck, and there was a collapse back to the pavilion with just 42 runs in the second innings. The problem was not in the bowling since Blythe took six for 129.

This hardly seemed like a side that would have a good season, but matters were turned around and Humphreys and Seymour led the batting to take the team to what was a very creditable finish by the end.

Possibly Marsham was suffering from the problem that inflicts "all would-be-captains," although his average in the previous season was his lowest at just 12.33 runs! However, such a dearth soon ended and during the next two months he came close to a century against Lancashire and Yorkshire, whilst he made 161 not out for the M.C.C. against Oxford at Lord's - his stand in the latter being with Ranjitsinhji who also made 142.

---

[3] The Marsham family owned Mote Park, Maidstone from 1690 and the first Kent game was played there in 1859 - regular county cricket took place in the park from the 1870s including a fixture against a W.G. Grace XI in 1871. The estate was sold to Marcus Samuel the 1st Viscount Bearsted in 1895 and was further developed with a pavilion in 1908-10. From that time it had more frequent use with a Week and two games a year, however was sold to Maidstone Borough Council in 1929. Mote Park has continued to stage cricket up until recent times.

No doubt this improvement in form helped inspire some confidence but it was his team-mates who lifted the side out of the doldrums. In the next game against Hampshire at Southampton, Humphreys and Seymour raised their batting and helped bring the Kent total to 142 runs, whereas Blythe excelled taking seven for 49 and the opponents were all out on 97.

In the second innings Marsham again went for a duck while H.Z. Baker and Murrell added 132 runs, but Blythe and Fielder showed how it should be done by scoring 34 and 33 apiece. The opponents returned and Blythe took another six wickets for 42 thus Kent won by 283 runs.

Such amelioration remained ephemeral and uncertain but the talent being shepherded by Marsham was clearly progressing, and in the next game at Maidstone Kent defeated Worcester by 204 runs. James Seymour did the double with 108 and 136 in each innings, but it seemed unlikely he would make the second as Fairservice and Blythe both succumbed.

Seymour remained resilient on 70 runs then Fielder joined him as the last man and made a stand of 37 in just 35 minutes, thereby allowing the other to reach the century (and the first "double century" for Kent). Blythe and Fielder did most of the damage bowling to secure the game.

The improvement taking place was then highlighted during an excellent performance against the champions Middlesex at Catford Bridge on 9-10 June. The visiting side which included the captain Gregor MacGregor and the bowler Bosanquet made 199 in the first innings with Fielder, Mason, and Blythe taking the wickets.

Kent replied with the lower score of 163 but there was then a dramatic change in fortunes as the champions Middlesex met their Waterloo, being thoroughly outplayed in every department. The newspapers speculated that one reason was the tricky pitch - a feature of some Kent grounds, since the opponents generally appeared on more "plumb" wickets.

A dazzling display of bowling ensued as Fielder took five wickets for 25 and Blythe did equally well taking four for 14 runs, the last man run out on nought. In fact, only two of the opponents managed to reach double figures and the side were all out for 45 runs.

One factor in the collapse was rain during the night - but then why did the Kent batsmen do so well? Amongst them the best was Dillon who also played rugby for Blackheath and England, whilst of the bowlers Fielder was hindered in his analysis by six over-throws and Blythe put "any amount of devil" into his deliveries nonplussing the visitors.

It was then an easy task for Humphreys and Seymour to make the runs and they won by eight wickets. Meanwhile, the result upset Plum Warner's honeymoon plans and he was hastily recalled for the next match.

A RECORD SCORE

However, Kent still suffered an erratic start to the season and Nottingham recorded their highest innings total against them at Trent Bridge on 16-18 June. The side featured A.O. Jones and J.R. Gunn and on the first day they made 418 for the loss of three wickets, whilst the main contribution came from James Iremonger who scored 272 runs. [4]

Not surprisingly Blythe's bowling figures were very poor on this occasion as he took three for 173 in the first innings. Eventually Notts were all out for a record of 602 and Kent came in to bat, however the home side left themselves quite short of time to secure the apparent victory.

Some of the foremost Kent batsmen failed to improve the situation but Humphreys the second bat put on a creditable 97 in the first innings. Play finished at the end of the second day with Fairservice and Blythe holding their ground at 17 and 15 runs apiece (the total 240).

Nottingham clearly fancied their chances, however the next day the two 'night-watchmen' stayed resolute as they both passed their previous bests by a considerable amount. Fairservice was dismissed on exactly 50 but Blythe could not be moved and was then joined by Fielder. Unfortunately the latter hit his wicket and went for 9, but Blythe was not out on 82 runs and may have been heading for a century.

This was Blythe's highest ever score and showed that he had some ability as a right-handed batsman, which disputed the comments of his detractors who said he was a "duffer" in that department. His previous high was 34 and in the game he reached 1,000 first class runs - while during the season he had his best batting average of 15.38.

In fact, the addition of 132 runs by Fairservice and Blythe took the Kent total up to 356 runs all out. During the follow on the batting was opened tactically with the free scoring Humphreys and Blythe - although the latter was caught on this occasion for just 3 runs. Humphreys, Seymour, and A. Hearne scored prolifically and at the end of play Kent were on 263 for 4 thus it was an honourable draw.

The spectators were undoubtedly provided with a master-class in cricket, and apart from Blythe's stunning display Humphreys came near to a double century since he also made 131 runs in the second innings.

---

[4] James Iremonger played for Notts in 1899-1914 and was "cricketer of the year" in 1903 with C.J. Burnup and a trio from Australia (including Victor Trumper). In the first innings his total took 375 minutes and included thirty-nine 4's.

During Tonbridge Week Blythe continued to improve and was not out twice against Lancashire, also scoring 20 in a victory over Gloucester. He then headed north (but not for the first time) since he had already played at those shared venues Bramall Lane, Headingley, and Park Avenue, whereas his next visit produced one of those peculiar sporting incidents.

St. George's Road, Harrogate was first used for a game between England and Australia in 1882 then for a few county matches from 1895, however when Kent arrived on 7-9 July 1904 they had little idea of what was about to occur. The exact details remain uncertain but the visitors made 177 with Rhodes, Haigh, and George Hirst taking the wickets.

Lord Hawke and H. Wilkinson opened for Yorkshire and Blythe clean-bowled Hawke on 14 runs, but with a good contribution from Haigh the home side managed to reach 212 for seven - Blythe's eventual figures being five for 125. However, during the night-time break there was some most unusual and clearly uncharacteristic jiggery-pokery.

When the teams came out to play on the third day it was soon apparent that "certain persons unknown" had doctored the pitch. There was clear evidence the wicket had been both rolled and watered, possibly with the aim of improving conditions for the last few batsmen.

"Law 9" was then invoked and the game was declared void as a first class fixture, although to their credit the players continued on the third day to entertain the crowd. The Kent side were eventually all out on 321.

This was followed by Tunbridge Wells Week with games against Sussex and the return against Yorkshire. Both of these games were draws although they produced some fine individual performances.

In the Sussex game Blythe led the bowling against Brann and Vine and in his first twelve overs they managed only one run! However, in the whole innings he took two for 32 although this did include the famous batsman Ranjitsinhji caught by Seymour on 13. But in the second innings the regal hitter replied with 135 and Blythe took just a single wicket.

Yorkshire then rolled up to the Nevill Ground which was prepared quite within the rules and the game started slowly, but in the first innings Kent scored 419 including Jack Mason on 138 and Marsham on 92 not out. In the second innings Yorkshire made almost 500 runs themselves including J. Tunnicliffe on 135 and George Hirst on 157.

With Yorkshire ahead by over 300 runs Kent came in and the openers Seymour and Fred Huish made almost 90, whilst Blythe came to the crease fourth and did well again finishing not out on 42 runs. In fact, he took his 600th wicket during the game and the teams remained un-separated.

WEST COUNTRY TOUR

Canterbury Week took place at the start of August and was a great success with victories over Essex and Surrey, whilst the side then headed off on an interesting West Country tour. Accompanying them was a "Canterburian" reporter who noted they arrived at Paddington looking fit as fiddles.

The train departed at 4.30 on Sunday, 7 August and the journey on the Great Western was notable for its speed and comfort, especially after the antiquated modes of progression found on the S.E. & Chatham lines. Upon reaching Bristol they had a good night's rest at the "Full Moon" hotel then went to the County Ground (Ashley Down) the next morning.

Before the match there was time for some practice and the recent success of the Kent side brought in an almost record crowd, although it was noted that (unlike the Kent supporters) they were partisan in the extreme. Kent won the toss and "Punter" Humphreys and Sam Day took the score along to 230 - although several were out quite unaccountably.

At the close of play Gloucester had reached 93 for 3 and the honours were about even. In the evening Kent were invited to a performance of "Sweet and Twenty" at the Princes' Theatre which was most enjoyable.

On the second day the opponents score reached an impressive '479 all out' not something the Kent supporter would really wish to see. Gilbert Jessop produced some "hurricane hitting" and Brownlee emulated him, although Dillon and Humphreys opened for Kent and brought matters around to reach 76 at the close of play on the Tuesday. Despite this they were in a tight position thus all of them went to bed early.

The openers returned in the morning and (with Day) displayed a degree of caution to secure the match - thereafter Day and Mason let themselves go and at one point put on 50 runs in just sixteen minutes. Day's innings was characterised by a number of magnificent strokes on the leg side and at the end of play he reached 152 not out with Kent on 383. It was an unlikely draw and a good start to the tour which only got better.

In addition, the reporter noted he had a tour of the large Wills' tobacco factory with Alec Hearne, and watched the game with Dr. E.M. Grace (a brother of W.G.) who continually contended that if only point had stood nearer to the batsman he would undoubtedly have caught him!

On Wednesday night the side travelled on to Taunton (known locally as Tawnton) and booked into some first class accommodation in "McCauley's Hotel." During the night and morning there was rain and before the toss both captains decided to put the other team in to bat.

Sammy Woods won the toss and duly obliged the Kent side who then found themselves in considerable difficulty. Nine of the wickets had fallen for just 80 runs, but Blythe took to the crease and saved the day with a degree of help from his fellow bowler Fairservice.

Indeed, Blythe hit out in a fashion which raised the enthusiasm of all the spectators (who were quite sporting towards him) and he managed to get a couple on the pavilion, one very near to the clock, and another through an adjacent factory window! This success came partly due to the fact that the County Ground was rather small in stature, being picturesque and located amongst a resplendent avenue of trees.

Blythe was finally bowled out on 70 by E. Robson of 98 added and the Kent total stood at 178. Somerset, meanwhile, failed to make their target the only good batting coming from Robson and S. Woods.

At the end of the first day's play (Thursday) the players visited The Park which was illuminated as part of the Taunton Flower Show, the highlight being a fireworks display and representation of the battle off Port Arthur along the river. During this time there was considerable fraternization with Sammy Woods and "his merrie men" making for a great evening.

Once Somerset were all out on the second day Jack Mason and Mr. Day put Kent into a winning position ably assisted by Alec Hearne and the captain Marsham. The performance was so good that Len Braund believed that Mason had become the best all-round player of the day, since he made a total of exactly 100 runs in a hundred minutes.

In the evening there was a game of American skittles between the Kent amateurs and professionals, in which Blythe applied his precise directional control to help the latter to a deserved victory.

However, the bowler failed to add to his first innings success and his side were all out for 401 on the Saturday morning, whereas Mason with Blythe took the first four Somerset wickets for just 16 runs.

The game looked all over at a whimper until Palairet and Braund made a substantial stand. The amateur Lionel Palairet played at his best and drove with power and precision to the boundary - there was just a clack and the next moment the ball was collected from beyond the line.

Braund, meanwhile, was more cautious and took three hours to make 73 runs having admitted he had suffered a recent loss of form, but hopefully this was a sign of imminent recovery so he could help England to retain the Ashes. For a while it looked as if Somerset would hold out for a draw but Humphreys then took four wickets for just 13 runs. As a result they were all out on 207 and Kent secured a victory by 210 runs with twenty-minutes on the clock - during the game Blythe took five wickets in total.

Several of the team attended a service the next morning at the beautiful old church of St. Mary Magdalene, and they then departed for Worcester and spent the afternoon sightseeing in the town.

The last game of the tour was played at the County Ground in New Road from 15-17 August. During the evening before the match Humphreys was unwell and looked unlikely to play - but made a fast recovery and then gave one of his better performances (with 143 runs). Blythe, however, was less effective although the visitors won by nine wickets.

With two wins and a draw under their belt Kent returned home and the reporter believed they were one of the strongest elevens in the country. This was largely due to the utmost good feeling existing between all members of the team, whilst most had still to reach their full potential. He confidently concluded that it would not be long before they stood triumphant at the top of the championship table.

Both Blythe and Kent were improving and the next game saw a stunning performance against Hampshire at the Angel Ground. The visitors won the toss but the bowler took nine wickets for 30 runs off just 22.4 overs with eight batsmen gone for 10 or less! - their innings total being 91.

Kent themselves managed only 114 with the highest score by Seymour at 38 runs. However, the visiting side were all out again for 85 and on this occasion Blythe took six wickets for 46 runs. Kent easily reached the total they needed to secure the game and won by eight wickets.

They failed to win any of their last three games away against Middlesex, Sussex, and Surrey and during the game against Warner's side they declared in the first innings on 280. This rather unusual decision opened the door for the home side since Kent were all out in the second innings on 83, and thus lost the game by one wicket.

But throughout the campaign they won ten games and lost four out of twenty-two played, finishing in third place. Blythe took part in all bar one contest and after the game at Hampshire was in the ascendancy having taken a stunning total of fifteen wickets for 76 runs - his record for the season being 138 wickets (and 134 for Kent).

The papers noted the side were very popular with the public but at the start of the summer their fielding let them down, especially off of Fielder. This they could ill-afford since Seymour and Humphreys were not in their stride, Marsham was yet to find himself, and Mr. Day and Mr. Mason were unavailable. This all changed around later on although in the Middlesex game an early declaration and a loss of fielding form led to defeat, however Kent cricket that season embodied the very best of ideals.

CRICKETER OF THE YEAR

During the season *The Star* newspaper ran a weekly contest to award the top cricketer a gold medal with only the professional players being eligible. Amongst those who had received the award that year were A. Knight, J.T. Hearne, Seymour, Iremonger, Braund, and Hayward. [5]

The last contest was under way and of those votes cast a high proportion were in favour of Blythe. Several stated that there was no contest after his performance against Hampshire, although in general it was concluded that the wicket was not at its best.

However, it was on such a wicket that Blythe provided his best trundling performances and in general was found to be unbeatable. There had been a proposition that the wickets should be widened but any such idea was now clearly obsolete, and others thought two stumps were more appropriate! Indeed, the success (at Tonbridge) was a real tribute to the contribution to the game of the local Kent Nursery.

One writer from Greenwich suggested that his performance the other Day against Hampshire should Hearne him the gold medal. No one could wish to Seymour skill and not only was he a useful bat but also a good Fielder. He always gave Fairservice to his county. Another gent from Paddington asked, "If Blythe beats brilliant batsmen by bowling break balls - where are the brilliant batsmen that Blythe's beautiful break balls beat?"

On a more serious note others indicated he produced fine bowling with a clever grasp of the situation. Combining pitch, pace, and flight variations he had almost every batsman in difficulty despite the fact Hampshire had some very good players. In fact, the game was more reminiscent of skittles and perhaps his West Country practice had paid off?

He was the mainstay of Kent's recent success and in the game surpassed himself producing the best bowling of the season. A dangerous trundler on soft wickets he patiently waited his chance, since earlier in the season the weather undoubtedly favoured the batsman.

The performance was spell-binding - a combination of sporting aspiration and natural skill, an individual effort which completely altered a game. The ball did not talk but positively hummed and Blythe, the fair-headed left-hander, produced a display that might not be matched for some time.

---

[5] T.P. O'Connor the journalist and politician founded the radical newspaper *The Star* in 1887. Amongst those who worked there were George Bernard Shaw and it was the first to have political cartoons, but the paper ceased to exist in 1960 due to a merger with the *Evening News*.

Some other readers muted that E.G. Arnold, E.G. Dennett, or Wilfred Rhodes might take the accolade, but there was in fact no contest and the gold medal was promptly sent to Blythe in the post. It was "a masterpiece of bowling" and the cricketing public had spoken.

After such success the season was capped off with some friendlies. Kent took on the South Africans at the St. Lawrence Ground on 25-27 August and scored 285, whereas the opponents were all out for 188 Blythe taking Tancred, Sinclair, and Snooke. Kent struggled in the second and despite good efforts from Day and Marsham only put on a further 196 runs.

South Africa clearly had a chance but the hero of the game was without doubt James Seymour who took six catches at slip off Blythe and Fielder. In fact, Blythe's figures were six wickets for 76 runs and Kent won the game which was a famous victory by 104 runs.

Frank Mitchell on this occasion played for the South Africans and in the first innings passed 8,500 runs, but in the second he was caught and bowled by his nemesis Blythe with just 1 run on the board.

Blythe also played in a North v South contest at the North Marine Road Ground, Scarborough on 5-7 September. The South included Warner and Bosanquet as well as Blythe, Fielder, Huish, and Humphreys of Kent while the North had Tyldesley, Hirst, Gunn, and Rhodes in their number.

The bowler took the wickets of Tyldesley (twice), Hirst, and Denton with the aid of Fielder and Huish, whereas Hirst scored a century and Bosanquet took five wickets but the match eventually ended in a draw.

Without doubt "Charlie" Blythe had raised his game (and the stakes) and was a Wisden *Cricketer of the Year* in 1904. Indeed, the others who received the award that year were John Gunn of Notts, Albert Knight of Leicester, Walter Mead of Essex, and Plum Warner of Middlesex.

HOME TEST MATCH

No doubt there was considerable delight in the Blythe household at these two accolades and they left Wotton Road for a more substantial property during the year. Their new home 374 New Cross Road was a plain-fronted four-storey terrace built as early as the 1860s.

Situated on a main thoroughfare just to the west of New Cross Station the house still retains the old name "Park Terrace" just above the façade. It was a suitable property for Walter Blythe and his large family since at this stage none of his children were married, whilst the younger ones are said to have attended the historic Addye and Stanhope School nearby and also went to the Greenwich Central School.

Meanwhile, Marsham continued to captain Kent but they faltered in the 1905 season. At this time the Angel Ground was secured by the local club and with such a set up better was clearly hoped for, however they lost by nine wickets to the M.C.C. at Lord's on 22-23 May and then by 50 runs to Oxford at the Christchurch Ground a week later. [6]

They also played their first game at The Circle in Hull on 29 June and although there were thunderstorms the day before, county-cricket weather soon prevailed once again. The inclusion of the Hull professional Rudston created profitable interest and there was an encouraging ring of spectators although the wicket was inclined towards the soft.

Hon. S. Jackson joined him at the crease just after 12.00 to face Blythe and Fairservice, but runs were difficult to obtain and Rudston fell to the former for nought in the third over. Due to considerable assistance from the wicket a revival under Hirst and Haigh did not take place, Lord Hawke also went for a duck and they were all out on 77. In fact Blythe had taken six for 40 and Fairservice the other four for 35 runs.

After lunch the attendance was up to 4,000 and Kent made an even worse start but eventually scored 124 all out. Yorkshire then fared better reaching 162 whereas Blythe took five more wickets and Kent won this significant game on the third day by a margin of six dismissals.

The season itself was generally quite undistinguished but for Blythe it was to include his first official M.C.C. test match and one played on home soil. The Australians arrived at Headingley for the third test on 3-5 July, having lost at Trent Bridge and secured a draw at Lord's.

England fielded a strong side including Tom Hayward, C.B. Fry, Johnny Tyldesley, B. Bosanquet, and A. Lilley; whereas Rhodes failed to take many wickets in the first two games thus Blythe was given his chance.

Hayward and Fry put on 50 runs between them at the start of England's innings, but Tyldesley and Denton went for a duck and Stanley Jackson had to steady the ship making 144 not out with eighteen 4's thus reaching 15,000 runs in first class cricket. Blythe, however, did not come close to emulating him and was bowled for nought by Armstrong in a single ball. Despite this England managed a total of 301 runs.

Reggie (R.A.) Duff was born in the Botanic Gardens in Sydney and was Blythe's first wicket on 48 runs (caught Lilley). Meanwhile, Trumper and Noble both went out lightly and only W.W. Armstrong's effort of 66 runs took the Australians on to 195 for the innings.

---

[6] The Angel Ground was named after a nearby pub and it staged county cricket from 1884 to 1939. A new soccer team Tonbridge F.C. took the lease in 1947 but the local council controversially developed a shopping centre there in 1980.

Hayward, Fry, and Tyldesley then batted well the latter making a century and England declared on 295 for five. Australia responded with 224 and Blythe took W.W. Armstrong, J. Darling, and A.J. Hopkins for 41 runs but the game was drawn. Blythe had not really performed in front of his home crowd consequently he was not chosen again during the series.

Rhodes returned to the team for the final two tests taking five wickets and none respectively during the two games whilst Hirst, Arnold, Brearley, and Jackson were all given a turn at bowling. Bosanquet, likewise, did not play again in either of these two matches.

In fact, England won at Old Trafford by an innings and 80 runs and drew at the Oval thus they were undefeated during the series. As a result they held the venerated Ashes at home for a period of two years - prior to the next test sequence which took place in the Antipodes.

THE 1905 SEASON

Meanwhile, Blythe was amassing some totals and at the end of July Kent took on Somerset at Mote Park. They won by an innings and 116 runs and Blythe took 2-59 and 6-76 reaching 750 first class wickets.

In the next game at Worcester on 31 July the Kent side put on 432 runs with Dillon on 117 - every player other than Blythe making double figures. Worcester batted on the second day their side including the three Foster brothers and closed on 271 runs with R.E. Foster on 47 not out. However, the next day he took his personal total to 246 and the home side achieved a record against Kent of 627 runs.

Blythe took just two wickets for 146 runs despite bowling for nearly fifty overs, and Kent made a further 167 but the game ended in a draw. Clearly this was not championship winning form!

The following game against Surrey at Foxgrove Road on 3-5 August was the last county match to be played at this leafy venue, with no play on the opening day. Surrey scored 148 runs in the first innings and Blythe took six wickets for 80 including Lord Dalmeny clean bowled on 60. Kent then managed to score 134 runs, but solely due to the efforts of Humphreys and Mason who added an excellent 108 between them.

However, this was followed by a complete collapse as Surrey endured a revolving door syndrome. Their highest scorer was Jack Hobbs on 16 and Blythe/Mason produced a combination to see them all out for 60 - their figures 6 for 30 and 4 for 27 (each in ten overs), including Lord Dalmeny caught and bowled by Blythe on 1. S.H. Day and F. Huish easily scored the 78 needed to win making an unlikely victory by ten wickets.

Despite this there was a bad defeat against Lancashire during Canterbury Week from 10-12 August - Kent losing by eight wickets. A combination of MacLaren, Spooner, and Tyldesley (with Jack Sharp making 142) took the visitors on to 479. Kent only managed 162 and had to follow on but took their second innings tally to 348.

It was a valiant effort and Blythe made one of his highest totals scoring 75 runs in the second before he was clean bowled by Walter Brearley. There was then a formality as Lancashire made 34 runs to win the match.

At the end of August there were games of further interest, and Kent lost by ten wickets to Sussex at Hastings then secured a draw with Middlesex at Lord's - either side of a contest against the Australians.

The tourists arrived at the St. Lawrence Ground from 24-26 August and put on a substantial 403 in the first innings. Their team included Trumper, Noble, and Armstrong but the highest scoring came from Joseph Darling with 114 runs to his credit. Blythe took three wickets for 73 whereas Jack Mason recorded four for 101, but Kent could not match their opponents and lost by an innings and 35 runs.

Undeterred by such setbacks Blythe retained his good form, and the last game against Surrey at the Oval on 31 August to 2 September was a contest most memorable to the slow bowler.

The visiting side lost the toss but were put in to bat and made 202 runs whereas Surrey with Lord Dalmeny replied with 125 runs - Blythe took five of the wickets for only 45 including Jack Hobbs on a meagre 6 runs. Kent, however, could not profit from their opponents rather low total and scored just 84 themselves in the second innings.

Surrey saw their opportunity and looked destined to win but Blythe was still on form and took six wickets for 47 runs off 26.2 overs. These included Lord Dalmeny (Rosebery) who was caught by Murrell on 0. As the innings progressed the scores converged closer and closer until they were level with just the last two batsmen W.C. Smith and Neville Knox at the crease.

Blythe then sent down a deceptive ball to Smith (who was on 21 runs) and he skied it high into the air. As it came down towards Joe Murrell Blythe is said to have stated, "This is the first tied match I have ever played in" just before Murrell caught the ball. Surrey finished on 161 all out. [7]

---

[7] A tie is a very rare occurrence and at the time there were 14 of which Surrey were involved in 6 - with the Oval having more than any other ground. The first was between Kent and Hambledon at Windmill Down in 1783, whilst Surrey also tied with Kent at the Oval in July 1847 and experienced two ties in 1868. The last was between Surrey and Lancashire at the Oval in August 1894, although Worcester also tied with South Africa at home in July 1901.

Yorkshire were champions that season and played The Rest at the Oval under their captain Lord Hawke on 14 September. Blythe was chosen to play in the game for The Rest with Hayward, Tyldesley, Quaife, and Lilley and took two and three wickets in each innings respectively, but Yorkshire including Hirst and Rhodes won the game by 65 runs.

However, Kent had a poorer season and despite winning ten games lost seven. They did not win a single game during the three cricketing Weeks and had no victories in their last four outings.

Blythe played in all twenty-two county games and took 140 wickets but he received inadequate support, whereas Huish the wicket keeper was in good form and caught 54 and stumped 23 (close to his record of 1899). But it was all to no avail as the side slipped down the table.

The newspapers were well aware of this fact and noted that the previous season Kent had stood third to the two great northern counties, but fell to sixth place swapping with Sussex. This was mainly due to an increase in defeats and they also opened badly losing four of the first five contests. Their Weeks were far from satisfactory but they had a great achievement at Hull and also the remarkable tie at the Oval.

One feature was the extraordinary success of the old Oxonian E.W. Dillon with an average of 50 runs an innings and several other players were also commended. In terms of the bowling Fielder had fallen away although it was another big season for Blythe, but generally the team were not as good as in the previous year.

The season was ended and many went off for a well earned rest warming their feet by the winter fires, whilst several of the number headed south for warmer climes and more practice. In Blythe's case it was practice that paid great dividends for Kent during the next season.

CHAPTER 7

South Africa 1905-06

In terms of football Scotland were the "olde enemie" whereas in terms of cricket the title certainly fell to Australia. In this respect South Africa came second, while the first "test" to take place there was captained by Aubrey Smith (the Hollywood actor) at Port Elizabeth in 1889. This was followed by three minor tours which were elevated to test status, the first M.C.C. visit being undertaken in the winter of 1905-06.

Without doubt South Africa were not rated on a par with the Australians or at least remained an unknown quantity, and had yet to play a test in England, both factors that were reflected in the choice of players for the tour. However, it was suggested that if South Africa did well their games should be elevated onto a similar level (with the Aussies), if they should come to England at a future date.

Plum Warner was placed in charge of a line-up which included only three players from the successful summer tests against Australia - namely David Denton and Schofield Haigh top batsmen from Yorkshire, and Blythe the sole representative from the Kent side. Without the likes of Hayward, Fry, Tyldesley, Jackson, Hirst, and Rhodes it was almost certainly a "B" side, a fact that was soon to be revealed in the performances.

No doubt Blythe was happy to receive another chance at test level and to represent his country on the first-ever M.C.C. tour to South Africa (having missed the inaugural one to Australia). In fact, England's only success was when he produced one of his better displays of bowling.

Before embarking on the trip the bowler took up a significant issue with the committee at the Kent club. During the closed season he was paid a holiday allowance of roughly 20 shillings per week, in addition to the money he earned working as an engineer in south-east London.

Regarding the previous tour down to Australia in 1901-02 the club gave him permission to travel, but declined to pay him the usual allowance since the tour organisers apparently reimbursed him 'quite well.'

Blythe considered this somewhat unfair and took the matter up with Kent on 6 November 1905. The committee again leaned towards a rejection but Lord Harris agreed to pay the winter allowance 'as long as he behaved,' in addition to any tour-money he received in South Africa. The latter stated that what he did with his allowance was his business, while this clearly set a precedent for other players and for the future.

The sojourn to Cape Colony (the Union of South Africa was not formed until 1910) was certainly not for the feint-hearted, since it continued from November 1905 to April 1906.

However, it provided a festival of cricket for the connoisseur with five test matches in Cape Town and Johannesburg, and a series of twenty-one local games in the provinces; it also furnished an opportunity for some sight-seeing within the beautiful colony. Meanwhile, a detailed record of the tour survived due to the efforts of two budding reporters.

Captain E.G. Wynyard was born at Saharanpur, India in 1861 and went to Charterhouse then fought in Burma in 1885-87 and was an instructor at the R.M.C. His family home was at North End House, Hursley thus he played for Hampshire from 1878-1908. Indeed, he and Jack Crawford of Surrey sent letters back to the papers chronicling the tour, whereas Blythe took the trouble to keep these thus recording the trip for posterity.

THE VOYAGE

There were animated scenes at Waterloo on Saturday morning, November 11, as the good and famous of cricket gathered to see the eleven depart. In one corner was seen Apted, the noted groundsman from the Oval, giving instructions to his comrades Hayes and Lees. In a most earnest manner he implored that the latter did not over bowl himself, since he would surely help Surrey to become champions the next season.

Further down the platform was the honoured cricketer A.J. Webbe of the M.C.C. and Middlesex, who first played for I Zingari at Phoenix Park in 1874. He was seen chatting with the umpire Jim Phillips and bidding him farewell as rumour had it Phillips would not return to England.

Warner was sauntering with Bosanquet who again expressed his regrets at not being able to join party, whilst O.R. Borrodaile the secretary of Essex came along to bid his captain F.L. Fane a fond adieu.

The Union Castle line ran a Royal Mail steam packet from Southampton to the Cape and Natal via Madeira every Saturday, and the London train deposited the cricketers by the harbour at midday. All were on board the R.M.S. "Kinfauns Castle" (9,664 tons) by 1.30, although the vessel was not underway until 5.00 allowing the party to enjoy a good luncheon.

Class decorum was preserved on this floating microcosm hence Mr. and Mrs. Warner and maid, Messrs. Crawford, Fane, Hartley, Moon, Leveson-Gower, and Captain Wynyard were ensconced in the first saloon. The other players including Blythe, Board of Gloucester, Hayes, Relf, and Lees of Surrey, and Denton and Haigh of Yorkshire went second class.

Other notable passengers on board were the artist and engraver W.H.J. Boot and his wife bound for Madeira, Lieutenant Colonel J.G. Fair D.S.O., Sir James Heath M.P., Mr. J. Norman Hill, Mrs. J.B. Lithgow and her maid, Sir William and Lady Milton (K.C.M.G.), and Mr. Henry B.W. Wynyard (who was a brother of the cricketer). With such an entourage the voyage was certainly destined to be entertaining.

Most of the team retired to bed early rather pale but confident, although awoke the next morning for tea and coffee looking a good deal paler and a good deal less confident! The Bay (of Biscay) was at its worst and the ship pitched and rolled in a most disconcerting manner, and although there were many good cricketers among them few were good sailors.

According to the latter assessment "the order of going in" from openers down to the tail-enders was as follows: of the amateurs Crawford, Wynyard, Warner, Moon, Fane, Leveson-Gower, and Hartley; of the professionals Hayes, Haigh, Lees, Relf, Board, Blythe, and Denton.

Blythe given his maritime ancestry might have done better (although he did improve later), while Phillips the umpire maintained absolute neutrality and with the ship rolling at its worst he was constantly found enjoying the best of the menu. As a sailor he certainly scored a six!

On Tuesday night the weather made an extremely popular decision to declare, and on the Wednesday the ship docked at Madeira to take on coal thus the party went ashore for several hours break. Meanwhile, the rest of the voyage was taken up with various sports and entertainments.

A committee was formed for the specific purposes of arranging several such pastimes with the patron Captain R. Winder, the president Sir James Heath M.P., and the secretary Mr. H. Leveson-Gower. The committee also included Mr. Warner and Captain Wynyard.

In the first instance the second class challenged the first class to deck cricket and won the game at a romp. With Haigh, Denton, Blythe, and Lees in the former "seven" the outcome was a formality and Denton's bowling gave the captain a headache, since he could easily have been added to the other seven first-class bowlers in the squad.

There was however a quite serious drawback. The deck was too narrow resulting in some collisions and for the same reason running between the wickets was restricted. In this way the game lacked any real exercise.

Deck hockey was found to be a much better prospect for this purpose with the stumps acting as hockey sticks. As a result the cricketers played hockey for half an hour every afternoon before their dinner, and Wynyard proved to be a good forward and Hartley a proficient goal-keeper. In this way the team prepared themselves for test cricket!

High jinx were soon afoot with sports days on Wednesday and Thursday, 22 to 23 November. Jack Board the Gloucester wicket keeper (who was later a coach in South Africa) came first in the potato race but narrowly lost out in "slinging the monkey," whereas Mrs. Warner took several prizes in deck quoits and other contests.

Wynyard, Hartley, Warner, Relf, Hayes, Lees, Board, and Blythe all won various prizes at indoor and outdoor games whilst Phillips proved to be the best cribbage player on board the vessel.

In general the team were "up for it" and Blythe played a violin solo at the concert whereas Board and Crawford also sang well - in addition Blythe was kindly 'chaperoned' by Hayes to the fancy dress ball and they danced a cake walk, winning first prize and a cake for their efforts.

On Tuesday, 28 November the ship steamed into Table Bay at 6 a.m., and the town clerk and various sports representatives came on board to greet them in the main dining saloon. The mayor was indisposed so Councillor G. Cunningham wished them an enjoyable but not too successful tour!

Pelham Warner replied for the tourists noting a great improvement in the South African's game since his visit of seven years ago, a fact most clearly revealed during their sojourn to England the previous year.

He was confident regarding his team's ability to win but would be first to congratulate the South Africans if they were to succeed. Indeed, the M.C.C. executive were monitoring events with some interest, and it was likely that when the South Africans next came to England three test matches would be arranged against a "full-strength" England side. He also looked forward to a future triangular tournament involving the Australians.

A toast was drunk to the team with numerous hearty cheers and they then climbed into brakes and drove off to the International Hotel, Cape Town which was to be their headquarters for the duration.

Later in the day they were entertained by Mayor Liberman to a luncheon at City Hall, and then repaired to Newlands below Table Mountain to begin some much-needed cricket practice. However, in the evening they paid a visit to Hall's Hippodrome both for the purposes of entertainment and to be displayed for the benefit of the cricketing public.

L.J. Hall was the proprietor of a large horse-show and hippodrome at Barrack Square near the City Hall in Cape Town; whereas the programme involved a grand parade, some of the last American buffalo, various horse acts, rough-riding displays, representation of a stagecoach hold up on the prairies, and a Roman chariot race. No doubt this was a fascinating and novel experience for the English cricketers.

CAPE TOWN

The first test match was not until the January hence several games were played against regional opposition in the December (some first class). Three pitches were provided at Newlands six miles west of Cape Town for the purposes of practice, and Captain Wynyard noted that their first efforts on these revealed a large degree was necessary.

Being accustomed to the good turf wickets in England the problems of batting correctly on matting pitches could not be under-estimated. It was necessary to watch the ball far more diligently than on normal grass since it would often do something unexpected - shoot a little, bump a little, turn a little, or fizz on a little quicker than usual.

Such conditions prevailed on many South African grounds and Warner and his side were anxious to forestall the critics. In fact, most had suggested they were an inferior side and had under-estimated the opposition which were soon to face (indeed, with some difficulty).

In the first game against Western Province at Newlands on 2-5 December the England side showed they had mastered the batting conditions. True, the opponents were not considered as good as Transvaal but had a number of fine bowlers including Kotze "the lightening flasher," G. Rowe the left-hander, J.G. Whitehead of Warwick, and Carolin who mixed his deliveries in a most clever fashion. The attendance was about 1,500.

Leveson-Gower, Moon, and the injured Lees were left out hence Warner and Captain Wynyard led the batting. The latter was run out but Denton came in and England then tackled the opponents bowling, and by the end of the day were 318 for just five wickets. Only Warner seemed to lack confidence and played a defensive game to reach his 56 runs.

On the Monday the last four wickets went for 35 runs but the M.C.C. had a total of 365 with Blythe bowled by Rowe for 0. Difford and Snooke then batted confidently to Blythe and Crawford, however Haigh was brought in and took five wickets for just 29 thus they were all out for 96 runs.

During the follow on the fielding was poor and at least four easy chances were missed off Hartley, while Blythe took two wickets in each innings and Western Province were all out for 142 runs. The outcome was a win by an innings and 127 runs but there was still room for improvement.

In addition two smoking concerts took place in the evenings at the Royal Hotel, Cape Town. The first was hosted by the York & Lancaster C.C. (on the 2nd) and "Charlie" Blythe provided a fine violin solo, whilst the second was held by the West of England Association (on the 4th).

A match was then arranged at Worcester fifty miles east of Cape Town and the team travelled there and back late in the evening. The opponents were a Country 18 and the arrival of the M.C.C. coincided with the opening of Boland Park, a new ground. Indeed, some of the enthusiastic spectators had travelled over a hundred miles to see the game.

Warner sent in twelve against fifteen in the field and the cricket was of a holiday-type throughout however there was a good degree of enthusiasm. Blythe was left out since he had cut his foot quite badly (although it was mending), whilst Captain Wynyard acted as a reporter. Not surprisingly the game was again won by an innings and Leveson-Gower was in great form scoring 82 and taking five for 14 (with three in the first over).

The team then travelled to Cape Town on the night mail and prepared for a return against the Western Province on 9 December. Blythe was left out due to his troublesome foot as were Board and Hartley, whilst Kotze was missing with a strained back. The wicket was poorer due to the absence of the matting and both teams failed to score runs on the Saturday.

However, a high wind then dried the pitch over the weekend and on the Monday Moon and Relf added 92 runs for the seventh wicket to reach a total of 272. Snooke and Horwood made a good effort for the Western Province whose score was 233 but the visitors won by ten wickets. Blythe was fit again by that stage (and had been missed), but there was still much room for improvement in their fielding.

MATTING WICKETS

On 13 December they left Cape Town at 11.30 on the "Bulawayo Express" hoping for stronger opposition en route to Johannesburg. The ticket cost £16 and they were bound for Kimberley "the diamond city," to play two games against Griqualand (West) in the intense heat of the interior.

Estimates of the temperature were quite correct although the deluxe train was fitted with every modern convenience. Soon after their departure they witnessed some of the rare Cape mountain-scenery and further on passed by the battlefields of Belmont, Graspan, and Modder River where Captain Methuen fought engagements at the start of the recent war.

Fifteen miles from Kimberley the train was brought to a complete stop by a large plague of "hoppers" (or young locusts) and Wynyard, Moon, and Crawford provided valuable service in helping to shovel them away from the track. In fact, all were probably in line for the D.S.O. for their efforts. The side then stayed at the Savoy Hotel, Kimberley and the first match was played the next day on 15 December in almost tropical heat.

This was a 12 v 15 contest with Blythe and Crawford sitting out, whereas the "Pirates Ground" at Kimberley was quite large and despite having no grass at all the wicket still remained fast and true.

The first to bat were the M.C.C. but runs came at some difficulty, though Wynyard gave a good display of the hook-stroke and Hayes bruised the hands of mid off and extra cover on the way to a fine century. Moon also showed that his form was no fluke and the side eventually reached 373 runs, this being a good total considering the number of fielders.

Griqualand had bowled and fielded well, hardly dropping a catch, but in their batting seemed determined to hit the cover off the ball. This was a pointless practice since the ground was like a road and the cover had already left the ball after thirty minutes of play! As a result a large number were out for below 20 runs and they followed on 199 behind.

Only the efforts of J. Powell, R. Bishop, and Rose-Innes took the game into the third day, but it was all over by the lunchtime since in the second innings the M.C.C. needed just 8 runs to win.

A return match took place on 19-21 December and Warner had a slight cold and Haigh needed a rest, thus they were replaced by Blythe whose foot was well mended and also Crawford. The same arrangement of twelve to bat then eleven to field was used, and the main change from the previous contest was the improved batting of their opponents.

The weather remained bright and warm although the slight breeze had a tendency to whip up the dust. Meanwhile, there was some debate regarding the length of matting laid on the wicket - sometimes the batsman stood behind the matting, but other times he had one foot on it.

Some among the number thought there should be legislation in the rules regarding this. A problem often arose in the latter instance since with one foot on and one foot off the batsman was clearly unbalanced, and in this way he had a bad start when leaning forward to play the ball.

The M.C.C. found themselves in the field for nearly six hours and Blythe and Crawford led the bowling against Eland and Maritz, the latter a good player who was soon to go up to Oxford. Bishop again did very well and Michell joined Eland to put on 60 runs, whereas the side recorded the same score as the Western Province namely 233.

Regarding the field Relf was again very good at breaking up partnerships and Board was great as wicket keeper whereas Hartley at slip, Denton at third man, and Gower at cover were especially praiseworthy.

The visitors batted rather well with some fine displays from both Fane and Denton, also by Hayes and Crawford of Surrey, thus they declared on an excellent high score of 432 for eight.

Griqualand, however, began to tire after six days of cricket and were all out for 187 thus the M.C.C. won by an innings and 9 runs. This was the fifth victory and they had made many friends in Kimberley but were now to travel to the stronghold of cricket in South Africa. Indeed, this would be the real test of whether they could maintain such good results.

There was a great send-off by the hosts on the platform at Kimberley, and Mr. Grimmer a prominent member of the De Beers Company presented the wicket keeper Board with a silver-mounted and inscribed cricket ball. He was most appreciative of this memento regarding their visit.

The party then embarked on a 36-hour journey which initially took them back to De Aar and Bloemfontein and then up into the Transvaal. There was some disappointment at not travelling on the new line (which was yet to be joined up) thus they went at some inconvenience on a slow train.

This was over-run with passengers in particular a Christmas crowd and at one point it looked as if they would go to bed without any supper. The train reached Kroonstadt at 10 o'clock and some victuals were obtained, thus they ate with considerable relish the tinned tongue that was provided.

It was a tedious journey but they finally reached Johannesburg at 7 a.m. on the Christmas Eve - Warner, Mrs. Warner, and Fane were already there and the whole party were soon settled down in the Victoria Hotel. Christmas Day was a quiet, cheerful affair and the professionals enjoyed a merry and extravagant dinner with the Mayor of the City donning party hats and other festive paraphernalia. Whether this really prepared them for the contests ahead was clearly a matter for debate.

A first class match was played against the Transvaal at the Old Wanderers Ground, Johannesburg from 26-28 December. Tancred and Shalders were the openers but the home side failed to score many runs and Lees took five for 34 and Blythe a further three for 41 - the total being 135.

In reply the M.C.C. did better although Warner who began well then trod on his wicket, while the best performance came from Denton who made 132 not out although he was nearly caught at cover on 65. Schwarz bowled well as did Faulkner who adopted the Bosanquet method (but faster), and the visitors were dismissed on 265 runs.

The deficit seemed to inspire the Transvaal with some strong and sound batting despite the loss of Tancred for just 14. Blythe was the best of the bowlers with Lees, Relf, and Haigh and in the second innings he took four for 92 runs - however Shalders and Faulkner both put on over 60 apiece and the Transvaal scored 305. The target of 176 was quite attainable, but Warner and Denton went out for small scores and Wynyard was brilliantly caught by the wicket keeper Sherwell low down at leg.

Three were gone for just 15 runs and it was down to Hayes and Fane to neutralize the bad situation. At lunch the score was 50 for three which was not an impossible position, but Hayes was caught at fine leg off a big hit and Fane went down lbw - both to Faulkner. Afterwards the wickets fell quite quickly and the M.C.C. side were all out losing by 60 runs.

The defeat was mainly down to a lack of determination in the tourists batting, combined with the brilliance of Faulkner and the great finger spin of Schwarz which was ideal on the matting wickets. Indeed, he took five batsmen for just 34 runs including Blythe on nought.

Six or seven of the side were to feature in the test team with the pick of the other South Africans and would clearly be a very hard nut to crack. In the meantime the visitors played a West Transvaal 18 at Witrand Cricket Ground in Potchefstroom on 29-30 December.

On this occasion the ground was in excellent condition and the wicket the best so far, however the home side played stonewall tactics and the first eight overs were maidens - with only 9 runs being added in half an hour. Towards the close of the innings Warner adopted "the block-house system" and Leveson-Gower at forward point was kept quite busy.

The Potchefstroom men were somewhat in awe of the bowlers and never tried to hit a ball beyond mid off, but this was not to their benefit and Hartley took six wickets for 30 runs and Blythe had five for 16 runs. As a result the "18" were all out for 92 off just under seventy overs and only three of them managed to reach double figures.

Warner and Fane took up the cause for the M.C.C. and the former was in good form thus he made his first century of the tour with 125 runs. Blythe was promoted to first wicket upon the dismissal of Fane, the latter having only failed to make double figures on one occasion.

In fact, Blythe had not scored a single run in South Africa and for that reason was promoted. When he got off the mark the applause from his team-mates was most enthusiastic and he eventually made 10 runs before being bowled out by A. Faunthorpe.

The order of the day for the M.C.C. was to play "the hard, high, and often game" to give the outfield practice and as a result they made 200 runs for just two wickets. They declared at lunch on the second day the score 317 for six - leaving the home side with four hours to bat.

C. Campbell put on 40 runs and gave them a slight chance, but they were all out for 115 in fifty-six overs and the tourists won by an innings and 110 runs. Hartley took four wickets for 34 including Campbell lbw and also made a remarkable running catch when Blythe bowled a ball to J. Donald. Remarkable, in that no one knew that he could run so fast!

The main matter of debate, however, was the defeat by the Transvaal with regard to the forthcoming test. After the reverse "a grand rumour" began to circulate in the Johannesburg Press - the English had sent an urgent cable home for Hirst to come and strengthen the squad! Such a rumour was of course a fallacy but the need was somewhat a reality.

INAUGURAL TEST

The test series began at the Old Wanderers Ground, Johannesburg from 2-4 January 1906 and England won the toss, but they had a disastrous start reminiscent of the Transvaal game (who formed the core of the side). In fact Warner, Fane, and Denton went for the addition of just 7 runs whilst none of them lasted more than twenty minutes at the crease.

Wynyard, Hayes, and Crawford steadied the ship in the middle order and at the end Blythe put on a creditable 17 runs before being bowled out by Jimmy Sinclair. The M.C.C. had made 184 in total and most of the damage was done by the bowlers Schwarz and Faulkner.

However, the wicket did not favour the batsman and at the end of the day South Africa were on 71 for eight wickets. Blythe took Shalders for just 4 runs caught by Haigh and also removed Snooke and Faulkner, then Nourse managed to add 16 in the morning to reach a total of just 91 runs.

On the second day England made a further 190 and looked on course for a victory whilst Warner made a half century in 100 minutes. But the home side then started to score freely led by Tancred and Shalders, and G.C. White made 81 and A.W. Nourse 93 to reach the target score.

South Africa had narrowly won their debut in test cricket by one wicket on the third day with Nourse and Sherwell not out. Indeed, in the second innings Blythe took only one for 50 and the M.C.C. used seven bowlers, as the game gradually ran away from them.

Sir Pelham Warner later described the contest in his book of cricket and declared that it was "the greatest match I ever played in," despite losing the game by the most narrow of margins. In the red-dust of the Wanderers Ground the drama was played out and the M.C.C. made an opening score far too low - although the opponents initially managed even less as Lees, Blythe, and Crawford bowled splendidly.

The game was a triumph for their fielding - Blythe and Lees sending down perfect-length deliveries from which scoring was extremely difficult. There was a great "shout" from the 10,000 spectators as the tall figure of Jimmy Sinclair arrived, but he went straight back to the pavilion, while the England tail went out quite easily and the home side needed 284 to win.

At first everything went the way of the M.C.C. and six wickets fell for 105, however Nourse and Sherwell then played extremely well (taking all their chances) and thereby won the game. It was their first test victory and one of the best rearguard actions ever seen, but the M.C.C. also received credit as they were handicapped by the absence of Haigh on the last day.

Warner then concluded, "Never have I witnessed anything like the scene at the finish. Men were shrieking hysterically. Some were actually crying and hats and sticks were flying everywhere. When the winning hit had been made the crowd 'tackled' Nourse and Sherwell and carried them into the pavilion, while for half an hour after it was all over thousands lingered on, and the whole of the South African eleven had to come forward on to the balcony of the committee room. And so we were beaten, but defeat in such a struggle was glorious, for the *First Test Match* will be talked of in South Africa as long as cricket is played there."

The victory was hailed with delight by every South African sportsman and most credit went to Sherwell (at the end), since his task might have shaken the strongest nerve. There was intense excitement and one of the keenest spectators was the High Commissioner, while the investment by Mr. Logan and Abe Bailey into South African cricket was clearly well justified.

It was then the duty of the team to win the rubber to put them on an equal standing with Australia, but they were warned against over-confidence as Warner had an extensive knowledge of "the science of the game." Practice, study, and training were needed to make sure that no chance was lost.

CULTURAL EXCHANGE

England also required more practice but in the meantime there was time for some leisure. Apart from Christmas there were several opportunities for swimming on the beach or at a local pool, some sightseeing, a trip to the race track for a "dead cert," and other cultural experiences.

Blythe clearly enjoyed being pictured with local black residents whom he made friends with and the whole team indulged in visits to local townships. On one occasion they were pictured with a group of black youths who were scantily clad (if clad at all), on another were pictured outside a mud/thatch hut with a group of teenagers wearing (the teams) cloth caps, and also were seen giving aid to the destitute beside shanty dwellings.

The contrast in their suits, ties, and umbrellas were striking compared to the inhabitants like the emergence of Stanley on Lake Tanganyika thirty years earlier. Their poses being similar to his polished boots and flannel suit as he uttered those immortal words, "Dr. Livingstone, I presume?"

Further to this there was considerable interest in a visit of Lord Selborne, the High Commissioner, to Maseru at the heart of the Basuto nation (now in Lesotho). Some fifteen to twenty thousand mounted horsemen gathered and encamped near the settlement during his sojourn.

With such interests in mind the team then played two regional games, one against Pretoria at Berea Park (in Pretoria) on 6-8 January and another with a Middelburg and District side on 10 January.

Pretoria asked to play fifteen but Warner was in opposition to this idea and they eventually fielded just eleven. The home side took a considerable amount of effort preparing the ground thus it was in capital condition, but the M.C.C. team were off to a bad start losing Board, Hayes, and Relf in quick succession. Matters then improved and Hartley made 77 thus with an opening total of 338 the visitors won by an innings and 80 runs.

The second game was at Middelburg and the ground was one of the best they had played on (and as good as Potchefstroom), although the fielding was at times still quite difficult. Blythe and Hayes continued to feel far from well in the climate and remained in Pretoria whereas Captain Wynyard was also left out of the fixture.

Warner made two good partnerships with Crawford who was "caught in the country" and with Fane thus he had a century by lunchtime. Eventually he reached 128 but like many of the team fell to the slow bowling of Major Barnes. Middelburg had fielded most of the day and had just one hour's batting but lost eight wickets during that period, whilst they became even worse on the second day.

Their second innings follow on was somewhat better and the match was finished just before a huge thunderstorm hit the ground. The result was an easy innings victory, but the small number of spectators remained keen and the visiting team greatly enjoyed the whole event.

Due to the latter match being finished in two days, a further contest was arranged against the British (S.A.) Army at Thare Tswana ("place of salt") in Pretoria on 12-13 January. Hayes, Lees, and Relf were left out whereas Captain Wynyard had departed for a three week trip to explore the Victoria Falls region, and as a result the services of Sir Godfrey Lagden were enlisted to complete the numbers. [1]

---

[1] Sir Godfrey Yeatman Lagden (1851-1934) joined the Civil Service in 1869 and was in the Post Office until 1877, becoming chief clerk to the State Secretary of the Transvaal in 1878 and the Government Secretary to Basutoland in 1884. He was then Resident Commissioner for the latter in 1893-1901 and a Commissioner for Native Affairs in the Transvaal from 1901-07.

All of the team were accommodated in the camp, although the amateurs were billeted with the officers and the professionals resided in the sergeants' messes - clearly, the shape of things to come for Blythe.

Warner won the toss for the M.C.C. and Board, Moon, and Denton made it a long day of fielding for the Army, thus at the fall of the second wicket the visitors had 150 runs. Denton eventually made 130 and Sir G. Lagden scored 21, whereas Warner came in towards the end and the following morning they declared on 480 runs with just seven wickets gone.

Captain Mitford and Lieutenant Davenport took to the crease against the bowling of Blythe and Crawford but they kept a good length and any runs came slowly. The first wicket fell to Blythe when Davenport was caught in the slips by Hartley, and thereafter a complete collapse ensued as Mitford made some 65 runs out of a total of only 97.

During the follow on Haigh was magnificent in his bowling taking four wickets for just 9 runs, although the Army did improve and reached 165 but lost the game by an innings and 218 runs. Blythe took two wickets in each innings and nine bowlers were used by the M.C.C. in total. The team then went on a trip to the coast, one that was full of interest both in terms of the culture and of the cricketing experience. [2]

---

[2] Blythe stayed in the "Transvaal Hotel" in Pretoria and his hotel receipts provide a taste of the journey ahead: Central, King William's Town; Hexagon, Queenstown; Masonic, Cradock; Steinmann's, Grahamstown (caterer to Sir W. Hely-Hutchinson the Governor); and the Grand, Port Elizabeth.

CHAPTER 8

Further Tests

After the first test South Africa were encouraged by the home newspapers to practice, and practice more, but England still had several tricks up their sleeve and soon engaged in further training themselves. True, they found it difficult playing on the matting wickets of the interior, but were more at home on the regular pitches of the Cape - in particular their favourite ground at Newlands where they often seemed to do well.

COASTAL SCENERY

Departing from Pretoria at the start of the year the side then travelled to the east through some countryside which reminded them of England, and arrived in the coastal-town of Durban on Monday evening, 15 January 1906. They were greeted by the mayor Mr. C. Henwood at the station and later on were introduced to several important sportsmen from the region.

Each part of South Africa where they travelled was a separate colony with vastly different roots and a conflict of culture - Cape Town was gentrified by the English, the Transvaal was the heartland of the Boers and Trekkers, and Natal presented a mix of cultures with some spice from India. In fact, the cricketers soon became accustomed to travelling about in rickshaws and enjoyed posing before them for photos with African natives.

Having established their bearings they also enjoyed some further cricket and the first contest commenced the next day against Natal at Albert Park (Oval) in Durban at 11 a.m. However, due to the heat Warner and his men in the field soon felt extremely tired and listless.

The home side sent in Rev. Robinson and Cooley to face Blythe and Lees but neither were "at home," thus Cooley went out to Blythe for 3 runs and the next man Thompson also fell to him caught in the slips by Hayes.

Dave (A.W.) Nourse the useful left-hander (born at South Norwood) was the hero of the first test and his arrival at the crease soon turned matters around. Square cuts were the chief feature of his innings and he was the last man dismissed on 119 with the total on 191 runs.

The M.C.C. came in at 4.45 and began rather badly thus Warner was gone for nought and Denton found it hard to settle, whereas bad light meant the stumps were drawn on 44. On the second day Denton made the only stand hitting six 4's and the team were all out for 175 - with Blythe on 7.

In the evening there was a complimentary dinner for the M.C.C. at their residence the Royal Hotel, Smith Street with a fine menu of sole, beef, turkey, plum tart, and ice cream. A lengthy series of toasts followed and the protracted list included the King, the Governor, the teams, cricket (of course), the press, and finally the chairman.

Back on the pitch the home side looked like making a high score but were all out for 159 at noon on the third day. The M.C.C. needed 176 to win but five wickets were gone for 57 and six for 97, then Haigh and Fane came together and made a stand for an hour until rain stopped play.

Just 36 runs were needed in a limited time and amid great excitement the duo held out to reach the target, although great credit went to Natal who pushed the M.C.C. very hard. Blythe was improving taking 3-35 and 5-41 including the danger-man Nourse clean bowled on just 5 runs.

A second game was arranged against Natal at the Oval, Pietermaritzburg on 20-23 January many of the opponents having played in the first fixture. Warner won the toss and put the opposition in for three main reasons:

(1) The matting was a new one and was likely to favour the bowlers for the first hour or two. (2) It provided an opportunity to become accustomed to the light and the surroundings. (3) Two or three players were below par due to the heat of Durban and were unlikely to do justice with the bat.

The same combination of bowlers led off as in the previous fixture, but there was a costly mistake when Blythe sent down the initial delivery to Thompson - and Hayes dropped him in the slips.

Afterwards Blythe bowled out both Rev. Robinson and A.W. Robinson whilst Hime fell to a yorker from Crawford. There was little of interest in the innings and Natal were all out for 117, whereas Thompson did well for his side but took two and a half hours to make his 48 runs.

Fane and Denton were the mainstay of the M.C.C. attack and the total was 121 for five wickets at the end of the first day. During the evening the local mayor and Pietermaritzburg Cricket Union gave a complimentary banquet at the Imperial Hotel with a meal of roast venison, mutton, and game, toasts, dancing, and regimental music, and a programme stating: *Play up! Play up! And Play the Game* (by Henry Newbolt).

Upon resumption the M.C.C. team were all out for 191 but the grass was extremely long restricting scoring on both sides, and even the hardest of hits only reached the boundary with the greatest difficulty. Natal came up against Haigh who took seven for 58 thus they reached 173 and the M.C.C. then put on 100 and won by six wickets. Blythe's figures were 4-51 and 1-32 although he did reach 850 wickets in the first innings.

Capt. Wynyard noted that this concluded their trip to the Garden Colony but added that the great heat had undoubtedly affected them, especially the change from the dry heat of the highland plateau to the damp heat of the coast. Such a change was, indeed, most enervating and only the resilience of Frederick Fane managed to save them.

The team then made their first acquaintance with the "Norman" one of the smaller vessels in the Union Castle line. A fond adieu was bid to their friends in Natal but the outlook was quite grim for their unhopeful band of sailors - the sea was very rough and this made the ship quite "fidgety," thus they were well relieved to reach dock at East London.

Arriving in the harbour at daybreak they disembarked as quickly as they could, and made their way across to the colonial looking Deal's Hotel with its opulent verandas and tower in the centre of town.

There were then a series of games against district opposition, and at East London the pitch was fairly good although the wicket had suffered from some heavy rain the week before. In Cape Colony the matting was generally stretched on grass with the benefit of fielding on greenery once again, but these wickets were not equal to those used from Kimberley onwards which had a foundation of either rolled sand or concrete.

The game began at the Jan Smuts Ground with East London batting and the fifteen players scored 120 runs. Hartley produced some good bowling whilst the M.C.C. side were just one run behind at the end of the day. This prompted the local press to suggest their bowling was completely mastered and lacked inherent variety, whilst in the evening there was a dinner of "welcome" which took place at the Belgrave Hotel.

On the second day Leveson-Gower came to the rescue (as he often did) and played some beautiful shots on the off - the score reaching 206. The opponents were then a mere procession and were all out for 73 runs.

Some right regal "Royal" fixtures followed and the M.C.C. side arrived at King William's Town on Thursday evening, 1 February. Denton and Fane again proceeded to bat superbly at the Victoria Ground and they declared on 415 runs but play was stopped on the Saturday due to rain.

In the evening there was a dinner at the Grosvenor Hotel which provided some diversion from the weather and play recommenced on the Monday. Despite the prolonged break there was time to get the XV out "twice" then take the night train to their next engagement at Queenstown.

In fact, this was a pattern in these games where the early batsmen scored heavily and the remainder made easy runs or went out to facilitate a victory in the time allotted. This was not a good spectacle, but most significantly did not prepare the team for the more important matches ahead.

Cricket in the border towns was not really flourishing since despite a fair number of supporters and good grounds there was little local interest. The players were keen enough, but there was a lack of coaching and a definite need for some good professionals to bring them along.

The game against Queenstown was played at the Sandringham Ground on 6-7 February, and was remarkable for a high score of 212 by Jack Crawford who was still in when the side declared on 400 runs. Indeed, the figures for this match bore out the previous and most pertinent hypothesis.

Blythe then carried all before him on the second day in the face of little resistance and the thirty-six batsmen made 224 in their two innings. The former took sixteen for 41, although the result was a close call as Hartley bowled the last man in the penultimate over but was "no-balled." Blythe then stepped up and finished the job during the final over.

At this time each member of the team received a presentation copy of *"Wisden's Almanac"* for the 1906 season forwarded by the courtesy of one Mr. Harry Luff. The volume was voted better than any of its predecessors and the gift was gratefully received by the cricketers.

With all the right facts to hand (about their opponents) the M.C.C. went to play the Midlands at the Standard Ground in Cradock. There was to be an early start at 6.30 a.m. on 11 February thus they slept in their "saloon" at the station overnight. They did not arrive until 9.30 in the evening, the town being of Dutch origin and a centre for agriculture 200-miles inland.

The game was limited to two days and as the Midlands side had 22 players a draw was the likely result. Indeed this proved to be the case. The home side made 256 and Blythe took six of the wickets although the three army-men in the team failed to score any runs. At the close of play the M.C.C. had reached 413 and it was a pity there was not another day.

There was a similar draw against Albany at Lords Ground, Grahamstown on 14-15 February with a meal at the Grand Hotel, and the side then went south to Port Elizabeth and played two games at St. George's Park from 16-21 February - concluding with a banquet at the Humewood Hotel.

The first contest against a Port Elizabeth 15 was won by an innings and 77 runs, whereas Crawford and Wynyard scored well in the next game as the M.C.C. beat Eastern Province by ten wickets - Blythe taking 3-48 and 5-30. A game against a S.W. District 22 in the mountains at Oudtshoorn three days later was drawn and featured the manager I. Difford.

A lengthy journey then ensued back to Johannesburg followed by two practice sessions at the Old Wanderers. The players batted in pairs and the others bowled and fielded, and by the end the M.C.C. believed they could reverse the one-wicket 'verdict' against them from the first game.

TEST MATCHES (2-5)

Regarding the second test the South Africans played the same side as in the previous encounter, whereas the M.C.C. had to do without the services of Hayes who had severely damaged his hand.

On the morning of the match (6 March) a heavy thunderstorm hit the Old Wanderers Ground which by 10 o'clock was mostly under water. However the weather shortly cleared and the hard, sandy soil rapidly recovered thus by 1 o'clock the only problem was some slowness in the outfield.

It was often hard to predict the South African wickets after rain but in general if the mat was not saturated or rain-sodden, and the ground on which it were stretched was not greatly affected, then there would be little variation in conditions of play. Captain Wynyard added that in this instance the dry mat was stretched over an even surface however the wicket was slower than during the first test.

Warner had been indisposed but declared himself fit and went in to bat with Crawford, whereas Percy Sherwell captain of South Africa used the fast bowler Snooke and Sinclair during the initial attack. It was a disastrous start since Warner was caught at short slip with only 3 on the board and Denton sent a slow ball straight back into the hands of Sinclair.

Fane himself began well but on 8 runs he likewise sent a fast ball back to Faulkner - who caught it one-handed. Only Moon and Crawford made any show of getting on top of the bowling, and Moon in particular batted in defensive style for an hour and a half saving a total collapse.

At the end Lees and Blythe provided "the sensation of the innings" and made a substantial stand, putting on 25 and 12 runs apiece, thus the final score of 148 runs was far more than had ever looked likely.

Tancred and Shalders led the home side's batting on the second day and they were not parted until 71 runs were on the board. Lees, Blythe, Haigh, and Relf provided some very accurate bowling and the situation might have been better but for two (unfortunate) dropped catches.

Crawford then came in to bowl and took both these batsmen within two minutes, and the bowling remained in the ascendancy until Sinclair and Snooke set up a partnership. The former sent off some great drives most of them low shots, one going clean over the ring, however once he reached a half-century he hit out at everything. This continued until Haigh stumped him on 66 when he tried to drive Blythe out of the ground.

The South Africans reached 277 runs and in the afternoon there was an unusual incident. A spider established a web on the wicket at the railway end and White, Nourse, Tancred, and Sinclair guarded their little mascot from any injury thus it remained intact until teatime arrived, whilst not one straight or curly ball succeeded in dislodging it!

Thereafter, a heavy rain-storm prevented the game from continuing and it recommenced on Thursday, 8 March. On this occasion matters were even worse - Snooke bowling very fast dismissed Warner with the first ball then Denton was caught by the wicket keeper with the score on 5 runs.

Fane began to make some kind of defence but Crawford produced a poor shot which went up in the air and was again taken by Sherwell the keeper. Moon was also caught with a low catch just a few minutes in, thus four wickets were gone for just 25 runs.

The best batting of the contest came from Fane who eventually scored 65, firstly with Captain Wynyard and then with Relf who also did well. In fact the former had seven 4's to his credit when he was finally dismissed by a good yorker. Schwarz then came in to bowl and rapidly removed the rest of the side leaving a target of only 32 runs.

South Africa won by nine wickets after just three days and were without doubt the better side, there being nothing in the wicket or light to explain the poor display by the M.C.C. Their batting was not inherently poor in form but lacked any real determination, whereas the bowling was adequate although Blythe only took one wicket in the first innings.

The all-round excellence of the home team showed them to be a side of exceptional merit, and very high class, and it was this that led to the easy defeat of the M.C.C. Whereas in terms of the fielding and wicket keeping there was little to separate the two elevens.

Only a one day break separated them from the third test in Johannesburg on 10-14 March, and there seemed every prospect of the same outcome. South Africa went in to bat and although Tancred and Shalders were gone before the hour was up, Hathorn made 102 runs with fifteen 4's. Every player had double figures and the score was eventually 385.

Each team provided an exceptional level of batting and Fane was again in good form making 143 with seventeen 4's out of a total of 295. The home side then scored freely with G.C. White reaching 147 and they declared on 349 with five wickets gone - near to the end of the third day.

Both Warner and Hartley went out lightly before the drawing of stumps, and on the fourth day the M.C.C. were all dismissed for 196 with Snooke taking eight wickets for just 70 runs.

The tourists had lost the game by 243 runs and with three defeats had also lost the rubber (which supported the theory of the critics). Blythe had taken just three wickets in the game and scored 10 runs in total.

With only their pride left to play for the M.C.C. travelled south to the Grand Hotel, Bloemfontein and played the Orange Free State at the local Ramblers Ground on 17-21 March. Blythe, Haigh, and Hartley took most wickets against the "fifteen" in a game that was ultimately a draw.

The M.C.C. then arrived back at Newlands perhaps in conditions more favourable and played the fourth test from 24-27 March. South Africa won the toss and batted but Blythe took the openers Tancred and Shalders both lbw which boded well, their scores 11 and 16 apiece.

G.C. White made a partial stand with 41 runs however Blythe then caused a collapse of the middle order dismissing Nourse, Hathorn, and Sinclair for a total of 5 runs. In addition he clean bowled Faulkner making his figures six wickets for 68 runs and the South Africans were all out for 218 - in fact this beat his previous best in a test match of 4-30.

Perhaps the home side were more relaxed after their earlier successes and the M.C.C. soon pressed home their advantage late in the evening of the first day. The tactics used by Warner were to use several night watchmen thus Board and Relf were the openers, but when the former went after just two balls Blythe came nonchalantly to the crease.

Promptly he put on 6 runs and Relf remained intact at nought thus the day was ended with England over 200 runs behind. The game was in the balance and no doubt both sides fancied their chances although the South Africans, being on form, were probably the favourites.

The next morning the unlikely couple of Blythe and Relf returned to the crease, and Relf proceeded to hit five 4's over the boundary before he was taken lbw by Faulkner on 28 runs. However, this was to be Blythe's game and with Fane at the other end the slow-bowler scored 27 runs in a stand lasting 75 minutes - his record batting score in test cricket.

Denton, Crawford, and Moon also added a further 100 runs between them and the side were all out for 198 finishing just twenty behind. In fact, there was every expectation they would lose yet again.

However, there was an unlikely collapse and after three minutes Crawford bowled to Shalders and Blythe took the catch. Only Gordon White made any kind of stand scoring ten 4's and a total of 73 runs, whereas Blythe bowled both Tancred and Nourse for small totals.

All resistance was gone and Lees clean-bowled Hathorn and Sinclair and Blythe gave similar treatment to Faulkner, Snooke, and Sherwell thus they were all out for 138 on the third morning. Warner and Crawford were both bowled by Sinclair for 4 runs apiece but Denton and Moon did well whilst Fane secured the game with 66 not out. England reached the 160 needed to win by four wickets in front of 3,000 spectators in fine weather.

The newspapers noted that South Africa only added 41 runs for their last five wickets, whilst Fane produced a fine all round performance without any chance being given to the fielders. However, with an admirable score of 27 runs, an important catch, and bowling figures of 6-68 and 5-50 much of the credit for the victory went to Blythe.

One might have expected this to prompt a revival but it was not the case. The last game of the tour was the final test at the attractive Newlands on 30 March and England went in to bat. Despite a good effort by Crawford and Fane with several 4's the total was just 187 runs, and South Africa then returned to form with all the team batting well to make 333.

It seemed that all confidence had finally expired with regards to batting by the M.C.C. and Nourse clean bowled four of the team, whilst the last five wickets went for only 36 added. Blythe alone remained at the crease having hit a four and scored 11 runs, as the side were all out for 130 and lost by an innings and 16 runs (in just three days of play).

SOME SPEECHES

The whole tour, however, encompassed an extremely good spirit, and the next day (3 April) there was a grand banquet for both sides hosted at the opulent Mount Nelson Hotel in Cape Town.

Prior to the toasts there was a meal of ox tail soup, fillet of beef (with garnish), mixed salad, bombe praline, fruits of the dessert, coffee &c. and some ambient music from Weber, Wagner, and Bizet. Indeed, this was in many ways a cultural exchange rather than just a sporting event.

Major General E.S. Brook C.B. was chairman of proceedings and in the room was one of the foremost sports gatherings ever seen in Cape Town. Initially a telegram was read from Sir W. Hely-Hutchinson the Governor congratulating the M.C.C. on their fine efforts.

The General then proposed a toast to the team and being from Yorkshire noted his natural interest in cricket, "that best of games." It was clear that such an interest was shared by many as evinced by the large crowds who had watched at Newlands, whereas with ominous portent he added - 'there was no true sportsman who would not make a good soldier.'

Warner responded for the tourists regarding the fine qualities of the South African cricketing side, and was happy to see that with regard to sport no question of racialism ever occurred. It was a lesson that politicians should take to heart (followed by laughter and cheers), whilst he preferred the term South African rather than that of "Afrikander" - since the former included the whole of the nation.

In general, no one asked where the player emanated from just that he was a cricketer for his country, and he thought the day was not far off when the entire nation would be united. [1]

Sherwell then spoke for the home team and complained that some in the press had under-rated the M.C.C. He was actually pleased that they had won a representative game, since this proved their strength and thus confirmed the achievement of the South Africans in their four victories. In addition, he admitted that there was some advantage in the fact that eight of the team regularly played at the Johannesburg ground.

He looked forward to playing against some good county players at Home in 1907, whilst he was proud to be captain of a side who Warner stated had made such improvements. There were few complaints about the selection from both centres of cricket, although the uncertainty of the turf wicket at Newlands meant only a few new players had been unearthed.

CONCLUSIONS

With many memories exciting and moving as well as new friendships the side boarded the "Norman" (a Union Castle vessel) which was smaller than the previous ship at 7,537 tons. Vogler was to accompany them whilst the other South Africans returned northwards. This was the 59th voyage and they left Cape Town at 5 p.m. on Wednesday, 4 April with 266 passengers who had embarked from both the Natal and Cape Ports.

The cargo included mails, raw gold, and sundry other items but the latter were of a negligible quantity as South Africa was backward in terms of her pastoral and agricultural resources. The weather was dull and dreary as they left Table Bay and that was how it stayed until they crossed the Equator exactly a week later (but fortunately it remained calm).

There was a degree of excitement since arrangements were made for the intermediate steamer "Gaika" to bring mail to the ship from the "Kinfauns Castle." This included letters from home, but a signal went up to the effect that the red and white "tub" of mail had been dropped overboard! A small boat was launched from the "Gaika" and the mail was safely secured whilst cheers went up from the passengers of both vessels.

---

[1] Warner was mainly referring to racial differences between the English and Dutch. In fact, the Boer War took place just before in 1899-1902 and the Transvaal and Orange Free State then came under British rule. Warner was not referring to the issue of Apartheid (1948-94) although there was already discrimination against the blacks regarding work, whilst the team took a great interest in the plight of black South Africans - the Union being established four years later.

On the Friday night, 13 April there was a grand concert in the first saloon before Commander S.C. Brown esquire. The band began with an overture of "Gypsy Life" followed by five songs humorous and grave and a violin solo "The Broken Melody" by Mr. Blythe. After a short interlude there was a suite of dances "Henry VIII," four songs, a clarinet solo, and a sketch by the band portraying the recent visit - "God Save the King!"

During the voyage there were several games and sports and Mrs. Warner consented to distribute some of the prizes, whereas on the Saturday there was a dance for first and second class on the promenade deck. This was in perfect condition for the purpose and the band provided a well executed ensemble of music to mark the occasion.

Both Denton and Haigh did well regarding games winning prizes at deck quoits, whilst Blythe won the wheelbarrow race with another passenger and Mrs. Warner came second in the egg and spoon race. The sports concluded on Easter Monday, 16 April with a tug of war and in the evening there was a Ju-Jitsu display by a leading exponent Mr. Bankier (or "Apollo").

There were frequent accounts from the outside world by *Rottar* which included details of Cambridge's victory in the Boat Race by three lengths, and of the Everton v Newcastle Cup Final at the Crystal Palace stating "all seats are booked." Meanwhile, the native rising in Natal was over.

Madeira was reached on the Tuesday and several passengers ascended The Mount (2,000 feet) on the cogwheel railway and then descended in sleighs. Others explored the capital Funchal whilst those on board watched local divers and bartered with vendors for lace, wickerwork, fruits, and photos. With the coal bunkers replenished the voyage continued.

In the evening there was a raffle organised by Jack Board - the prize being a bat used during the tour and signed by both teams who had played in the final test match at Newlands.

The winner on this occasion was Mr. J. Cansfield whereas the proceeds of £7 10s were to go to the Bristol Royal Infirmary. A souvenir of the voyage entitled "The Norman Observer" included details of the M.C.C. tour and noted there had been 26 matches - 16 won, 5 lost (four test matches and one against Transvaal), and 5 drawn.

Fane, Crawford, and Denton led the batting averages with Fane on 42.46 whilst Crawford and Haigh were the best bowlers for the M.C.C.; although Blythe bowled by far the most overs at 689 (with 241 maidens) and took the largest number of wickets at 113 (average 12.88).

The "Norman" sailed into the Solent on Saturday, 21 April and Warner then had to face the press who came on board, and initially a reporter for *The Sportsman* asked why the side had failed in the test matches.

Warner's reply was to the point and succinct in the extreme, "I have no excuses to make. We were beaten by a better side." Indeed, his opinion of South African cricket remained very high since they had now reached a standard of equality with the British sides:

"On matting wickets the South Africans are capable of beating an eleven of the calibre that we send to Australia, and especially on the Wanderers' ground at Johannesburg are they strong. Perhaps we should beat them here because the wickets would suit us and we should be able to pick our best men at the top of their form.

But out there, when we have only a certain number to select from, they certainly have the better chance of winning. Since I was last in South Africa their strength has increased quite fifty per cent. Mind you, we had a good team, but they fairly beat us. They were stronger in batting, better in bowling, and fielded just as well as we did."

Some suggested the fielding was the problem but Warner disputed this and said it was actually the batting. The wickets were very fast and the likes of Schwarz produced tremendous breaks on both sides, some of them turning by two or three feet. It was a paradise for leg break bowlers and the home side had eleven batsmen and nine bowlers, thus Shalders who was not a regular bowled some of the finest balls ever seen.

In Warner's opinion White was the best all-rounder with the hitting power of Sinclair and the defence of Charles Fry, whilst Nourse was also highly commended. For the tourists Crawford looked like being the next Jackson, Fane and Denton did well, and Blythe and Lees bowled splendidly, whereas the South African spectators were cordial and impartial.

D. Denton concluded by stating how difficult it was to play on grounds devoid of grass and noted that the fielders collected nails full of grit when picking up the ball, while he praised the opponents saying their attack was more difficult to face than the M.C.C. With that the players took the boat special to Waterloo, although Haigh headed directly for Yorkshire!

CHAPTER 9

Champions 1906

Blythe barely had time to unpack his travelling valise back at New Cross Road before the new cricket season started, and what a season it was to be for Kent with the bowler playing a leading role.

Meanwhile, Surrey had last won the championship seven years earlier and believed they were favourites to take the title for a seventh time. Before the tour Apted showed concern that Lees might over bowl himself and thus inhibit his side's chances, and in some way this was true since he bowled 589.3 overs (behind Blythe) and had the lowest M.C.C. average at 15.16. But, no doubt, other teams were to have a say in the matter.

Marsham continued to captain the Kent side and Blythe settled back into county cricket which was his *piece de resistance*. Although he did well in certain test matches (more of this later) he was clearly most at home in first class cricket, and the 1906 season provided the chance for his bowling to come together with the batting of his team-mates. The promise was already there and the promise was soon to be fulfilled.

However, there was an inauspicious start against the M.C.C. at Lord's on 14-16 May when Kent lost by 69 runs. Blythe started well and took five wickets for 55 runs and three for 57, but it was the middle order including Marsham who failed to make the runs in the second innings - although the bowlers Fairservice, Blythe, and Fielder all made double figures.

He then played on his home turf against Yorkshire (the champions) at the Private Banks Sports Ground, Catford from 17-19 May. It was a stiff early test and the opposition included Lord Hawke, Hirst, and Rhodes as well as Denton and Haigh who had done so well in South Africa. Yorkshire batted first and Denton put on 46 and Hirst made 101 before they were bowled by Blythe - their final total being 229 runs.

The Kent batsmen were then besieged by Haigh, Hirst, and Rhodes and only Humphreys and Seymour made any kind of stand, whilst the lower order had a complete collapse thus they were all out for 178 runs.

Blythe soon made a game of it (in front of his home fans) and Yorkshire recorded only 137 in their second innings. He took seven wickets for 63 in 28 overs with ten maidens, and only Denton made any impact reaching 68 runs before he was bowled by Fielder. Kent clearly had a chance but were all dismissed for just 69 with only two in double figures, and it was Hirst who did the damage taking seven wickets for just 33 runs.

This was not championship form and in the next game against Essex at the County Ground, Leyton there was a draw; although Kent pressed on and made 366 in their second innings with Blythe scoring 23 runs.

The first hint of a reverse in fortunes came in the next contest against Sussex at the County Ground, Hove on 4-5 June. Fielder took six wickets to see the opponents all out for 124 then Punter Humphreys lived up to his name and made 109 - whereas Dillon, Seymour, and Burnup were all free scoring as they led the batting.

By the end of the first day Kent had 294 and they were all out on the second for 414, whilst Fielder took another five wickets and the visitors were removed for 173 losing by an innings and 117 runs. This was the start of a great improvement for the team but it came at a cost.

In the second innings Blythe took two wickets and dived well to catch Robert Relf off a fast delivery by Fielder - Sussex were in trouble and had lost five wickets for just 53 runs thus the game was for the taking. Blythe then tried to catch Albert Relf (the brother) with a similar attempt however sustained a bad hand injury that saw him miss three games.

A disappointment for one player was, however, to be a most propitious opportunity for another. Kent arrived at Old Trafford to play Lancashire on 7-9 June without their left hand orthodox bowler, thus the game saw the debut of Frank Woolley who was later to take all records before him. He had a similar style to Blythe but mixed this with a left hand medium pace, although in his first game he did not inspire. [1]

Archie MacLaren and his men blasted their way onto the pitch on the first day and Johnny Tyldesley (at number three) scored 295 not out. Woolley had the misfortune of dropping Tyldesley twice and took one wicket, and before the stumps were pulled the home side had reached 531 runs.

Kent had a mixed bag and the normally reliable Humphreys went for a duck (and Woolley followed suit), although they achieved a creditable 282 runs which normally would have been considered a success. In the follow on Woolley revealed his great all round ability, an ability that took him beyond Blythe in the batting department, and scored 64 before he was out lbw to Willis Cuttell the leg break bowler.

His side made a further 302 but Spooner and MacLaren soon put on the 56 runs needed to win and had a victory by ten wickets. It was Lancashire's day as Tyldesley made his highest ever score, MacLaren passed 19,000 runs, and Cuttell reached 750 first class wickets.

---

[1] Frank Edward Woolley was born in the High Street, Tonbridge on 27 May 1887 opposite to the Bull Hotel and a blue plaque records the event. He also has a plain memorial in St. Peter and St. Paul's, Tonbridge above one to Colin Blythe.

NEW COINAGE

Kent appeared to be in the doldrums however hindsight shows this was the last defeat of the season, since the Kentish horse was only down at the bit for a short time and reared up again in the next match.

On 11 June, Somerset arrived at Gravesend but the day after went home having lost by a similar ten wickets. Fielder then Woolley took six wickets in each innings and were equally successful in the next game at the Oval. They dismissed Tom Hayward and Jack Hobbs for only 8 runs during the first innings and Woolley scored 72, the Kent side winning the contest by a narrow margin of just one wicket.

Tonbridge Week came around and Blythe returned to his home turf to play Hampshire at the Angel Ground on 18-19 June. The combination of Blythe, Woolley, Fielder, and Fairservice were integrated to some effect as the opponents were beaten by an innings and 12 runs.

Hampshire made 131 in their first innings and Fielder took six wickets for 67, although Blythe bowled 17.4 overs and took no wickets at all whilst he conceded 32 runs. In reply Kent made 365 and Woolley achieved his first century of 116 whereas Blythe and Fielder added 24 and 19 apiece. Woolley then took six wickets for 46 as Hampshire were all out for 222.

Blythe clearly had a problem with his hand injury and was not recovered thus he missed a further four games. Middlesex then arrived at the Angel Ground led by Blythe's old friend and mentor Plum Warner, whereas Ken Hutchings (more of later) made his first appearance of the season.

This was a very high scoring game which provided excellent entertainment for the spectators and the lowest innings score was 253. However, the man of the match was clearly Hutchings who made 125 and 97 (not out) in a game that was ultimately a draw.

The series of four games missed by Blythe included a few other events of interest, and in the game at Bramall Lane on 25 June there was an unusual incident with the bails. Fielder bowled to Lord Hawke who was distracted when the wind blew the bails off and the ball promptly ploughed into the stumps. It then became a matter of honour, and although Marsham asked Hawke to continue his innings he politely refused the kind offer.

The game likewise ended in a draw and the side then travelled south to the Aylestone Road ground in Leicester (another venue also used for soccer). The match took place from 28-30 June and was of some moment since it was the first ever contest between the sides. Leicester made quite a small score in this instance and Kent won by eight wickets.

Meanwhile, there was a small matter of probabilities. The 'northern' tour came to an end at the attractive New Road ground in Worcester, with the pleasant ripple of water and the reassuring echo of cathedral bells.

A number of people had supplied the captain Marsham with new coinage in the hope that he would finally win the toss. Some eleven times he had spun the coin since the start of the season and on only one occasion was he successful. That success was during the Somerset game at Gravesend but without the advantage of foresight he elected to field.

The probability of losing the toss ten times in a row was over one in a thousand, and perhaps Marsham looked to Heaven as he spun the coin in the shadow of the cathedral tower. A moment in time was lost as it fell to the ground, there was a pause for breath, and he finally won at last.

Kent then led the batting for the first time that season and Alec Hearne and his fellow hitter Humphreys were first to emerge from the pavilion. In fact, the former made 154 before he was run out and Kent scored 576 although the game was eventually another draw.

Fortunes continued to ebb and flow and from the middle of July they embarked on a series of six home matches, including both the Tunbridge Wells and the Canterbury Weeks.

However, in the first instance there was an epic encounter between the Gentlemen and Players at Lord's on 9-11 July. The former won the toss and led the batting with Reggie Spooner of Lancashire and Henry Foster of Worcester. Arthur Fielder of Kent was one of five bowlers used by the professional team but as it turned out no one else was needed.

He soon dismissed the openers both clean bowled and then proceeded to take all the other eight wickets. The long procession back to the pavilion included such notables as Jackson, Bosanquet, Hutchings, Crawford, and Jessop however despite his efforts this was still a tight game.

The Players side included Hayward, Tyldesley, Denton, Rhodes, J. Gunn, Lilley, and Haigh but they only managed to move 32 runs ahead and in the second innings Fielder took just four - the Gentlemen winning by 45 runs. However, it was the bowler's game, and he received a memento from the Men of Kent and Kentish Men in honour of his fine record.

Blythe was two years the junior of Fielder who came in past him and was yet to be chosen for this classic contest (which started in 1806), however in terms of Kent's progress both players were vital.

There was then another first as the side played the West Indies at Catford on 12-13 July. The match was notable for three reasons - namely it was the first game between the teams, Lord Harris appeared (for the penultimate time) at number eight, and Blythe returned to the squad.

The opponents fielded players who emanated mainly from Barbados and Trinidad although one was from Guyana, but by all accounts they had a lot to learn regarding their cricketing aptitudes.

Kent went in to bat first and A.P. Day made the best score of 82 whilst Lord Harris came in after Marsham and added an additional 33 runs. The side recorded a first innings total of 471 on the first day, although Blythe only managed 2 before being bowled by R. Ollivierre. On the second day the returning bowler set about the opponents taking seven wickets for 86 as they were dismissed for 248 runs.

In the follow on Blythe, Fairservice, and Hutchings took the wickets as the side were all out again for 209 - thus Kent won by an innings and 14 runs. From the first it was evident the county were the better side and the West Indies main deficiencies were in terms of slovenly fielding, plus a tendency to try impossible runs while neglecting to take safer ones.

Despite this the tourists had scored well on a good wicket against some formidable bowling. Woolley took a bad knock from the ball during the first innings being replaced on the pitch by Fielder (as a substitute). The Kent bowling and fielding was to a high standard throughout, although most praise was accorded to Blythe who was clearly well recovered and bowled some sixty overs during the match:

"All through he maintained a splendid length, and varied both pace and pitch with excellent judgement. He only hit the stumps on two occasions and was largely indebted to the field for most of his success, but it was a really fine example of how to get men out, for the wicket played hard and true and afforded him no assistance."

SURREY COLLAPSE

In fact, with the return of Blythe and the great form of Fielder Kent won the next eleven county games! In the first instance they beat Essex and Gloucester during Tunbridge Wells Week, at which time the bowler may have become acquainted with his future wife (see next chapter).

There was then a ten wicket victory over Leicester at Mote Park however there was even more success to come. Indeed, one of the most significant encounters was against their rivals for the title Surrey which took place at Rectory Field from 30 July to 1 August.

Kent won the toss and went in to bat with Burnup and Dillon but only the former made any score and they were all out for 136, with Lees and Knox taking the wickets. Surrey had a strong side under Lord Dalmeny including Tom Hayward and Jack Hobbs, and Hayes, Crawford, and Lees from the

South African tour. Hence, it was no surprise when Hayward scored 124 (from a total of 219) with six of the wickets falling to Arthur Fielder - the other bowlers being Blythe, Mason, and Woolley.

Kent did much better in the second innings reaching a total of 327 with the main scorers being Hutchings, Woolley, and Humphreys (all with over 60 runs). However, when Kent lost their fifth wicket they were only 57 ahead and Surrey were in a strong position, but Knox was unable to finish off the good work begun by Lees. In general the last five (or tail-enders) go out quite easily but Humphreys in particular was immovable.

For a time it looked as if the game would not continue into the third day however the Surrey side were left needing a total of 245 runs to win. By all accounts they fancied their chances, but later events made it questionable why they ever remained so optimistic.

The game shortly began to slip from their hands and the main factor was the difference in approach by the two sides. Surrey relied on the genius of Tom Hayward to make a base on which to build a tower of success which was like building one's house on a foundation of sand, whereas Kent based all of their advantage on a rock of uniform excellence.

Indeed, the newspapers stated, "No champion team could have shown to greater advantage than Kent did in the field yesterday," whilst a number of factors were put forward to account for the imminent collapse of Surrey which took place on the last day.

In the first instance they had lost Hobbs for 2 runs the night before and had to reshuffle the order, there was a trouble-some morning dew on the pitch, and the weight of superstition weighed upon them regarding the 'jinx team' of Kent. Something was always said to account for a collapse by way of excuses but in this case there were several influences.

The main one was undoubtedly the superior bowling by Blythe who made it seem that the pitch was the most treacherous surface imaginable. But it was not. Goatly and Strudwick had remained in resolutely at the end of the second day, and when the former was bowled by Fielder with the score on just 28 runs - the latter lost his head.

Bert Strudwick, the diminutive wicket keeper for Surrey, had refused to score the night before but managed to put on 6 runs in the morning and should have remained cautious. However, he skied a ball up into the air off Blythe and as he tried for another run was easily caught out.

Tom Hayward at the other end probably raised his eyebrows but was soon in trouble himself. A finer piece of bowling than that provided by Blythe had seldom been seen before, as he asked serious questions of the Surrey batsmen during all of their forty overs.

Hayward had barely got into his stride when a ball from Blythe eluded him, but Huish failed to stump him with an uncharacteristic miss. Fifteen minutes later the bowler sent down a beautiful ball, which moved across and took away his off stump thereby completing the earlier job.

Huish was the first to congratulate Blythe who basically had the honour of beating Hayward twice in a short space of time. This was some accolade and during the innings Blythe eventually took five wickets for 25 runs (the others Hayes, Crawford, and P.R. May), whereas of the twenty overs he bowled twelve were very economical maidens.

Jack Mason had stood in for Marsham as captain during the game and his choice of bowlers was commended, but it was the application of Blythe that won the contest. Surrey were all out for just 80 (a collapse reminiscent of four years earlier) and Kent had a victory by 164 runs.

During the first two days of the encounter there were an estimated 10,000 spectators at Rectory Field (on each occasion), whereas half that number turned up at the start of the third day. Some of the absentees were soon observed climbing up nearby Westcombe Hill, but on arriving many were left speechless to find the game was almost over.

Blythe had actually taken his five wickets for just 10 runs added (in his last thirteen overs), and was easily the best of the slow bowlers - while no other was deemed to get more finger work on the ball. But most of all it was a great team effort and Kent were the best side in the country, winning the game through their bowling and fielding plus a little bit of luck.

With regard to this one supporter wrote to the papers and put forward a theory for Surrey's collapse. The wicket was clearly in good order and he expected the best batsmen to score well once the bowlers had tired.

However, while sitting opposite the pavilion he noticed that a fresh wind was catching his face, and observed that it also blew directly against the sweep of Blythe's arm. This had the effect of making the ball hang in the air thereby accentuating the break when the ball finally landed.

On such a wicket it was hard to explain how a bowler had great success but in his opinion the wind was the significant factor. There was a similar example against the Australians at Canterbury some years earlier - Burnup and the others bowled well against the wind from the pavilion end, and a large number of catches were taken at slip. But wind or no wind, Blythe won the latter game with some brilliant bowling on an easy wicket against some of the best batsmen in the country. [2]

---

[2] This probably refers to Kent v Australia at the St. Lawrence Ground on 10-12 August 1899 when the home side won by two wickets. Burnup's bowling figures were 3-7 and 5-44 whereas Kent had "sixteen" catches off the visitors.

Meanwhile, this was not an isolated victory and he was in the ascendancy when Kent took on Sussex in the first game of Canterbury Week (at the start of August). Marsham returned to the championship fray as captain and his side went in to bat with a confidence born only of success.

Sussex found themselves in all kinds of trouble and just the wicket keeper Harry Butt failed to bowl. Nothing would work for the ten bowlers (!) and Burnup put on 141 followed by Hutchings on 51. Dick Blaker who scored over 5,000 runs in a Kent career from 1899-1908 made 123, and Marsham partnered him to score another 119.

The records were for the taking and at the end of the first day Marsham and Huish were guarding the fortress. In fact, the wicket keeper made 30 before he was out the next morning, and Blythe then joined Marsham and scored 53 runs before he was bowled by Cox - the total 568 runs.

Sussex could not take advantage of the good batting conditions and were all out for 176 and 261 thus Kent won by an innings and 131 runs. Blythe took five wickets in total and a number of bowlers were used.

The newspaper headline promptly stated, "*Marsham and Blythe Electrifying.* The two indulged yesterday at Canterbury in cricket sufficient to almost put Jessop (of Gloucester) in the shade. Laying on to everything they put on 111 runs for the ninth wicket in less than thirty-five minutes.*"

Despite taking all kinds of chances, neither were said to have received a lifeline until they reached almost three figures. Marsham had made his first century of the season in just 85 minutes with nineteen 4's, whereas Blythe followed this with some good bowling and frequently puzzled the batsmen with his outrageously insidious deliveries.

A strong Lancashire side then came to Canterbury and were given similar treatment. Marsham kept winning the toss and in a stunning first innings Kent raced to 403 at the end of the first day - Burnup made 94, Seymour 50, Hutchings 176, and Mason 88 to establish a total of 479 runs.

Archie MacLaren and Lancashire had a strong side including Spooner and Tyldesley but only made 169, whilst Blythe took 5-80 and Fielder 4-81 the other wicket being a run out. In the follow on the first four wickets went for 20 runs and only Sharp and MacLaren made any kind of stand being on 30 and 28 respectively at the end of the second day.

However, the next morning the Lancashire side were all out for 115 and Blythe took 3-27 whereas Fielder did most of the damage with 7-49. Kent had beaten the 1904 champions by a substantial innings and 95 runs.

They then travelled to the West Country and had a ten wicket victory over Gilbert Jessop and Gloucester at Cheltenham, and a 354 run win against Sammy Woods and Somerset at Taunton.

THE FIRST TITLE

Back at the St. Lawrence Ground on 23-25 August they defeated Worcester by seven wickets with another century by Burnup - and with two games to go sat at the top of the table. Other results went their way and the pressure was clearly on - Was this finally to be their year at last? [3]

They then entered into a tough engagement against Warner's Middlesex (the 1903 champions) at Lord's on 27-29 August. The home side batted first and only made 143 runs with Fielder taking five wickets and Blythe three for 52 runs. Kent had reached 129 for seven at the end of day one when Blythe was dismissed for nought leaving Blaker on 7 runs.

The next day the latter took his total to 86 before he was bowled by Jack Hearne and thus saved the innings - the Kent total being 266. Middlesex started well with Warner and J. Douglas but the captain was run out and the rest of the side collapsed for a score of 181 on the third day. This success was mainly down to Blythe who took seven wickets for 66, including four clean bowled and a stumping - the other wickets to Fielder.

Kent made the 61 they needed to win for the loss of just three wickets and thus cemented their position at the top. However, there was little time to relax and that evening they took the train down to Bournemouth, since the last game was to commence the following day.

Hampshire won the toss at Dean Park and scored 163 with Blythe taking six wickets for 67 runs. Kent then secured their highest score against the home side as Burnup (who opened with Woolley) made 179, followed by Ken Hutchings on 124. Blythe managed to add 15 runs of his own at the end to make a final total of 610 all out.

There was a valiant fight back and C.B. Llewellyn recorded 158 not out in the middle order but they were all dismissed for 410 runs. Blythe had taken another six wickets for 123 including Phil (C.P.) Mead on 4, and his side had a victory by an innings and 37 runs.

It was September 1906 and the Kent side who for several years had given such great promise were finally the champions of England. They had won sixteen games out of twenty-two, eleven of them consecutive victories at the end of the season, and no one could question their pre-eminence. There were just two defeats and the whole team was to be commended.

---

[3] Gloucester played Yorkshire at Ashley Down, Bristol on 23-25 August. It was a crucial game regarding the final destination of the championship, and on the third day the visitors were bowled out and finished just 1 run behind.

Of those who came in for special mention were Hutchings who scored 1,454 runs with an average of 60.58. He was also a good fielder and Victor Trumper the Australian said he was "the sensation of the season."

The new arrival Woolley played in sixteen matches and made 779 runs whilst taking 42 wickets. He was renowned for his off drive and bowled up to the same standard as Blythe, and was later to become a good test player. Burnup also headed the batting with 1,207 runs and an average of 67 while Marsham made some fine performances, and wicket keeper Huish was one of the best in the country especially regarding stumpings.

In terms of bowling Fielder took 172 wickets and Blythe some 111, while the captain Marsham received a large number of letters and telegrams to congratulate him, and to reverse of the general order of things it was now time for the talking to commence!

The victory was in fact a rather tight one and three teams finished on 14 points with Kent achieving a percentage of 77.77, Yorkshire second on 70.00, and Surrey third on 63.63. Both the latter teams played twenty-eight games but lost the title by virtue of suffering more defeats.

At the start of the season there was some debate that the game was in a moribund state, and the arrival of the lack-lustre West Indians did nothing to allay this fear. However, such a statement was proven to be a fallacy and as Fred Huish remarked, "Give us good weather and plenty of sunshine, and there is little amiss with the game."

Dame Nature may have played a part in the excitement and in August the games took place under meteorological conditions that rendered soccer an absurdity. However, it was the contest itself which was most responsible as for some time all eyes were on Surrey and Yorkshire. It was only near the end that Kent overtook Yorkshire, taking the championship south of the river for the first time since the "nineties."

In fact, a neck and neck struggle kept the tension right up to the last and on the final day three games decided the title. For the first half of the season Surrey were the best until N.A. Knox fell lame, whereas Yorkshire were not as good as before due to an over reliance on George Hirst. In addition the absence of the Hon F.S. Jackson, the appearance of a "tail," and the reduced success of Rhodes all added to their failure, but they often got out of tight spots through both pluck and determination.

Meanwhile, the Kent team were considered a great side with some form batsmen, an array of good bowlers, and a phalanx of both smart and safe fieldsmen. They were very popular with the public as they played to win and were most sporting in their approach, whilst they had a bond between amateurs and professionals that was rarely seen.

Snapshots - Blythe's first South African tour of 1905-06

Some early race relations in South Africa

Boulder Beach - near Cape Town

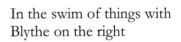

In the swim of things with Blythe on the right

"Tickled Pink"

The effervescent John Hartley tries to wake Jack Board from his slumber

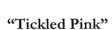

Plum Warner leads his team out at Newlands

(The Members' Stand)

A small colonial gathering - smoking the pipe of peace

What chance this price at Lord's?

Per season!

The M.C.C. Bench - "modern" hi-tech comforts for Hartley & Co.

Professionals Only!

Dinner at the mayor's place in Johannesburg, Xmas 1905

The team at leisure

South Africa were a revelation and the tourists won just a single test match

Albert Park, Durban
(17 January)

Above: After lunch at 143 for 7 - two wickets had just gone leaving Hayes 27 and Hartley 0

Right: End of M.C.C. 1st innings - They won by four wickets, Blythe taking eight in total

M.C.C. travel arrangements, Royal Hotel, Durban

Some by carriage, some by rickshaw, but note the rather interesting drivers

Telephone Nº 42.
P.O. Box 110.

Telegraphic Address
"DEAL".

DEAL'S HOTEL.
EAST LONDON.
(South Africa)

27ᵗʰ Jan. 1904

East London

The M.C.C. won the game by an innings - but Blythe took just one wicket against the "Home XV"

"Charlie" Blythe - after the South African tour of 1905-06

He recorded a best of 27 runs in the 4th Test at Newlands, and also took 6-68 with eleven wickets in total

In first class games he made 94 runs, and took a storming 57 wickets

Kent - County Champions 1906

Back: Burnup, Humphreys, Woolley, Huish, Seymour, W. Hearne, Blythe
Middle: Fielder, Blaker, Marsham, Mason, Hutchings
Front: Hubble, Fairservice

Below - Grand celebrations took place at the Hotel Cecil and Corn Exchange (right), but the professionals had their own "do" at the Bull Hotel, Tonbridge on 25 October

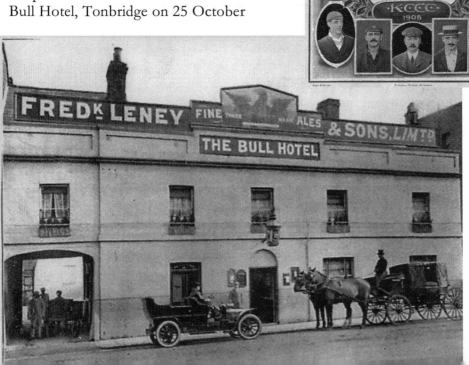

The Tyke (to Blythe): If yer please, our Wilfrid 'ere 'ud like ter know 'ow yer does it. He's a bit of a bowler 'isson.

1907 - A vintage year for Blythe

Top Left: He married Gertrude Brown in March

Top Right: His record of 17 for 48 against Northants on 1 June still remains unbeaten in county cricket

Below: A study of Blythe that same year - showing "the ball that goes with the arm"

Australian Tour 1907-08 - The "Ophir" departs from Tilbury (20 September)
Scenes of enthusiasm from the quayside, and the wives (including Gertrude)

The Team   Back: Hobbs, Barnes, Rhodes, Fielder, Blythe, Hayes,
Braund, Humphries **Middle:** G. Gunn, Major Trevor (man.), Jones (captain),
Fane, Crawford, Hutchings **Front:** Young, Hardstaff

Adelaide Oval v South Australia - Tuesday 12 November

End of the third day of a four-day match - The M.C.C. declared on 660 for eight wickets but Blythe took just three during the game which was won by an innings and 183 runs

PARLIAMENT HOUSE   BELLE VUE HOTEL

Belle Vue Hotel,

W. PETERMANN, LATE OF LENNON'S, PROPRIETOR.

TELEPHONE No. 136.

POST AND TELEGRAPH OFFICE
IN PARLIAMENT HOUSE.

QUEENSLAND CLUB

Brisbane, from 28th Nov. to Dec. 1907

Opulent lifestyle - Two games were played in Brisbane against Queensland and an Australian XI - the first was a victory and Blythe had figures 11 for 83 whilst the second against stiffer opposition ended in a draw

FAREWELL DINNER
Given by
MR W.H.BURGESS
to
A.O.JONES ESQ
and his English Cricket Team.

Luncheon
Given by
MR JUSTICE CUSSEN.
President of the Melbourne C.C.
to A. O. JONES ESQ.
AND HIS ENGLISH CRICKET TEAM.
GRAND HOTEL
W.H.BURGESS MANAGER

Grand Hotel, Melbourne

Blythe and the M.C.C. were invited to a "farewell" dinner and also to a luncheon in February 1908 (note the menu on the left upon the table)

Regarding the season in general Tyldesley scored the highest total at 295 runs - strangely this being during a game against rivals Kent whilst Denton, Hirst, and Hayward (twice) scored two centuries in one game.

The latter also reached over 200 runs on two occasions and with twelve centuries to his name beat Fry's record of nine in 1901. Further to this he recorded an amazing 2,814 at an average of just over 70 and only Tyldesley, Hirst, P.A. Perrin, and Hayes came anywhere near to him.

These were definitely the high days and holidays and the team were soon basking in their profligate success. They were the best in the country and as was the tradition they took on the Rest of England at the Oval from 10-13 September. During the four days of play some 40,000 spectators came to watch the cricketing elite and the best they undoubtedly were.

Indeed, The Rest comprised of Spooner, Hayward, Tyldesley, Fane, Hirst, Warner (captain), Rhodes, Buckenham, Lees, Haigh, and Humphries and they scored 392 in the first innings. Blythe took the first wicket Spooner and also Fane who was stumped by Huish, whilst Fielder took a further five wickets - however the game followed a predictable pattern.

Kent managed a creditable 365 runs whereas The Rest declared with eight wickets down on 344. Blythe had taken just one wicket and Fielder four but the champions were then all out for 120 and lost by 251 runs.

There was a surplus of £825 raised from the game and this was paid to the Cricketers Fund and London Playing Fields Society, but the honour of the achievement could not be valued. Kent had finally won the title and after a brief respite the real celebrations began.

HOTEL CECIL

The first event was at the Corn Exchange, Maidstone on 10 October 1906 the mayor Mr. W. Day (jun.) Esq. presiding. Included in the banquet were turbot, whitebait, beef Anglaise, salad Romaine, bombe glace, dessert, and coffee followed by toasts to King Edward, Queen Alexandra, the Prince and Princess of Wales and sundry royal persons.

The mayor then presented silver cigarette boxes to all of the team from the inhabitants of the town and Mr. C. Ferguson (High Sheriff) toasted the Kent Eleven. In reply Marsham thanked the enthusiastic supporters and in terms of the cricket praised the batting of Burnup and Hutchings, and the bowling of Blythe and Fielder as the chief reasons for their success.

Marsham also expressed his wish that the Mote Park Ground would soon be levelled so that it could hold a cricket week, whereas Alec Hearne and Fred Huish responded on behalf of the players.

Sir Marcus Samuel then proposed "The Club" but stated that Mote Park was already a good sporting ground, and he would hesitate to disturb the turf which had lain for over 100 years. With this slight dispute between the new and old owners resolved Lord Harris took to the stand.

He recalled the formation of the present club just a few yards from where they sat and spoke at length about the history of Kent cricket. In fact, two hundred years ago a man from Harrietsham near to Mr. Marsham's home first took a team out of the county. [4]

Lord Harris then eulogised on the club's forty-year struggle to win the title and noted how gratifying it was they had achieved their purpose at last. Mr. Hoare of Staplehurst (see later) also toasted the visitors and explained that Col. Warde M.P. had subscribed to ninety-eight cricket clubs.

The latter then replied as did Craig "the Surrey poet," whilst there was a programme of waltzes during the feast and afterwards there was a musical entertainment performed by Mr. Harrison Hill.

With barely time to digest the meal there was a further dinner at the very grand Hotel Cecil, London on the evening of 11 October. This included a programme of marches played by the Royal East Kent Imperial Yeomanry, a menu of saddle of lamb and roast pheasant, and speeches by a whole host of dignitaries connected to the Kent club. [5]

The grand hall was secured for the purpose and despite its size was well pressed to accommodate the "six hundred" guests. Proceedings began at 6 o'clock but with a lengthy list of speakers it was likely to end very late.

Mr. Cloudesley Marsham and his team were ensconced in the position of honour at the middle table, while the company included every captain since 1850 - with only one or two exceptions. The Earl of Darnley then stepped up and proposed "The Eleven." [6]

---

[4] The first club was formed at the Mitre Hotel, Maidstone in 1859 and combined with the Beverley Club at the Bull Hotel, Rochester in 1870.

[5] The Hotel Cecil was built in the Wren style in 1890-96 and was once the largest in Europe with 800 rooms. It was between the Embankment and the Strand and was later the first HQ of the RAF but was demolished in 1930. The façade is now part of Shell Mex House between the Savoy Hotel and Adelphi.

[6] Ivo Francis Walter Bligh (1859-1927) played for Cambridge University and Kent from 1877-83, and led the team that beat Billy Murdoch's side to bring back the Ashes from Melbourne and Sydney in 1882-83 - England won the series 2-1 but a fourth game a defeat was not recognised. He was president of Kent in 1892/1902 and 8th Earl of Darnley in 1900, whereas his father John Stuart Bligh (6th Earl) presided over the meeting when Kent were formed in 1859.

Darnley, who captained the most brilliant university eleven, one of the best Kent players, and captain of the side which brought back the Ashes, stated that in the first instance Kent had played in the best traditions of English cricket and secondly had managed to improve the game's appeal in the eyes of the cricketing public.

They were splendidly led by their captain, had half a dozen of the best batsmen, and also three bowlers of the highest class "in our time." In fact, Kent had always been fortunate regarding their captains, and Darnley had the honour of playing under Lord Harris whom he believed was the most able and resourceful captain he ever played for.

Mr. George Marsham, uncle of the captain and chairman of Kent County Council, then made a short speech and invited Lady Harris to present the eleven with enamelled sleeve links as a memento of their success. After this the captain responded and commended all of his players for their special effort - in particular noting their vital understanding.

Sir W. Hart-Dyke then proposed a toast to remember the Kent successes from 1700-1900 and recounted achievements from earlier times. Linking these to the current victory he believed the side would uphold the county motto of "Invicta" for many years to come!

He was followed by W.S. Norton who was captain from 1859-70, and the Earl of Dartmouth who then proposed "The Committee" and in particular talked of the efforts of Lord Harris. Once the latter was seated there was a rendition of "*Swing, Swing Together*" (the Eton Boating Song).

Lord Harris also took to the rostrum and brought a tone of amusement to his speech which was lacking from the one made at Maidstone. He read out a few letters from well-wishers including one from another county who he was not prepared to name, stating, "It is a splendid thing for cricket that the championship should have fallen into the hands of Kent?"

After some rapturous applause he said that Lord Alverstone (president of Surrey C.C.C. from 1895-1915) had suggested, "But for one catch dropped Surrey might have been champions." This was met with a large degree of laughter thus Harris added that somebody else might have said, "But for one leg before Yorkshire would have been champions!"

Once the merriment subsided, he finished by commending the attitude of the side in particular the sporting way in which they took both victory and defeat to their hearts (rather like King George's maxims).

As the celebration continued late into the evening there was time for the guests to read their complimentary programmes. These included a picture of the team with Pawley as manager and a rather unusual Canterbury Week Ode (from *The Tatler*) which omitted to mention Blythe!

It also showed that Burnup and Hutchings had by far the highest batting averages at 69.75 and 64.06 whereas Blythe, Fielder, and Woolley led the bowling with figures of 19.16, 19.74, and 20.04. The two batsmen recorded four centuries while Humphreys made two and Hearne, Blaker, Marsham, Seymour, and Woolley scored one apiece.

In terms of batting the side had used seventeen players plus Lord Harris and Mr. S.H. Day who both appeared once. Of these Burnup, Hutchings, Dillon, Mason, Blaker, Marsham, and A.P. Day were gentlemen; whereas the players comprised of James Seymour, Woolley, Humphreys, A. Hearne, Hubble, Fairservice, Huish, Blythe, Fielder, and Hardinge.

Eleven bowlers were used during the season although the bulk of the work was done by six men: Blythe, Fielder, Woolley, J. Mason, Fairservice, and Humphreys. Blythe had taken some 90 wickets in county games whereas Fielder had 158 to his name, while Woolley who bowled half their number of overs only took 42 wickets.

The club were clearly up with the times and at the end of the programme there was a very important sales advertisement: "The Official History of Kent County Cricket edited by the Right Hon. Lord Harris."

This was available from the printers at Fetter Lane in the City and was priced at £1 1s, with important new facts about the history of early cricket and contributions from previous captains viz. Lord Harris, W.S. Norton, F. Marchant, J.R. Mason, a founder H. Knatchbull-Hugessen, and the cricket historian Frederick S. Ashley-Cooper.

Handsome and profusely illustrated the book was full of records of Kent matches and an early history of the game (never before seen), while the nett profits were to be devoted strictly to a fund "for the benefit of deserving Kent professionals!"

BULL HOTEL, TONBRIDGE

However, these two grand affairs held by the County and the Club were followed by a more cosy local celebration closer to "home," which took place at the Bull Hotel in Tonbridge High Street.

This was situated on the east side just below the castle and River Medway while a short distance to the rear was the Angel Ground. Indeed, it was a chance for friends of the professionals to express their gratitude, all the more so since Woolley's family once resided just opposite.

The dinner was on the evening of 25 October and the chairman was Mr. George Webb a coach at Tonbridge School, who was also responsible for bringing on so many of the players at the local Nursery.

W.C. Wilson the proprietor sent out the invitations and Craig "the Oval poet" joined them. The latter penned a short prose praising the host and the efforts of McCanlis and George Webb (at the Nursery), which he claimed by then had become a familiar household name. [7]

The committee for the night included T. Ives a local councillor (and a cricket ball manufacturer) and E.O. Howis of Tunbridge Wells, whilst the professionals present were Fielder, Blythe, Seymour, Fairservice, Woolley, Humphreys, Hubble, and R. Munds (a member of the 2nd XI).

Meanwhile the rest of the company included local cricket enthusiasts from Hadlow, Sevenoaks, Marden, Plaxtol, Ightham, Boro Green, Tunbridge Wells, and Penshurst and several other dignitaries. Names that stood out were Fielder from Plaxtol, Charles W. Woolley (cycle maker and father of the cricketer), and the groundsman H. Day (see later). A capital meal was provided in the ancient hostelry followed by the loyal toast.

Councillor Ives was then very sporting and sang a rendition of "Admiral Tom" followed by a clarinet solo by Mr. Dray which called for an encore. Mr. Howis also proposed a toast to the Kent club and said how happy he was they had risen to a place where they played "All England."

He had first gone to Canterbury Week at the age of ten in 1864 and only missed one gala since, and was proud to note that Kent were the first to stage such events which soon afterwards spread all around the country. He recalled how the initial games were played against Canterbury, the M.C.C., the Gentlemen of Kent, and the I Zingari club.

Having given considerable praise to the Kent team he introduced an old player who once hit balls from Tunbridge Wells Common to the adjacent 'Brighton' Railway Station! Mr. C. Payne arose and said he did not deserve such accolades, but remembered the days when Alfred Mynn and Fuller Pilch featured in the side. He was only too glad to see the progress of the team from those times as well as their firm financial position.

George Webb, the chairman, then proposed a toast to "Our Guests" and noted they had many players fit to appear for England, and that two had already done so in Australia and South Africa. But although the side had some splendid batsmen in Burnup and Hutchings it is unlikely they would have won the championship without Blythe and Fielder.

---

[7] Albert Craig (1850-1909) was born in Huddersfield and worked as a postal clerk but came South in the hope of making a fortune with sporting verse. He went to both cricket and soccer and then printed broadsheets which he sold to the crowd. His verse was not of great merit, but he still became very popular with the public for his good humour and great wit. He was mainly connected with the Oval and resided in Clapham.

Generally he did not wish to say too much since they were not a mutual admiration society, and explained that "the guests" were not only there as professional cricketers but as friends of the private company present. With that he concluded and there was considerable applause all round.

After a short musical rendition by Mr. J. Carr there was a response from Blythe, and in the first instance he commended George Webb as the first of three coaches who had taught the professionals. Webb had done more for him in his career than most people thought - whilst he was very proud to be in a team which included his friend Arthur Fielder.

The latter also spoke and said it was a pleasure to come to Tonbridge where most of them learnt their cricket. He was one of the first to arrive there under George Webb and thought he should also be congratulated on bringing along such a fine cricketer as Ken Hutchings. Finally his colleague Humphreys made a short speech to conclude the response.

There was then another song, a toast to the chairman and visitors, an amusing recitation by Mr. Craig, and a violin solo "The Broken Melody" by Blythe (one of his favourites) which met with vociferous applause. [8]

Craig responded for the visitors and thanked Mr. Wilson for the invite noting that he cancelled two other invitations to be there. He was in no way *pessimistic* about Kent's future success although some were (which caused laughter), thus he added that the last time he used such abstruse language in Brighton the local booksellers sold every dictionary!

No men of learning would ever agree that a team lost the championship because they dropped just one catch, although he had heard of someone losing a wife because he missed out on one proposal! The players in Kent never made any excuses for a missed century or a dropped catch, and they played simply for the love of the game.

He (Craig) had adopted them as a county and shared a secret. In his living room he had a piece of furniture given him by the professionals, one that would not disgrace Lord Alverstone's front room! Mr. Knight then added that they were very proud of Fielder up at Plaxtol, and during the winter months he was a prominent footballer amongst them.

Finally Mr. Thompson thanked the host and hostess for providing the Bull Hotel. Indeed, all the more so since Tonbridge had failed to come forward to entertain the professionals in honour of their great success.

---

[8] Auguste Van Biene (1850-1913) was born in Rotterdam and studied the cello then came to London in 1867 and busked in Hanover Square, but soon played at Covent Garden starting an opera company. He composed "The Broken Melody" as part of a three act play in 1892 - which was an instant success.

The final celebration came a month later at the 9th Annual Dinner of the Association of Men of Kent and Kentish Men at the King's Hall, Holborn Restaurant, London, on 6 November.

John Henniker Heaton Esq. M.P. was the chairman and the menu came from all over Kent including scalloped turbot Ramsgate, sole from Dover, mutton from Sheppey, potatoes of Sevenoaks, pheasant of Cobham, salad from Minster, pudding Harrietsham, and Canterbury bombe.

After a toast to the King the famous soprano Miss Carrie Tubb sang the "National Anthem" and "Let Me Dream Again" by Cowen, while the Right Hon. Alfred Lyttelton M.P. proposed "The Team." He was supported in this respect by Lord Dalmeny M.P., C.B. Fry Esq., and P.F. Warner Esq. and this was followed by a humorous sketch.

A reply came from the captain C.H.B. Marsham whereas Col. Warde M.P. was on hand to propose "The Association." W. Pett Ridge spoke on behalf of the visitors and G.L. Jessop provided the response.

Blythe was a guest of honour at some of the most lavish feasts and was feted by some of the most eminent gentlemen in the land. No doubt his head was reeling from the experience and it must have been hard to settle to work as an engineer in the winter months, thereby supplementing the small amount of pay he received when not playing.

But that was not all. Whilst Lord Harris was giving his speech at the Hotel Cecil he suggested the club commission a painting to celebrate their success with three stipulations: (1) it was to be an action picture, (2) it must show Canterbury, and (3) the bowler must be Colin Blythe.

Indeed, the commission was given to A.C. Tayler (R.A.) in the autumn since he was a cricketing enthusiast and had done paintings and lithographs relating to the game. To achieve accuracy members of the Kent side sat at his London studio, and "the innings-victory over Lancashire" was then on display at Canterbury for over ninety years.

CHAPTER 10

Matrimony

Blythe then spent a last Christmas with his family at 374 New Cross Road and in the local environs must have been quite a celebrity. However, he had five younger brothers of very similar appearance and one wonders if they were ever mistaken for him?

There was indeed a large contrast between the opulence of the Hotel Cecil an environment of the gentlemen players, and the less salubrious setting of New Cross with its frequent trains and trams rattling by. Little wonder that the bowler collated his experiences since he had been taken to a different world through his cricketing talents.

During the winter months Blythe had more on his mind than engineering and planned to engineer a little project of his own, which involved a few trips down to Tunbridge Wells in the closed season.

Perhaps he also spent some time with his family and no doubt there was varied entertainment to be had at New Cross Road. None of his siblings were yet married, his brother Wally a general labourer was aged twenty, and his other brothers and sisters were just teenagers.

His father Walter still worked as an engineer although this was to change later on, and perhaps Colin entertained them around the fire with his violin. Maybe there was some socialising in the locality, a visit to see his cousins, or a trip under the river to watch Millwall at North Greenwich. Meanwhile, there was someone waiting for him down in Kent.

GERTRUDE BROWN

The Brown family came from Frant on the border with Sussex and their only child Henry was born in the village in 1858. The father Alfred was a local bricklayer and stonemason and with his wife and son moved a short distance east to the nearby town of Tunbridge Wells.

By his twenties Henry Brown who worked as a painter resided in London and married Deborah Wright at Wandsworth in September 1880. His wife was born in Hadlow, Kent out of wedlock and was the granddaughter of Samuel Wright the local farrier and his wife Jane.

The latter a straw bonnet maker raised Deborah in the village, hence the couple initially went to Hadlow and had a son Henry, then spent a brief period in Stratford, Essex where a son Edward was born.

However, they soon returned to Tunbridge Wells on a permanent basis and had two daughters: Alice Rose (December 1886) and Janet Gertrude (1 February 1889) the latter born at 19 Rochdale Road northwest of the town. The family then moved to a nearby property 24 Dukes Road two years later however the father "Harry" died in 1894 aged 33.

This was clearly a difficult situation for the family thus Deborah took on washing work at home, and formed an association with a local man John Underhill who worked as a fitter and smith. Indeed, the couple lived at 104 Shatters Road, Tunbridge Wells in 1901 with daughters Alice a laundry girl and Janet (aged 13) a pupil at school.

The address was then re-designated 104 Silverdale Road and they moved around the corner to 10 Denbigh Road in 1903-07. Matrimony was in the air and Rose married Harry John Walter a carman in the parish church on 25 February 1905, whilst Gertrude met Colin through the local cricketing circles - probably at one of the popular Weeks in the locality.

There was soon a second marriage but this took place up in London, the likely reason being the bride had little family in her home town. Indeed, Colin Blythe a civil engineer of 374 New Cross Road married Gertrude Janet Brown of 130 Silverdale Road at Greenwich Registry Office on 11 March 1907, the witnesses being J. and R. Walter (her sister).

At the time of the marriage Blythe was aged 27 and his bride was 18 and she was by all accounts a great local beauty. There was little money around since the bowler had yet to improve his position despite the foreign tours, and they initially moved to 40 St. Mary's Road, Tonbridge which was south of the Angel Ground and railway across the Pembury Road.

The house was a small semi-detached cottage in a long line of properties with a single front room on each storey, and the name "Ivybank" adorned the roof-line. The couple lived there for the next four years and it remains today although it is still a rather modest abode.

From that time onwards Blythe appears to have adopted cricket as a more full time profession and as shall be shown several of his neighbours were in the "industry." Indeed, two months later the new cricket season started and unlike teams of today who have 'strength in depth,' the Kent side found it a struggle to maintain their high standard of success.

Alec Hearne played in some of the early games in the previous season but was dropped from the side due to his age (44 years), whereas Burnup only played in three matches that year despite scoring 1,207 runs previously. In addition, Ken Hutchings ("the sensation") was injured and in a wet summer there was every prospect that the team would struggle. Blythe, however, was unerring and improved on his form by some considerable degree.

THE 1907 SEASON

Despite such difficulties the Kent side were off to a good start and took on the M.C.C. in the opener at Lord's on 9-11 May. They began their account with Hardinge and Woolley but the latter was out for nought, and Seymour and Hutchings went for 9 and 11 runs apiece. It did not at this stage look promising since the visitors were all out for 99 runs.

The M.C.C. side were led by Warner and featured a number of players from South Africa who included Sibley (S.J.) Snooke, Charlie Llewellyn, and their captain Percy Sherwell. Despite this they recorded only 76 runs and Blythe took six wickets for 29, including Warner clean bowled on 4 and also the duo of Snooke and Llewellyn.

Kent then provided a better account of themselves and reached a total of 184 with Blythe not out on 18 runs. Fielder also took over from Blythe and did most of the damage taking seven wickets for 51 in a row (at one stage four wickets for 10 runs), of which six were clean bowled and one lbw. The M.C.C. were all out for 114 and Kent won by 93 runs.

The initial championship game was against Northampton at Catford on 13-14 May. This was of some interest to cricket history since the opponents only entered two seasons earlier and it was the first ever meeting between the sides. Indeed, it began a challenge that Blythe was to relish.

In the home-tie Kent went in to bat and made 259 runs quite early on the first day - Woolley made 99 but was bowled by George Thompson who was a Wisden *Cricketer of the Year* the previous season. Northants then made a meagre 73 runs and Fielder took 8-42 and Blythe 2-29. The follow on saw them all out for 86 and Kent won by an innings and 100 runs, whilst Blythe took 4-37 and reached 1,000 wickets with his third victim.

This was an important milestone in his career and having played just over seven full seasons, he had averaged (with the foreign tours) more than 140 wickets each year. However, his figures against Northants although good gave no real inkling of what was to come in the return match.

Kent continued their championship form and won the next two games against Somerset and Sussex both by a considerable margin. In the latter game Wally Hardinge (from Greenwich) made a career best of 129, but his opening partner Woolley suffered the ignominy of being out again for 99. In both these games it was Blythe and Fielder who took all the wickets.

There was then a tough test against Lancashire at Old Trafford on 23-25 May, and the game was in the balance as Kent finished some 7 runs ahead after the first innings was completed.

Lancashire with J.T. Tyldesley then improved slightly and made 171 while the wickets fell to Blythe, Fielder, and Woolley. Clearly the visitors were in with a good chance and Ken Hutchings and Jack Mason put on the runs to bring them within striking distance. Blaker also did well to add 26 runs but Blythe was caught on 6 - leaving just Fielder not out on 3.

As a result the game was lost by a demoralising 6 runs but this did not witness an immediate downturn in their fortunes. In the next fixture they beat Derbyshire by a good innings at Chesterfield on 27-29 May, the latter side including Charles Ollivierre the West Indian player, however it was the following game when the records really began to fall.

ALL TEN WICKETS

Kent travelled the short distance south that same evening and the next day Thursday, 30 May (his birthday) Blythe awoke suitably refreshed. At this stage the press were certainly enamoured with the team and stated, "Kent have preserved their reputation for finishing matches."

They were the only county-team to have won five matches and it was surmised that if games were limited to two days, 99 out of 100 cricketers would choose Kent as the side most likely to win. It was their knack of quick runs and wickets that made them such firm favourites.

On the day of the Northants game there were several interruptions at the County Ground due to some intermittent rain. But the outfield and crease were probably in fair condition, since although soccer was played there it never took place after the month of April.

Woolley, Hardinge, Seymour, Hutchings, and A.P. Day were the first five batsmen for Kent and between them scored 211 runs, and at the end of the first day the side had reached 212 for four wickets. However, there was no play the next day due to the weather and this factor no doubt contributed to some sensational cricket on the Saturday. The tail-end added 39 runs in the morning thus with extras their total was 254 to the good.

Northants then came meekly to the crease and were the reverse of a good batting side producing a shocking display with the willow. With just 1 run showing on the scoreboard three wickets were gone and this state of affairs was solely down to the immense bowling of Blythe:

"The batsmen faced him as if he were a great magician against whom their chances were less tangible than the sunshine!" Charles Pool their best hope was out first ball (caught by Fielder) whereas G. Thompson, Kingston, and Crosse also failed, and when East went for the seventh wicket there were just 4 runs on the board (of which 2 were runs and 2 were extras).

A.R. Thompson and George Vials (not out on 33) averted a record low score and approached the bowling with some considerable pluck. In fact, there was quite a sensation in the crowd when Thompson managed to hit a ball from Blythe to the boundary. Driffield also made a small stand at the end and shortly after lunch the side were all out on 60 runs.

The most significant fact, however, was that like Fielder the previous year Blythe had taken all ten wickets for the addition of just 30 runs. It was a truly colossal effort off sixteen overs including seven maidens, whilst the other bowlers in the innings were Fairservice and Fielder. [1]

Meanwhile, in the follow on there was a decided downturn in the batting! Vials was put in at 'number one' in the hope of continuing his success but was out for 1 and the rest of the team were all gone for 39 runs. Indeed, Blythe had taken another seven wickets for just 18 runs in 15.1 overs, the other wickets being down to Fairservice and Humphreys.

Kent had won a notable victory in a match which concluded on 1 June by an innings and 155 runs, but it was certainly "Blythe's game" and the newspapers were full of reports regarding his amazing feat.

They noted that in the first innings he had taken seven wickets in just thirty-six balls, but his overall performance of seventeen wickets for 48 runs was of equal moment and received several plaudits:

"Blythe, by this feat on Saturday last, had not improved his reputation for the simple reason that it stood so high before. Regardless of weather forecasts he would be the cricketers' choice for bowler-in-chief, and could get the best of batsmen into difficulty on a good wicket, while being merciful in his quick despatch of the rabbit!"

Some debate then ensued as to whether he might have taken all twenty wickets and thus secured an even higher status in the cricket record books. One theory surmised that under the strain of nearing such a target he lost his nerve and thus failed to achieve this ultimate feat.

The statistics suggest otherwise. True, any sportsman nearing such a goal would have muscles and nerves stretched to the limit, although presumably it was the batsmen who were the more nervous. Blythe was probably just enjoying the cricket and praise from his team-mates and supporters.

---

[1] The newspapers quoted several instances of players taking all ten wickets in an innings (twenty-five in total): William Clarke for Nottingham in 1845, E. Hinkly the only other time for Kent in 1848, John Wisden in a North v South game in 1850, E.M. Grace for the M.C.C. in 1862, W.G. Grace for the M.C.C. in 1886, Sammy Woods for Cambridge University in 1890, plus Fielder and Dennett (of Gloucester) the previous season. Meanwhile, only H. Verity and G. Geary have taken ten wickets for less runs than Blythe in county cricket.

In fact, Fairservice clean bowled Vials for just 1 run which took away any possible chance that he had. There is little evidence of a loss of nerve since Blythe promptly took the next three batsmen two of them stumped by Huish and the other out lbw, this being an exacting degree of precision which belied any shaking of the hand.

Blythe had achieved a record of the highest quality for wickets in a match that was to stand the test of time for a hundred years. Only the famous Jim Laker, F.W. Lillywhite, H.A. Arkwright, F.P. Fenner, and J. Wisden rank above him in this respect (the first three with more than seventeen wickets), but "none" of these were for county cricket games.

Regarding the latter his closest rivals on seventeen wickets were C.W.L. Parker Gloucester v Essex for 56 runs (1925), A.P. Freeman Kent v Sussex for 67 runs (1922), and W.G. Grace Gloucester v Notts for 89 runs (1877). Other examples at the time being C.T.B. Turner against an England XI in 1888, W. Mycroft for Derby in 1876, Walter Mead for Essex in 1895, and finally Walter Brearley for Lancashire in 1905.

Such figures clearly reveal the great achievement made that summer, but all the more so since Blythe was the only one to achieve this feat in a single day (later matched by H. Verity and T.W.J. Goddard). In fact, Kent were well disposed to continue their success with Blythe and Fielder leading the rather impressive bowling attack.

A MIXED (CRICKET) BAG

The team then arrived at Headingley on 3 June to play Yorkshire but their star bowler was pronounced "a little under the weather" and was thus unfit to play. Marsham, the captain, rejoined the side after missing the Northants game whereas Samuel Day played in place of his brother Arthur.

Some cartoons then gauged the humorous (albeit truthful) mood of the cricketing press regarding his form and his enforced absence. Hirst and Haigh gazed forlornly at the averages and the former said, "Fancy us down there, in June too, us that's always been at the top."

Blythe, however, was found in bed and the Tyke suggested he was much safer there. The latter also asked him if he could tell our Wilfred "ow yer does it, as he's a bit of a bowler imself." In fact, Fielder offered a duck to Rhodes as a token of their esteem in the absence of Blythe.

During the game Yorkshire made 150 in their first innings although as the press humorously indicated Rhodes (an opener) was bowled by Fielder and caught by Hardinge for a duck. The visitors, however, were then all out for 78 runs and the bowler Haigh took six of the wickets.

Meanwhile, the weather affected the pitch as well as Blythe's health and Yorkshire only had time to score another 65 runs and the match concluded in a draw. In fact, the star bowler also missed the following game which was an "away" against Hampshire at Southampton.

But with his alka-seltzer and lemsip duly imbibed (or equivalent remedy of the day from Mrs. Beeton partaken of) he was fit again and played in the game against Leicester at Aylestone Road on 10-11 June. In fact, Fielder and Blythe took five wickets apiece as the home side were all out for 66 runs and Kent won the contest by eight wickets.

The team then returned to their home turf and Blythe played for the first time before his local fans since his marriage. It was Tonbridge Week but in the first game against Warner's Middlesex there was a humiliating defeat by ten wickets, and Blythe took only one wicket off the opponents.

However, in the second game against Hampshire there was a very good innings victory, and in the first Kent made 596 with Seymour on 204 and Hutchings on 101. Blythe was put in to bat at number four but was bowled for nought and only took three wickets in total.

Possibly he was still a bit under the weather - although regarding the team they were clearly on top and had won seven games of the eleven played. But this was to be the high point and thereafter a slump ensued.

This began with a very narrow defeat against the touring South Africans at the Private Banks Sports Ground, Catford on 24-26 June. Most of the side whom Blythe had played against in the Cape arrived duly padded-up and no doubt he was pleased to renew such former acquaintances.

Kent won the toss and batted producing a creditable 273 runs against a strong side, whereas Blythe notched up 33 before he was bowled by a fast ball from Schwarz and caught by Shalders. In fact, the highest total of the innings came from Fairservice who departed on 61 runs.

The South Africans had already played a series of county teams since their arrival in May, whilst their captain Percy Sherwell also made a number of appearances for the M.C.C. Despite such practice they were all out for 95 as Blythe took five wickets for 46, however in the follow on there was a turn around and they made a total of 281 - Blythe taking 5-114.

Kent then required an easy total to win the game and Woolley opened to make 29 runs, but they were soon in some serious trouble with the loss of Hardinge, Seymour, and Humphreys for just 2 runs added.

Only J.C. Hubble made a stand on 25 and there was a collapse with Blythe out for a duck. Hutchings came in at the end but they were all out for 101 and lost this closely fought contest by only 2 runs. The newspapers then carried the obvious headline *"Dramatic Finish at Catford."*

At one point it looked as if only rain could save the South Africans, but the game resulted in 'a slump in cricket profits' as the visitors won through their own efforts. It was a nail-biting prologue to the first test and the sun and a drying wind resulted in a splendid pitch.

They had demonstrated their right to meet the best in England as some fine batting turned the tables. A different outcome might have occurred if Fielder had bowled nullifying the need for a second innings, or Fairservice had taken Snooke on 54 with the side on 193 - indeed, the only down side was that the latter did not achieve his century.

HOME TESTS

South Africa had proved themselves able in all departments during the tour by Warner and his men, and had earned the right to a full test series on a par with the Australians, thus three games were played in the summer. The contests were spread out through July and August and R.E. Foster an old Oxonian who played for Worcester was made captain of England.

At the time he was aged twenty-nine years and had made centuries in the varsity match and for the Gentlemen v Players (in both innings). He also held the record score during a test match of 287 against Australia made in 1903-04, and was in addition a brilliant slip fielder. [2]

His opposing captain Percy W. Sherwell was his junior by three years and was making his second visit to England. He was not considered to be a great bat and during the tour his highest innings was at that stage 74 runs, but he was significantly a first class wicket keeper.

Foster and Sherwell stood at the wicket with the umpires at Lord's on 1 July and the former won the toss and took England in to bat. C.B. Fry and Tom Hayward were the openers and lasted for an hour apiece adding 51 runs, whereas Tyldesley followed up with a good half century.

---

[2] Reginald Erskine "Tip" Foster (1878-1914) was educated at Malvern College and was one of seven brothers who played cricket. With his brother Wilfred Foster both scored a century in each innings for Worcester against Hampshire in 1899, this being the side's first season in county cricket. He was Wisden *Cricketer of the Year* in 1901 and his 287 against Australia was the highest by an Englishman there, but in latter years business commitments took precedence.

He also played soccer for the Corinthians and appeared five times for England from 1900. In fact, during a game against Ireland at Southampton he scored twice and C.B. Fry was a full-back. He then captained England in a game against Wales at Wrexham in March 1902 the score 0-0 (8,000 attendance), however he suffered with diabetes and despite a trip to South Africa died at Brompton in 1914.

Foster, however, suffered from that problematic captain's malaise and was bowled by Vogler on 8 runs. Len Braund then made 104 and G.L. Jessop reached 93 whilst Lilley just missed out on his 50 - consequently the home side were all out for 428 at the end of the first day.

Shalders and Sherwell opened for South Africa but the captain hit a four and was then run out soon afterwards. Only Nourse and Faulkner had any success hitting seven 4's between them and the side were all out for 140. In fact, Blythe clean bowled Nourse on 62 runs and took Snooke lbw for 5 runs - his figures being 2-18 whilst he bowled just eight overs.

He only scored 4 runs and his peer (the idiosyncratic Fry) may have had one eye on his performance? Meanwhile, in the follow on Hirst quickly took Shalders for nought, but Sherwell made 115 before he was clean bowled by Blythe - who also took Hathorn on 30 runs (caught by Fry). Thus at the end of the day Nourse and Faulkner held the fort on 185 runs.

South Africa thus required 103 runs to avoid an innings defeat and the papers confidently predicted an England victory. They praised Sherwell for his efforts in trying to save the game, and although the remaining batsmen might cause trouble only the weather could avert an England success. As it was there was no play on the third day and the game was drawn.

Blythe had bowled a further twenty-one overs in the second innings and took two wickets for 56 but made a limited contribution. Without doubt it was the same old story, since he soon returned to form on the county stage in the first game played at the Crabble, Dover on 11-13 July.

This natural amphitheatre was laid out in a hollow north of the port, and was a perfect "circle" with steep banking and a fine pavilion (which is still present today) being situated on the far side.

It was a grand setting for county cricket and Blythe was so impressed that he kept pictures of the ground showing the hills just beyond, detailing the sedate rows of Victorian housing, the marquees, and the many spectators with their uniform boaters and female finery.

His old friend Gilbert Jessop took to the crease with Gloucester and the side made 165 although Blythe took seven of them for 62. In reply, there was a good performance from Seymour who scored 70 runs, but there was a complete collapse beginning with Marsham and they were all out on 182. Gloucester did much better in the second innings and Jessop reached 74 whilst Blythe and Fielder took the wickets - the total 249 runs.

Kent could not match this effort and they were all out for 136 losing the game by 96 runs. Tunbridge Wells Week was to be a mixed bag and they beat Worcester but then lost to Essex (both times by several wickets), then had a return to form against Surrey at Rectory Field on 22-24 July.

Blythe really enjoyed playing the latter who batted first and the openers Hayward and Hobbs made few inroads, whereas only Lord Dalmeny saved their blushes scoring a total of 70 runs. Blythe took seven wickets for 56 in sixteen overs and the side were all out for 136 runs.

Kent improved on this making 187 with Dillon and Seymour leading the way, whilst Fairservice made 33 and Blythe was 23 not out. Surrey did not have a collapse in the second innings since to have a collapse there must be something to collapse from! In fact, Blythe and Woolley combined to see the first five wickets gone for just 27 runs on the board, and Surrey reached only 79 in total thus losing by ten wickets.

In the second innings Blythe took five wickets for 34 runs and during the game reached 1,100 wickets in his career. With such form Kent may have fancied their chances, but during the last eight games they managed one victory and the championship went away over the Crabble hill.

This change in fortune was more down to the batting since bowlers such as Blythe and Fielder remained in form. Indeed, the former was chosen over his team-mates and Rhodes of Yorkshire for the next two tests. It was during the first match at Headingley on 29-31 July that some controversy surfaced which was ultimately to end his test career (see later).

England got off to a terrible start and only Hayward, Tyldesley, and Hirst reached double figures whereas Fry was gone for 2 in just five minutes and there was a complete collapse at the end. Blythe finished on 5 not out but the total was just 76 runs and Faulkner did most of the damage.

South Africa promptly came in to bat but Tancred was bowled by Blythe for nought (stumped Lilley), however the captain Sherwell proved more resilient. He made 26 runs in seventy minutes before he was dismissed lbw to Blythe - his side being all out for only 110.

Eventually the bowler took eight wickets for 59 runs in fifteen overs which was his best analysis in test cricket, while reaching fifty test-match wickets on taking G.C. White who made only 3 runs - his previous best being six for 68 also against South Africa at Newlands.

At the end of the day the openers Hayward and Fry held the crease with England on 25 runs for nought. But the next morning they improved the whole situation and Fry scored 54 including four 4's, whilst England were eventually all out for 162 on the third morning.

The bowlers Blythe, Hirst, and Ted Arnold of Worcester then had their chance and set out to punish the South Africans. Possibly the tourists were happier on their home soil with matting wickets and under the onslaught of Blythe soon capitulated. Tancred was run out on nought whereas Sherwell, Nourse, Hathorn, and White were gone with 18 on the board.

The middle order of Faulkner, Sinclair, and Snooke were the only batsmen to achieve double figures but all fell to Blythe and the others collapsed all out on 75. Indeed, it was a fine victory by a small margin of 53 runs and was undoubtedly the Kent bowler's game.

His figures for the second innings were seven wickets for 40 runs and in total he took fifteen wickets for 99 runs. In fact, the only English players to beat this test record were J.C. Briggs at Cape Town in 1889 (15 for 28), G.A. Lohmann at Port Elizabeth in 1896 (15 for 45), Sydney F. Barnes at Johannesburg in 1913 (17 for 159), and Jim Laker at Manchester in 1956 (19 for 90) - Hirwani, Massie, and Muralitharan also took sixteen.

These statistics alone cement Blythe's position in the history of cricket and his performance undoubtedly won England the test match, while since the other games were draws it was this victory that secured the series.

Following on from this it would be expected that adulation was in order but there was some dissent, and C.B. Fry stated he was under considerable strain being completely 'knocked up' at the end. True, he did have a loss of form in the matches played immediately afterwards and missed one game, but significantly the selectors still chose him for the final test.

END OF SEASON

In August Kent drew with Worcester and Sussex, lost to Lancashire and Gloucester, but finished the sequence with a good victory over Somerset at Taunton by an innings and 103 runs. In the first session Blythe took seven for 45 runs including Len Braund for a duck and was clearly back on form. Regarding the batsmen Seymour made 164 and J.R. Mason 119.

This was followed by the third test against South Africa at the Oval on 19-21 August the team being little changed from before. C.B. Fry produced the best performance and made 129 runs with seven 4's, whilst the captain R.E. Foster scored a useful 51 but they received little support.

Tom Hayward the opener was bowled out by Vogler with his first ball and Jack Tyldesley managed only 8, whereas Len Braund reached 18 but was clean bowled by Schwarz. The middle order Hirst, Jessop, and Crawford added only 10 runs between them and this left Fry on 118 and Lilley on 16 at the end of the first day.

It was an erratic sequence and the next morning Lilley reached 42 before being bowled by Nourse, and Blythe added 10 runs to close the innings on 295 - the last man left in being Neville Knox of Surrey.

South Africa were off to a poor start and lost Sherwell and Faulkner for just 8 runs but Snooke, Nourse, and Sinclair did well to leave the score at

149 for five wickets at the end of the day. The next morning Shalders also put on 31 but there was then a rather rapid collapse and they were all out for 178. Of the bowlers Blythe had the best figures of five wickets for 61 runs the others being Hirst, Crawford, and Knox.

England then hurried through their second innings and made 138 all out but at the finish of play South Africa reached 159 for five wickets and the game was drawn. In the second innings Blythe bowled Snooke and Vogler and the most notable incident was when Jack Tyldesley reached 1,500 runs in test matches, but was bowled with no addition to his score.

There were then draws for Kent against Yorkshire and Middlesex, and in the last game against Surrey at the Oval on 29-31 August there was a severe reverse. Hayward and Crawford made the best scores to take Surrey to 426 and Kent used six bowlers but made a poor return. During the follow on Marsham saw his side lose the contest by an innings and 13 runs.

Throughout the season Blythe missed just four of the twenty-six county games - two through illness, one against Derby at Maidstone as a result of the second test, and a game against C.B. Fry and Sussex in early August when his colleague Dick Blaker replaced him.

However, with twelve victories and nine defeats Kent fell to eighth place and looked up to Nottinghamshire who were champions for the first time, which left just Gloucester and Sussex of the "founding eight" who had yet to win. Seymour made 1,547 runs in a wet summer which favoured Blythe since he took 157 wickets for Kent out of a total of 183, although he was to better this figure on two occasions.

EPISTLE TO BLYTHE

C.B. Fry may have had some personal reason for bringing Blythe's health in to question, but he was probably in the minority and during the season the papers carried *"An open letter from Gilbert Jessop to Charlie Blythe"* with a comparison to Wilfred Rhodes (dated June 1907).

The famous Gloucestershire right-hander then eulogised as follows: "It is clear that comparisons are rather odious, however Bobby Peel and Johnny Briggs had already gone when you came on the scene, whereas I know nothing of Peate except for the old record books. But of the bowlers that came afterwards you Charlie are certainly the greatest.

For years Wilfred was backed up by the best hands in the country and Kent did not have the fielding side of today. In fact, you are probably the best bowler on a hard wicket, but as an all-round cricketer Wilfred clearly has the advantage - indeed, you take your choice.

I remember well your first appearance against Gloucester at Catford (in May 1900) when you looked just sixteen, but already with an old head on your shoulders, and in particular displayed a peculiar run up and delivery. It was a gentle amble followed by a last final hop.

Regarding batting you have occasionally done well including in Sydney and Nottingham, whilst you bowled well for England at Leeds, but have played in few representative games and not yet for the 'Players.'

Wilfred always came ahead in this sense due to his batting ability and fine fielding, although you did catch most balls that came your way. Certainly, Charlie, you are a first choice for your country and it is odds-on you will appear in both England and Australia this coming year.

You have a great reputation with the horses to the benefit of yourself and of your friends, whilst your popularity was raised with both song and violin across the Australian Bight - despite the great rolling of the boat!

Further to this you have earned honours in the Association game with Hayward, Quaife & Co. Sadly you are now in-disposed (with flu) and have had to stand down for two matches, but are much needed with easy wickets to be had despite those left-handers Humphreys, Woolley, and Hardinge. We have three weeks before the first test match, and with MacLaren and Spooner unavailable and Jackson and Fry in some doubt, the England side can hardly take to the field without you.

We should not under estimate the strength of our opposition as we did on our last trip to South Africa. Well, my dear Charlie, I trust it will be many a year before that hop, skip, and jump is no longer familiar to us and that you will claim one or even two hundred wickets a season. However, I pray that I may be spared from becoming one of your victims."

Yours very sincerely, *Gilbert Jessop*

CHAPTER 11

Australia 1907-08

The matter of test cricket was now commonplace to Blythe, and with such good bowling figures he was chosen to go on a second trip to Australia in the winter months. This time he was to represent the M.C.C. or England rather than an "eleven" and joined a team that was captained by A.O. Jones the successful leader of Nottinghamshire.

Blythe collected fewer papers regarding this tour than before suggesting the experience was less of a novelty in one regard, and that his place in the team and his selection was more of a certainty in the other. Despite the fact he had described himself as an engineer his position in the mainstream of professional cricket was now verily assured.

Major P. Trevor was the manager of the touring side and George Gunn and J. Hardstaff of Notts joined their captain. Indeed, Kent also received more recognition and Blythe was accompanied by Arthur Fielder and Ken Hutchings, whereas J. Crawford, E.G. Hayes, and Jack Hobbs represented Surrey. Other tourists included F.L. Fane of Essex, R.A. Young of Sussex, Len Braund of Somerset, and J. Humphries of Derbyshire.

Wilfred Rhodes was in fact the sole representative from Yorkshire and in the previous season scored an average of 22 runs taking 177 wickets. Like previous tours there were some obvious omissions, whilst an unexpected addition was Sydney Barnes who after the MacLaren tour only played for Lancashire in 1902/03. In fact he then appeared for Staffordshire and took ten wickets for 26 runs against a Yorkshire 2nd XI on 10 July 1907.

A souvenir programme was printed to celebrate what was the 18th visit of the English cricketers to Australia (by Anthony Hordern & Sons, Sydney) with pictures of the early teams and profiles of the players.

At the end, several statistics showed that Jack Hobbs of Cambridge and Surrey had made the most runs at 2,135 with the highest average of 37.45, followed by Ernie Hayes and Ken Hutchings. In the bowling department Blythe had the most wickets at 183 with the top average of 15.42 and not far behind were both Rhodes and Fielder.

The introduction noted it was a relatively long time since the previous visit under Warner in 1903-04 mainly due to "the subsequent cricket troubles." These, they added, were started at the onset by the Australians rather than the English, and both factors they thought would add considerable interest to the forthcoming contests.

However, they then had to explain a rather familiar problem the supposed weakness and representative character of the side. Fry, Jackson, Hayward, and MacLaren were absent (not to mention Warner) and they might well have been improved in the batting department, although their "varied and bowling strength" was deemed to be in their favour.

Regarding Blythe it was stated that he was the best bowler in 1906, and using great accuracy was especially skilful in making the ball come from the off. However, the unusual feature of his delivery was the habit of taking (and hiding) the ball behind him just prior to its release.

He maintained a variety of pace and breaks both ways which troubled even the best of batsmen, whilst one of his top performances was the year after his last visit to Australia. He bowled thirteen wickets at a cost of less than 5 runs per man against Yorkshire's best viz. Brown, Tunnicliffe, Denton, and Hirst - then again in an innings against Surrey in 1906.

In the last season he ran close on the heels of Rhodes and Fielder and if the name of Barnes were added then, "a strong quartette [sic] of bowlers is visiting us." With reference to the recent tests against South Africa Blythe had an average of 10.38 and excelled "top-notchers" like Arnold, Hirst, and Braund although little was expected of him in the batting department.

PERTH, W.A.

With the Aussies left suitably "in awe and trepidation" at the description of such players in the souvenir, the members of the M.C.C. gathered at St. Pancras station to take the train to Tilbury. The party was for the most part complete although Hutchings, Fane, and Rhodes were to travel overland to Marseilles and R.A. Young was to join them in Plymouth.

Jones, Braund, Fielder, Barnes, Blythe, and Rhodes had previously been to Australia, whereas G. Gunn was going "principally for his health" and was only to appear in an emergency. The captain gave a brief interview before leaving the station and noted that he had a good team but could not say if they would win - however they were a fine bunch of players.

A large crowd gathered at St. Pancras to provide a send off and a select band of cricketers bid them farewell i.e. F.E. Lacey secretary of the M.C.C., W. Findlay secretary of Surrey, members of Essex, T. Pawley the manager of Kent, Rev. J.C. Crawford and two sons, P. Warner, W. Brearley, W.G. Quaife, G.F. Hearne, and officials from the Rugby Union.

The party reached Tilbury on 20 September and joined the "Ophir" part of the Orient Line a 6,814 ton vessel with 426 passengers. She was to sail for Sydney under the master A.J. Coad the voyage taking 56 days.

Before setting sail there was a luncheon on board and the success of the side was proposed by Mr. C.E. Green. There was a response from Arthur Jones who said that whatever the outcome it would be a good experience for the young players in the side (although twelve were over 25 years and five were over 30 years). Thereafter, the vessel left the dock and there were further scenes of enthusiasm emanating from the quayside.

The "Ophir" initially arrived at Perth a month later and the side stayed at the Palace Hotel, St. George's Terrace with its grand entrance/dining room (built in a gold boom in 1897). The first game was against Western Australia on Saturday, 26 October and being the first international in the province it excited the keenest of interest amongst the public.

The Western Australians over the previous two years had produced some creditable performances against South Australia and New South Wales, and thereby earned the opportunity to play in the series of games that took place every "third season" against the English in Australia.

It was apparent that cricket had done a great deal for raising the profile of Australia whose population was then just 4 million. That they were able to match England in cricket, a country with ten times the number of people and centuries of experience, was truly remarkable - whilst in turn this had raised the profile of cricket around the world.

Up to that time South Australia, New South Wales, and Victoria had been the premier states regarding the game, and every aspiring young batsman hoped for the day when he would play on the other side of the world. In fact, Australia had secured considerable success both at home and abroad and players such as Hill, Graham, and Trumper went to England as boys, whilst many colts appeared in the "Sheffield Shield" matches.

A significant factor was a three day limit in England which had produced models in terms of the English batsmen, batsmen who knew the necessity of making runs and also quickly all the time they were at the wicket. Fifteen years earlier A.C. Bannerman, Donnan, and Moses of New South Wales had been a by-word for dreariness in batting and lack of initiative.

This old stone-walling type of play was by then virtually extinct and they abandoned the philosophy of - 'stay there sonny and the runs are bound to come!' Instead, they had batsmen who were both dashing and positive in their approach. A good example was W.W. Armstrong who for many years pottered about in a timorous irritating fashion, but on his return home went for the runs and used his height and strength to great advantage.

Western Australia had now earned its place with the other states and large crowds came to the "WACA" to watch their players practice, but they had few accredited batsmen unlike the tourists who had several.

The ground at Perth was beautifully green and play commenced at noon, then Mr. James Gardiner president of the local association entertained the visitors with a luncheon in the pavilion. Frederick Fane led the attack with 133 whereas Braund, Jones, Hardstaff, and Crawford also had good scores and at the end of the day the M.C.C. were 350 for seven wickets.

Blythe spent his time with his feet up just outside the pavilion and in the evening went to a special event. A letter was sent to him (on 25 September) by J. Murray secretary of the Amalgamated Society of Engineers in Perth, inviting him to their annual dinner and "smoke social" at the Shaftesbury Hotel that evening. They hoped he could see his way clear to attend and added that it would do them the greatest of honour.

All the players had a break on Sunday (as was the tradition at the time) and on the Monday the M.C.C. were all out for 404, whilst the total was scored in just 315 minutes. A number of bowlers were then used and the western side were beaten by an innings and 134 runs.

PROVINCIAL TOUR

With the first job completed the players boarded the packet and soon had a formal public welcome at the Town Hall, Adelaide. Jones said that the spectators might miss Tyldesley and Hayward but his players were some of the best, whereas England could produce three fielding teams.

Major Phillip Trevor then added that since the M.C.C. had taken over the tours they had increased in importance and this had strengthened the bond between the two countries. He sat down to many great cheers.

Five players from the previous M.C.C. visit in 1903-04 turned out for the South Australians, and the two sides played a game at the Adelaide Oval on 9-13 November. Joe Darling a veteran player led off the batting with E.R. Mayne but it was Clem Hill who was most successful scoring 104.

The Australians looked in a good position and had reached 274 for five wickets at the end of play on the Saturday. When play recommenced on the Monday they took their total to 343 all out, but the M.C.C. were to reply with a staggering score that went way beyond the probable.

Initially the captain A.O. Jones made 119 and at the end of play Braund and Hardstaff were not out and going well with the score on 233 for four. This allowed some time to relax and Blythe and his team-mates then linked up with another Australasian tour and attended a concert.

Dame Clara Butt the famous contralto from Sussex had arrived with her husband Kennerley Rumford and performed at Adelaide Town Hall on the Monday evening, supported by pianist Frank Merrick. This may have been of some interest to Blythe since there were several violin solos as well as various arias, a solo on the pianoforte, a rendition of "Abide with Me" by Madame Butt, and a concluding duet of an olde English air.

The "singing" tour was to involve two more concerts in Adelaide, but the cricketers were not put out of their stride by the entertainment and on the Tuesday they reached a total of 660 runs. Jones, Hardstaff, Braund, and Crawford all made centuries whilst the innings lasted 465 minutes and they declared at the end of play with eight men gone.

Braund and Crawford took most of the wickets as the Australians were all out for 134 the next morning, and the M.C.C. won by an innings and 183 runs. It was indeed a most promising start. Blythe played in both of these games although made no major contribution, but was absent from the next fixture against Victoria at Melbourne on 15-20 November (a draw).

The side soon moved north and stayed at the Hotel Metropole, Sydney, a six-storey building on a major thoroughfare with two conical corner towers. The M.C.C. then took on New South Wales at the Sydney Cricket Ground from 22-25 November and had a good first innings, whilst all the players made double figures to reach a total of 304.

In particular, Blythe was not out on 27, and yet again contradicted those who had talked of his weakness in the batting department. He then joined Barnes and Fielder to tackle the home side who opened their account with the right-hander Victor Trumper.

The latter stayed in until he was bowled by Blythe caught Braund on 38, but players such as Monty Noble and R.A. Duff went out lightly. The others followed the same pattern and were all dismissed for 101 runs.

Meanwhile, the M.C.C. put on another total of 301 and this time Blythe scored 23 to bring up his half century in the match. New South Wales had no answer and were all out for 96 losing the contest by 408 runs.

During the MacLaren tour there were a large number of provincial games but on this occasion the M.C.C. remained cautious in this regard, and they restricted practice mainly to the more serious first class matches. Indeed, for this purpose they made the long journey north to Brisbane, Queensland, and stayed at the grand Belle Vue Hotel in the centre of the city from 28 November to 10 December. It was a long sojourn and the players spent some of their time boating on the river below the bluffs. [1]

---

[1] The Belle Vue Hotel was erected on the corner of George and Alice Streets in 1885-86, and had a series of decadent verandas and attractive cast iron supports. It sat between Parliament House and the Queensland Club by the Botanic Gardens becoming a prominent landmark for many years. The Government purchased the hotel in 1967 and after a lengthy fight it was demolished in 1979.

The first fixture was played against a Queensland side on 30 November at Woolloongabba, Brisbane (or the "Gabba") but the home team were all out for 78 runs after an hour and a quarter. Only two bowlers were needed in the twenty-four overs played and Blythe took five wickets for 35, whereas Braund took a further four wickets for 43.

Hutchings, Rhodes, and the captain Jones all scored nearly 70 and the latter two held the crease at the end of the first day. In the evening there was a banquet for the players just opposite their hotel at the Government House, Brisbane and the following day was the Sunday.

Upon the resumption of play Rhodes and Jones added to the score but the others went out easily and Blythe was stumped on nought - the total 308. Queensland then improved making 186 but lost the game by an innings and 44 runs whereas Blythe took a further six wickets for 48.

This was followed by a fixture against an Australian XI under the captain Percy McAlister (of Victoria) on 6-9 December. It was a much stronger side including players such as Armstrong of Victoria and Gregory of New South Wales and the home side began with an innings of 299.

In this instance Braund took most of the wickets (7-117) and Blythe took just one for 60 whereas England replied with 223 runs. Australia had made a further 110 at the close of play on the second day but there was no play on the third and the game finished as a draw.

TESTS (1-4)

The M.C.C. then returned to Sydney and after seven weeks in the country they finally played a test match on 13-19 December. Regarding the earlier discussion of the three-day game this was in fact a timeless match.

Clearly there was some kind of *emergency* regarding previous comments since the captain Jones was absent from the team, and George Gunn came in as third bat after the openers F.L. Fane and R.A. Young. Perhaps he was just itching to play and actually put on the best score of 119 including twenty 4's as the visitors were all out for 273.

In reply Australia reached 50 runs at the end of the first day's play and the best scores went to Trumper, Noble, and Clem Hill who reached 87 runs. The side finished on 300 and the M.C.C. used six bowlers in total whilst Blythe bowled twelve overs but failed to take any wickets.

Rhodes and Fane then went in to bat and had added just 19 runs when play finished, and there was a break until the Monday. In the evening the players travelled to Sydney Town Hall and enjoyed a concert with Madame Melba the famous soprano (and her 1907 tour).

She was supported by her troupe who included Miss Una Bourne on the piano, Mr. Bryce Carter on the cello, and John Lemmone on the flute. The music itself was by Chopin, Puccini (from La Tosca), and Liszt. [2]

Returning to the crease Blythe managed to make 15 runs in the second innings and the M.C.C. also reached 300, but Australia scored 275 and won the game by two wickets. In the second instance Blythe took just a solitary wicket for 55 runs and clearly did not have the best of matches.

This was followed by two provincial games, the first against a Victoria XI at Albert Park (or South Melbourne Cricket Ground) on 21-24 December. The game also ended in a draw and Blythe did not play.

Once the Christmas festivities were completed the side travelled inland to Bendigo and played a local "18" from 26-28 December. This was clearly a holiday game and Crawford, Hobbs, and Hayes put on a display of batting to take the M.C.C. total to 213. No play took place on the second day and the opponents were then all out for just 55.

The game was ultimately a draw but Blythe took seven wickets for 31 runs and Crawford took six wickets for 15 runs. Played at the Upper Reserve it was basically an exhibition match and the team most likely stayed nearby at the opulent Hotel Shamrock (as on the last tour).

With the New Year beckoning the series began in earnest, but Blythe was not considered to be on form and played in no further test matches - a fact that may have raised doubts about his inclusion on the tour.

Wilfred Rhodes was chosen in his place although as it turned out he also failed to register many wickets. However, this was a significant choice since Rhodes who was also a slow left-arm orthodox bowler represented England in several later tests when Blythe was overlooked.

The M.C.C. won the second test at the Melbourne Cricket Ground from 1-7 January, with the most important performance by Ken Hutchings who scored 126 runs. In general the game was high scoring and the tourists won a narrow contest by one wicket, whilst most of the bowling was down to Barnes and Crawford although Fielder was also present.

In fact, Armstrong bowled the last ball to Barnes who played it to Hazlitt at point. The latter tried to throw the wicket down but missed and Fielder got home and only stopped running when he reached the pavilion!

---

[2] Dame Nellie Melba was born Helen Porter Mitchell (1861-1931) near Melbourne and met John Lemmone who was later her accompanist and manager, but made her name as a soprano in Covent Garden, Paris, and New York. Una M. Bourne was born at Mudgee and first performed at the Bechstein Hall (Wigmore Hall) in London, then was chosen to join the 1907 Australian tour. Bryce Morrow Carter a rising star was born in Melbourne and then educated at Haileybury.

Next came the third test played at the Adelaide Oval on 10-16 January, and following the old adage of 'stay in and the runs will come' there were some high scores over six days. Fielder bowled Victor Trumper on 4 runs and removed W.W. Armstrong taking 4-80, but it was Clem Hill's 160 for the home side that helped them to a 506 run second innings. As a result the game was won by Australia with a margin of 245 runs.

A trip to Tasmania followed which must have been of some interest to Blythe, while the team stayed at the Launceston Hotel and initially played at the North Tasmania Cricket Ground from 18-21 January.

The first innings saw Jack Hobbs make 104 out of a total of 321 and the opponents Tasmania replied with 276, but Blythe took no wickets in his twenty overs although he then had an important role.

It was nearing the end of the second day and Blythe was put in to bat with R.A. Young but the latter was promptly bowled for 1. The next morning Blythe stayed in with Jack Hobbs to see 34 added and when he was finally bowled he had scored a creditable 21 runs. Hardstaff also did well making 85 and eventually the M.C.C. total was 249.

Tasmania then failed to make the runs and Blythe did slightly better taking three wickets for 35 and the game was won by 120 runs. However, it was Braund and Crawford who took most of the wickets.

Soon after the game they travelled south and stayed at Heathorn's Hotel in Hobart which was a short distance from the railway, wharf, and domain. A second game was played against Tasmania on 24-27 January but this ended in a draw - Hardstaff and Rhodes both made centuries whereas Blythe and Fielder took just two wickets each in the first innings.

There was also a game against Victoria in Melbourne on 1-4 February and it was Joe Hardstaff of Nottingham who again led the way making 122 runs out of 338. Victoria were bowled out for just 77 runs whereas Blythe took four wickets for 41, and reached a milestone of 1,200 wickets with his first wicket taken. Jacks Hobbs soon added another 115 and the side declared on 241 winning the game by 330 runs.

The fourth test then took place at the same venue on 7-11 February and in the first innings Australia reached 214 with M.A. Noble on 48 and V.S. Ransford on 51. Jack Hobbs of Surrey was playing in his first test series and scored 57 and G. Gunn made 13 with the side on 88 runs for three wickets. There was then a complete collapse and they were all out for 105!

In the second innings Australia made 385 with W.W. Armstrong on 133 while Fielder took four wickets in both innings. However, it was all to no avail and despite the arrival of Jones as captain (Fane held the position in the first three tests) the game was lost by 308 runs.

During the evening there was a "farewell dinner" at the Grand Hotel held by W.H. Burgess Esq. the steward of the Melbourne Club and long term manager of the hotel during its modernization. This was a sumptuous affair with cricket bats adorning the table and fine French menu, but was unusual in description since the tour was yet to be concluded.

JOURNEY HOME

Blythe was then back in the team for another provincial game against New South Wales in Sydney on 14-20 February. This was also a timeless match and allowed for some lengthy displays of batting - in particular 132 not out by Len Braund. Eight bowlers were used by the M.C.C. during the game which was a draw and in the first innings Blythe took five for 93, including Victor Trumper who he clean bowled on 14 runs.

By that stage the test series was well and truly lost - the M.C.C. having suffered defeats in Sydney, Adelaide, and Melbourne with just a single victory to their name at the latter location. However, their honour was at stake at the Sydney Cricket Ground on 21-27 February.

Jones, the captain, won the toss and decided to field which seemed to be a good decision as Australia were all out for 137 runs, and the aptly named Sydney Barnes took seven wickets for just 60 runs. Crawford and Rhodes assisted him in the bowling, whereas George Gunn played in all five tests although he only came along to benefit his health!

Despite the loss of Fane, Hobbs (65) and Gunn (50) took the score up to 116 for just one wicket at the end of the first day. Indeed, Gunn eventually made 122 with seven 4's and a 6 and the M.C.C. reached 281.

However, it was all change in the second innings and to the delight of the home crowd Victor Trumper (of Sydney) scored 166 in 241 minutes with eighteen 4's and the side were all out on 422.

Hobbs and Fane started well in the final innings but Charles Macartney a slow left arm bowler then damaged any hopes for the M.C.C. He dismissed Gunn on nought and Hutchings on 2 runs, and despite a good later effort by Rhodes (with 69) the game was eventually lost by 49 runs.

There was much travelling back and forth and the side then attended yet another "farewell luncheon" on 28 February, given by Mr. Justice Cussen the president of the local cricket club back in Melbourne.

The meal again took place at the Grand Hotel and the invitation displayed a picture of the M.C.C. side on the front, and the ground on the back with a full crowd attending. There was another good menu followed by some loyal toasts to the King and also to A.O. Jones and his cricket team.

A number of notaries were present including Sir Reginald Talbot who was Governor of Victoria, Mr. Deakin the Federal Premier, and Mr. Weedon the Lord Mayor which gave some idea of the status of the players and the tour. Mr. Cussen stated that a three-two victory would have been a fairer reflection of events, and noted that the weather was especially trying to the visitors whose bowling was equal to any that went before.

In reply Jones noted that his main hope was that the next side to come would be the best that England could provide. Up to that point the M.C.C. had never sent their foremost players due to certain difficulties existing with regard to arrangement of the visits.

With the 'shouting' almost over there was a three day match against South Australia on 2-4 March, which was Blythe's last game on Australian soil. It was high scoring with George Gunn (102) and Wilfred Rhodes (78) not out for a total of 404 runs. However, the home side then made 445 and Blythe scored 9 runs whilst taking just one wicket. The M.C.C. reached 134 on the third day and the game ended in a draw.

During the return voyage there was a stop over in Perth and a three day match was played against Western Australia from 13-16 March. The home side put on 256 runs but the revelation was Gunn who again made a century with 122 - Sydney Barnes also scored 93 from a total of 362 while the side declared on the third day. Western Australia continued to improve making a further 265 but the game also ended in an honourable draw.

The main conclusion about the tour was that England had struggled again in the different conditions of climate, and needed to address the problem of sending a truly representative side if they really wanted to win. Any business commitments of the gentlemen needed to be put to one side and only in this way could they challenge the improving Australians.

Regarding Blythe he had played in fifteen test matches at this stage, but had only been a member of the winning side on three occasions (once with MacLaren, once in South Africa, and once at Headingley). Being recently married he no doubt missed his wife which probably affected him, but he did have further test successes in the near future.

CHAPTER 12

Kent's Revival

Blythe returned home to his wife at St. Mary's Road in April 1908, feeling somewhat disappointed that he only played in one test match during the tour - and clearly failed to perform to his county potential. Indeed, so many sportsmen since have experienced such peaks and troughs and it has been down to their character if they could bounce back.

In the case of Blythe he had plenty more regarding both test and county cricket and continued to perform right up to the end of his career, although a degree of controversy was soon to enter the debate. It was a controversy that overshadowed some stunning performances.

There was some surprise at Kent's lowly finish of eighth the previous year, largely due to the absence of Burnup and A. Hearne as well as the injury of Hutchings. Meanwhile, Hardinge and Woolley were now established in the side and with further consolidation matters could only improve.

Cloudesley Marsham again led the eleven, who were clearly a formidable team in terms of county cricket, but in the opening game against the M.C.C. at Lord's on 14-16 May there was a draw. Warner was the mainstay of the attack scoring 64 not out and Blythe took three wickets for 43, however no play took place on the second day.

There was then an early test as the Kent side travelled up to Yorkshire to play at Park Avenue, Bradford beginning on 18 May. This was not for the connoisseur and was a low scoring game with the visitors all out for 77 runs, and only A.P. Day and Marsham on double figures.

The weather affected play and that was how the score remained at the end of the first day. Yorkshire then suffered a similar fate and despite 45 by the opener Rhodes, Denton went out to Fielder for 10, Hirst was bowled by Fairservice on 1, and S. Haigh was caught and bowled by Blythe for nought. Indeed, the latter had figures of 4-24 including Lord Hawke on 0.

Yorkshire were all out for 101 but Kent reached a dismal total of just 46 with the highest scorer being Ken Hutchings on 16. Not surprisingly the home side won the game in two days by nine wickets.

A short break then ensued before the next fixture and Blythe revealed his involvement in local events when he attended *a dinner and smoking concert* at the Bull Hotel, Tonbridge on 22 May. This was in honour of Tonbridge F.C. who over three seasons had been champions and runners-up in the local league, and twice finalists in the related charity cup.

The local footballers included Blythe, Fairservice, and Woolley who all played for the team. The event started off with an appetising meal of roast beef and lamb, Yorkshire pudding, rhubarb tart, and cheese salad whereas there was some assorted music played by the "Cecilian Concert Party" and diverse other contributors.

After a toast to the King and to the Kent F.A. there was a presentation of medals followed by several varied speeches. The chairman A.F.W. Johnson Esq. J.P. initially proposed Tonbridge F.C., the response coming from the hon. secretary A.F. Lawrence and also the captain who was none other than Bill Fairservice of Kent. Councillor G.F. Stacey then proposed "kindred clubs and sports" and Mr. C. Blythe provided the response.

THE 1908 SEASON

Certainly the next fixture was viewed by Northampton with a degree of trepidation, but there was no repeat of the previous year's events as Kent arrived at the County Ground on 25-26 May. The visitors still won by an innings and 54 runs and Blythe scored 15, but he only took four wickets for 64 and then two wickets for 33.

There was also another first for the Tonbridge bowler as he played for Kent against Cambridge University at F.P. Fenner's Ground on 1-3 June. It was to be an interesting struggle against an old colleague. [1]

Cambridge went in to bat and R.A. Young of the Australian tour and a Sussex player led the way. He scored 106 in the first innings and 89 in the second before being bowled by Blythe on both occasions. All of the innings saw scores of over 200 and Woolley reached 2,000 runs in the first, while Blythe took four wickets in total and the game was drawn.

The Kent side continued to do well and won four of the next five games including a victory over Lancashire at Old Trafford on 11-12 June by 213 runs. In the second innings Woolley made 79 and Blythe added a useful 24 from a total of 280 - leaving Lancashire needing 319 to win.

In fact, the home team included players such as Walter Brearley and also A.F. Spooner and W.K. Tyldesley (brothers of the England duo) however they were all dismissed for 106. Blythe had taken six wickets for 46 runs whereas three were taken by Fielder and the other was a run out.

---

[1] Francis Phillips Fenner (1811-96) played for Cambridge Town in 1829-56 with games against the University and M.C.C. at Parker's Piece (the Cambridge Rules for soccer were established there in 1848). Fenner also played for England against Kent at Lord's, Town Malling, and Bromley in the 1840s and first leased the F.P. Fenner Ground in 1848 - the freehold being purchased in 1896.

Soon after, there was an absorbing performance against Northampton at the Bat and Ball Ground, Gravesend on 22-24 June. Marsham started well with 65 runs but there was an amazing fourth wicket stand by Hutchings and Woolley of 296. During the stand both scored over twenty 4's and the players finished on 132 and 152 runs apiece.

This combination of first class batting followed by definitive bowling was to prove irresistible on this and many other occasions. Kent finished on 561 runs and Northants replied with 146 and 129 thus losing the game by an innings and 286 runs. In terms of the bowling Blythe (with some help from Woolley) was unstoppable and took 7-57 and 6-54.

However, in the next two months he missed a couple of games against Somerset and Essex due to a problem of water on the knee. In addition his partner Fielder was also injured, and the latter only took 86 wickets rather than the 159 he amassed during the previous season.

Kent then went on a northern tour to Worcester and Leicester and ended the trip at the County Ground, Derby on 2-4 July - the adjacent Racecourse Ground staged a Cup Final replay in 1886. The visitors won the toss and scored a record against Derby of 615 including Marsham (91), Hardinge (127), Seymour (171), Hutchings (102), and Woolley (46).

On the second day the home side batted and recorded 253 which under normal conditions might have been a good score. Blythe took three wickets for 102 and a further three fell to A.P. Day, whilst in the follow on the side were all out for 128. Kent had won the game by an innings and 234 runs, and the bowler Blythe took another four for 74 runs and reached 1,300 wickets with his last dismissal.

There was then an important game against their opponents Yorkshire at the Crabble, Dover on 6 July. In the first innings Blythe took two wickets for 61 as the visitors made 401, while Kent replied with 242 although the bowler was then "absent hurt." The game ended in a draw and he missed the next fixture against Somerset (also played at Dover).

Meanwhile, the club maintained their good record against Surrey and won at Rectory Field by 206 runs on 23-25 July. In the first innings Blythe took five wickets for only 65 including Hayward, Hobbs, and Lord Dalmeny then added to this with a further three wickets in the second.

Next month the momentum was continued and Kent played Somerset at Taunton on 13-15 August. Blythe took three of the wickets as the home side went out for 186, however Kent then went into overdrive again and scored 601 including J. Seymour (129), Woolley (105), A.P. Day (118), and E. Humphreys (149). The latter two made a record of 248 for the seventh wicket putting on 201 in 75 minutes.

In reply P.R. Johnson who was born in Wellington, N.Z. scored 126 and Len Braund made a good 53, but there was then a middle order collapse under the onslaught of Blythe and Seymour. The former took six wickets for 115 runs and reached 150 for the season, whereas Kent won the game by an innings and 114 runs.

Kent were destined to win a second title but suffered a surprise defeat at the hands of Surrey in the next fixture at the Oval on 17-18 August. After winning the toss the visitors chose to bat but only made 111 runs and the home side promptly went on the offensive.

Tom Hayward made 54 however Jack Hobbs then scored 155 and Alan Marshal, from Queensland, added 167 runs in as many minutes. A. Ducat also scored 77 not out and Surrey declared on 532. The normally reliable bowlers made few inroads and Fielder sent down several wides or no balls while Blythe took two wickets for 181 - each bowling 35 overs.

It was time to call it a day on this occasion and in the second innings Kent basically conceded at 103 all out. They had gone through eight bowlers in their attempts to change the course of the game, but ultimately lost by the extremely large total of an innings and 318 runs.

This surprise defeat saw the title go away from them although they soon bounced back with victories against Leicester and Middlesex. In the latter game at Lord's on 24-26 August they won by 117 runs however for a long time it was a close-run contest. The first three sessions produced scores of just over 200, but Middlesex collapsed in the fourth mainly due to Frank Woolley who took six wickets for 8 runs in 4.3 overs.

Kent had finished as runners-up to Yorkshire and but for losing the head-to-head and the Surrey defeat might have won. They recorded seventeen victories and lost just three games, whereas Blythe played in all but two of the twenty-five fixtures. His figures were 174 wickets for Kent in the season (197 in total) and clearly he was undaunted by any criticisms.

Indeed, it was a combination of formidable batting and guile from their bowlers that put them on the brink of further success in "the golden age of cricket." During the season Hardinge made 1,341 runs and Woolley 1,244 with another 71 wickets, whereas Marsham had almost reached a total of 1,000 - although he resigned as captain at the end of the season.

The M.C.C. took a team to America in 1905/07 and Bart King and the Philadelphians came to England on their final tour in 1908. Arriving in July they played their first game against South Wales at Cardiff Arms Park followed by some county fixtures, then went to Dublin and Belfast in early August. Indeed, with the more serious contests out of the way there was simply a chance to enjoy playing cricket.

GENTLEMEN'S TOURS

Philadelphia also played against the M.C.C., had a trip to Derby/Notts, and lastly travelled to Durham, but the tour concluded with a match against Kent who clearly held a special place in their affections. The side included John Lester their captain ably supported by Mr. Bart King and F.S. White (a member of the Colts) who were all prominent back in 1903.

Once these old friendships were renewed the teams took to the pitch at the St. Lawrence Ground on 27-29 August. The visitors did quite well in their first innings and reached 188 - while King removed Seymour, Mason, Hutchings, and both the Days leaving Kent on just 102.

But the Philadelphians were soon all out for 37 the home side winning the contest rather easily by four wickets. Blythe was a just spectator and on the first evening went to a dinner at the County Hotel, Canterbury with Lord Harris - the toasts to the "King" and to the "President."

There was then another reunion and Arthur Jones collected together the M.C.C. Australian team (of the previous winter) and went on a brief tour, the first game played against an England XI at the Central Recreation Ground, Hastings on 3-5 September.

A whole host of stars were displayed by the opponents and in some ways this was the first against the second eleven, perhaps the side who should have gone to Australia. Fry and Warner opened for England but Blythe sent them both back to the pavilion with only 21 runs between them.

Samuel Day, Gilbert Jessop, and Jack Mason fell quite easily to Rhodes whereas only the famous Ranjitsinhji (he became the Maharaja of Nawangar on 10 March 1907) had any success reaching 64 runs. A.F.A. Lilley and Ted Arnold also fell to Blythe and the England side were dismissed for 161. All was quite symmetrical as Blythe took 5-77 and Rhodes 5-78.

The touring team which included many successful batsmen from Australia such as Hobbs, Gunn, Rhodes, and Crawford could only manage 107 due to the efforts of Ted Arnold who took seven for 51 runs.

However, the weather upset the fixture with no play on the second day and England declared in the second innings on 87 runs. Blythe managed to take just two more wickets - Ranjitsinhji on 5 and A.F.A. Lilley on 3, while the tourists then added 41 runs and the game ended in a draw.

The Gentlemen v Players took place at the North Marine Road Ground in Scarborough on 3 September; and a number of the participants then came together as Lord Londesborough's XI to play at the same venue against the M.C.C. touring side on 7-9 September.

Some good scores were made and Jack Hobbs and J. Crawford both had half centuries, whereas Ranjitsinhji was bowled out by Hutchings on 101. Blythe also bowled Spooner, Hayward, and Tyldesley; Bosanquet and Hirst put on substantial scores but Leveson-Gower didn't bat and they declared. Indeed, the weather meant the game also ended in a draw.

C.B. Fry and some of the other players such as A.E. Knight, C.P. Mead, and G.L. Jessop then headed off to Broad Halfpenny Down for a nostalgic game between Hambledon and an England XI. Fry led the batting for the village side making 84 not out and they won by five wickets.

At the same time the M.C.C. Australian team took on J. Bamford's XI at the Oldfields Ground, Uttoxeter, Staffordshire, on 10-12 September. The players including Blythe stayed at the White Hart Hotel which was an old 17th-century coaching inn and latterly home to "The Automobile Club of Great Britain and Ireland." One can imagine the gentlemen arriving in their touring cars with running boards, although perhaps at this early date the majority came from Scarborough by train!

A. Marshal, E.G. Arnold, and A.F.A. Lilley (wicket keeper) appeared for the opponents who made 180, and Blythe was on good form taking seven wickets for 75 runs. The M.C.C. then scored a reasonable 201, but Blythe improved his game with figures of six for 39 runs and J. Bamford's were all out for just 80. The bowler had now reached 1,400 wickets in his career and his side won the contest by nine wickets.

The main feature of such games were the ever-present rain showers, water dripping down from pavilion eaves, puddles lying around the wickets, fresh smelling greenery in the air, and a feeling that Blythe had joined a rather distinguished club. Indeed, there seemed little question of his fitness to be included with the "elite" gentlemen of cricket.

THE 1909 SEASON

Blythe continued to live a ten minute walk from the Angel Ground and in the next season he helped take Kent to a new level, establishing a record for wickets taken. In addition he had a very successful "benefit year" after ten full seasons, although this was tinged with disappointment in the fact his marriage had yet to produce any children.

Kent maintained their progress from the previous year and in the first instance they appointed Ted Dillon, a student of Rugby and Oxford, as the next captain. He was a left-hander who had played for the side since 1900 and was also an international rugby player, and was to lead Kent into the most successful period in their history.

One surprise introduction to the squad was Douglas W. Carr a right-arm medium pace bowler and advocate of the googly. The latter played for the Kent 2nd XI in his younger days and a couple of matches for Oxford, but appeared on the scene for the Gentlemen in July 1909.

Carr had played games with Bosanquet and thereby honed his skills, but recently regained his form with regard to both the leg break and the googly. As a result Dillon brought him into the side and his innovative style proved a revelation, despite the fact he was already 37-years old at the time. Dillon was very successful as captain although business sometimes kept him away at which time Jack Mason acted as his deputy.

Indeed, Kent were off to a good start and defeated the M.C.C. at Lord's by 97 runs, with Fielder taking thirteen wickets and Blythe five. The line up of batsmen and bowlers available to Kent was quite literally awesome and in the game Seymour scored 81 and Woolley made 97.

Kent then travelled up to Aylestone Road to take on Leicester on 17-19 May and went in to bat first. Dillon led the way with a score of 84 runs and by the second day they were all out on 334, providing the latter with an extremely difficult early-season task.

Cecil Wood and Albert Knight started well for the home side adding 54 runs between them, however Blythe produced a fine display of bowling to bring about a total collapse. He took nine wickets for just 42 runs and they were all out for 104 resulting in the follow on.

In the second innings Blythe set about Leicester yet again and by the close of play on the second day he had taken another five wickets - making a total figure of fourteen for 56 runs in one day. Leicester had just two wickets remaining and he took these the next morning as they were all out for 149 thus his final analysis was seven for 60.

Kent had won the contest by an innings and 81 runs and Blythe had a return of sixteen wickets for just 102 scored, the other dismissals falling to Bill Fairservice and Henry Preston. With such bowling taking place the batsmen must have wondered if they would ever get a chance.

This "problem" was borne out in the next two games and initially Kent played Derbyshire at Queen's Park, Chesterfield. Winning the toss they set up a total of 357 with Blythe on 22, and the home side lost by an innings and 141 runs. Then came Northampton on 24-26 May and Blythe produced his usual impressive performance against the cobblers.

Dillon took his side in to bat and Seymour made a half century, whereas Arthur Day made 133 in as many minutes with twenty 4's and a 6. Blythe also scored 24 and the Kent side were all out for 326 runs, with the game following the same tried and trusted formula of the previous two.

Northampton were unable to get going and were all out for just 88 with Blythe taking five wickets for 31, the others falling to Fielder and Woolley. In the follow on Blythe moved up a gear and took nine wickets for 44 runs in just eighteen overs, whereas Northants were all out for 78 and lost the match by an innings and 160 runs.

Blythe had reached 1,450 wickets in first class cricket during the game and the papers noted Northampton collapsed solely as a result of his bowling. He was in fine form on both soft and hard wickets and they were convinced of his place in the forthcoming test against the Australians.

During the Northants game he got through a tremendous amount of work with the ball, and assisted by the state of the pitch played havoc with the Midlands batsmen. Indeed, his aggregate for the match was some fourteen wickets at a little more than five runs a piece - no play took place on the second day and the game was soon finished on the third.

EDGBASTON TEST

The newspaper predictions were promptly fulfilled and despite any earlier controversy regarding his stamina, Blythe was included in the side for the first test at Edgbaston on 27-29 May. It was definitely a good decision as the slow bowler reproduced comparable form for his country.

Australia won the toss and their captain Monty Noble decided to bat, the other batsmen in the side including such notables as W.W. Armstrong and Victor Trumper. It was to be a remarkable contest greatly affected by the weather and most certainly the rain-sodden Edgbaston pitch.

Despite the array of famous batsmen appearing on each side the game was fought to a thrilling finish in almost a day and a half. On the Thursday only an hour's play was possible and the tourists made 22 for two wickets leaving Armstrong and Trumper holding the crease.

However, when play resumed Blythe (6-44) and Hirst (4-28) "skittled" them out for 74 runs. Blythe bowled the opener A. Cotter for just 2 and also took Trumper and Noble to catches for limited scores. [2]

England came in to bat on a wicket favouring the bowler and despite a strong side captained by MacLaren with Hobbs, Tyldesley, Fry, A.O. Jones, Jessop, and Rhodes they were all out for 121. Australia then made 67 runs for just two wickets at the end of the second day, the undoubted highlight being a diving catch by Jones at slip off a fast ball from Hirst.

---

[2] The papers noted that this was not the smallest test match score, since Australia were all out for 36 runs at Birmingham in 1902.

The crowd were then driven to a great level of enthusiasm that was little dented by the approaching rain. On the third morning there was no sun to dry the pitch resulting in a "sticky" wicket which rolled dead, whilst hard driving was needed to make any ball travel over the sodden outfield.

Initially, S. Gregory and V. Ransford made a stand using patient cricket but Blythe and Hirst retook the initiative. Ransford was cleverly bowled by the former, although when Gregory came in Australia had a lead of 50 that should have been a winning one unless something extraordinary happened. The newspapers happily noted that, "It did."

Trumper, Armstrong, Carter, and Bardsley scored just 8 runs between them and although the tail wagged briefly they were all out for 151. Blythe and Hirst had identical figures of five wickets for 58 runs, which meant that the Kent bowler took eleven wickets (in total) for just 102 runs.

The bowling of these two men was the significant factor and they left England needing 105 runs to win. In fact, Blythe bowled just one more ball than Hirst in a second innings that saw some fine fielding - in particular a catch by Tyldesley right up to the pavilion railings.

Under the poor batting conditions the Australians might have expected to hold the English down but that was not the case. The batting was opened by Hobbs and Fry who hit the ball with the greatest of freedom perhaps aided to a degree by 'a drying of the pitch.'

This was the first time Jack Hobbs of Surrey had played for England on his home soil, although he was a member of A.O. Jones touring side which went to Australia the previous year. His nerves showed in the first innings as he was out for a duck, but backed up by Fry in the second it was clear he had completely mastered the opponents bowling.

Fry himself was likewise out for nought on the first occasion and started slowly, but Hobbs eventually scored 62 and Fry recorded 35 as England won the first test by a ten-wicket margin.

A scene of great enthusiasm marked the end of the match and a crowd of many thousands congregated outside the pavilion. After repeated calls the captain MacLaren and Hobbs came out onto the balcony and the cheering they received was quite deafening. Blythe was no doubt taken up with the euphoria of the occasion but soon found he was in some difficulty.

This began with a game against Middlesex at Lord's immediately after the important test match triumph. There had been a long-standing tradition for Middlesex to play Somerset on the Whit Monday, however that year the position was filled by another Metropolitan county in the form of the more attractive Kent eleven. Indeed, the game was also a benefit for J.E. West one of their most successful wicket keepers.

Due to this change of fixture, Blythe and his team-mates arrived at the Lord's ground to play in front of an expectant crowd of 15,000 on 31 May. Kent went in to bat first and a pattern soon developed with an uneven game of rather attractive cricket.

The visitors scored at a good pace before lunch making 157 in under two hours with the loss of only Dillon and Humphreys. However, the last eight wickets were gone in eighty minutes for the addition of just 70 runs.

John Hunt an amateur for Middlesex took four of the dismissals and was delighted with his fast bowling performance. Indeed, he supplied a cheery word to all of his opponents as they came to the crease and (again) as they departed for the pavilion soon afterwards!

Blythe, though, was less cheered by the atmospheric charged situation. He came in as the last man to rapturous applause following his test match success and joined wicket keeper Fred Huish at the crease. However, the degree of adulation seemed to unsettle him completely and Patsy Hendren, who was in his first full season, caught and bowled him for nought.

After making the long walk back to the pavilion he soon returned to the fray with the Kent fielders. Plum Warner and Frank Tarrant led off the batting but as Blythe went in to bowl there was another standing ovation, whilst the papers stated, "This and the heat seemed to upset him, for his temperament makes him dread that sort of thing."

Meanwhile, they also added, "He seemed on the point of collapse but did not leave the field." As a result Dillon rested him from the limelight of the bowling maelstrom, and brought him back when he had recovered and the crowd had settled into a more ambient slumber.

He was then fully fit to bowl again and rescued Kent from any further fireworks by M.W. Payne, removing him with his second ball to leave the score on 62 for two. Fielder was out with a strain, Carr was unavailable, and although Mason appeared for the first time that summer Blythe's input to the visitors bowling was undoubtedly critical.

Despite such difficulties he then revealed his genius once again on any kind of pitch - he eventually took six for 37 and had five maidens in his seventeen overs. The papers were convinced he would be required for the next test "wet or fine" although this was not in fact the case.

Warner fell to a fine catch by Fairservice, Tarrant guarded his wicket well, and Payne made hay whilst Blythe was inactive, however there was little resistance thereafter and they were all out for 158 runs.

This left Kent some 69 runs ahead at the end of the first day, and it was suggested that West would sleep soundly regarding his benefit-takings since the game was still clearly in the balance!

On the second day Kent came out fighting and scored 393 runs with Humphreys making 105 and Seymour 88 - they declared at eight wickets whilst Middlesex replied with 31 runs. There was no play on the final day and a game of so much drama concluded with a draw.

Regarding Blythe, the incident with the crowd exposed two sides to his character. In the first instance he enjoyed his success and any measured or generalised congratulations, but was less able to handle the more intrusive full-scale adoration of a huge crowd (in common with many others).

There was, however, a second less obvious conclusion. Some may have wilted under such pressure, but Blythe had a determination of character that saw him not only continue to play but to produce bowling of the highest calibre thereafter - contrary to claims about his nervous nature.

HEALTH MATTERS

The Edgbaston test was a great success for the M.C.C. and for Blythe but it was soon to turn on him. Indeed, there were conflicting reports and some said that he went off faint during the Middlesex game.

It was a tough series of matches for any player and the next Kent fixture was against Lancashire at Old Trafford on 3-5 June, meaning that in a week Blythe went to three major test match venues. The game itself was a draw but the captain Dillon apparently held Blythe back to the eighth over, due to concerns that he was in poor health and not on form.

However, a look at the bowling figures completely disputes this assertion. In the first innings he took seven wickets for 57 which by any standards was "good form," including Tyldesley caught and bowled on 25, whilst in the second innings he clean bowled MacLaren (England's captain) on just 3 runs. There was then no play on the final day.

Whatever the case the problems he'd experienced did not go un-noticed and the Kent Committee were worried, so they sent him to a specialist for a check-up. After careful consideration the eminent doctor told the club he should not play in the next test at Lord's on 14 June, and Lord Harris sent a telegram regarding this report to the selectors.

Despite this he continued to play county cricket with two further games taking place in early June. The first was against the champions Yorkshire at Fartown, Huddersfield (also a Rugby League venue).

Kent had only beaten Yorkshire four times since the county championship began the last time being at The Circle, Hull, in 1905, and this result was long overdue for a renewal. Radcliffe the home captain decided to put the visitors in to bat but it was a decision he would regret.

Seymour, A.P. Day, and Hardinge all made good scores as Kent reached 319, whilst Rhodes was left on nought at the end of the first day since his fellow opener Benjamin Wilson was run out on 1 run. There was an erratic performance on the second day as Yorkshire were all out for just 69, with Fielder taking six wickets and Blythe a further three.

In the follow on Wilfred Rhodes recorded 101 and George Hirst 61, but Fielder took another seven wickets and Blythe just two as they were all out for 364 runs. The score was clearly far more respectable however Kent eventually won the game by seven wickets.

This was followed by a draw against Essex at Catford then Tonbridge Week began on 14 June. Worcester arrived at the Angel Ground and made 240, whilst Blythe took five wickets for 77 but was over-played and bowled for some 37 overs - far more than any of his team-mates.

In fact, both Blythe and Fielder had a poor return in the two innings, and the former had to retire on the second evening and went home. At that stage Kent were in the final innings and had a chance being on 51 runs for one wicket. However, Blythe returned to play the next day (scoring nought) and there was a partial collapse to lose the game by 108 runs.

Meanwhile, MacLaren, who was in charge of his last test series, captained England at Lord's for the second test on 14-16 June. Despite the previous success there was a complete change in line-up and in addition to Blythe both Fry and Rhodes were omitted. G. Gunn, J.H. King, A.E. Relf, and S. Haigh entered the side in their place but they lost by nine wickets.

The test was a disaster and this put the M.C.C. selectors under a large degree of scrutiny, both from the press and the public. An alteration to the line-up was the obvious reason for the failings and blame seemed easy to apportion, but as is often the case with human nature there was an attempt to deflect such discomfort by looking elsewhere.

They then took action which in the modern climate would be completely illegal and released the medical report regarding Blythe to the press. This was done to show that they had to leave the bowler out and thus exonerate themselves, but this involved some highly sensitive personal information being placed within the public domain:

C. Blythe whom I have seen this morning suffers severely in a peculiar way from the strain on his nervous system caused by playing in a test match, and the effect lasts for a week afterwards. It is desirable that he should have a temporary rest from this work and should not play in the coming match at Lord's. If this can be arranged there is good hope that with treatment his difficulty will pass away. It does not exist in the case of county matches.

Undoubtedly the absence of Fry and Rhodes was also quite critical and it appears they simply required a scapegoat. Indeed, the bowler must have been less than pleased at this very public exposure the very thing they said he did not like, and it was to his credit that he rode the storm and played much excellent cricket in the future.

But that was not all. His colleague C.B. Fry was introduced into the debate and brought up the game against South Africa at Headingley in 1907. When asked about the matter originally he said that Blythe was exhausted by the strain, but now changed his story and said that he had a fit and that other players were aware of this problem.

However, there is good reason to dispute such observations by Fry. In the first instance the famous sportsman altered his story, and in the second he had an ongoing dispute with Blythe over other matters (see later). Further to this Fry soon had his own problems and became paranoid, developed a fear of Indians including his good friend Ranjitsinhji, and was even seen running down Brighton beach naked!

Clearly such a testimony had some degree of doubt and even the doctor's report made no mention of either epilepsy or fits. The papers collected by Blythe about his career were also strangely quiet on this matter, whilst the evidence placed in its favour was conveniently vague.

At a latter date Lord Harris alluded to a delicate temperament but did not mention fits, and more recently Martin Williamson stated that the problem was more likely to be the stress of the occasion. Whatever the case Blythe would wish to be remembered for his cricket not his health, and in the modern era this would be politically correct.

Kent then took on Lancashire in the second game at the Angel Ground but Blythe showed a poor return despite reaching 1,500 wickets, including the wicket of Mr. K.G. MacLeod who made 41 runs in three overs. Indeed, the home side were undone by the bowling of Walter Brearley who took twelve wickets and they lost by 312 runs.

Eventually the two home defeats were the only ones of the campaign and the slump was the prelude to a remarkable season, one that brought further rewards to Blythe and the Kent club.

CHAPTER 13

Benefit Year

The 1909 season continued with back-to-back games against Gilbert Jessop and his graceful Gloucester side. The first contest was at Catford on 21-22 June and Fielder took six wickets for 34 while Blythe took four for 20 as the visitors were dismissed on 61 runs. Kent, however, replied to this with a staggering total of 593 (which was beaten again the next year).

Punter Humphreys was most impressive making 208 with thirty-two 4's, James Seymour scored 86 runs, and Ken Hutchings reached exactly 100 in just 50 minutes. The innings took four and a half hours and Gloucester were left needing 532 just to draw level! However, Fielder took another six wickets and Kent won by an innings and 314 runs.

There must have been some trepidation as Kent arrived at Ashley Down in Bristol for the return match on 28 June but on this occasion Dennett, Jessop, and Parker restricted the Kent batsmen.

Blythe then produced a very good performance and took six wickets for just 6 runs (including Jessop) in the first innings, the eventual return on his bowling being 37 runs. He finished the job with Fairservice and Woolley in the second as Kent won by a rather narrow margin.

The newspapers reported on this match in some detail stating that Blythe was the first bowler past a hundred wickets - going from 97 to 103 during the game leaving him 30 ahead of W. Brearley. Such success made it all the more regrettable that he could not assist England in the third test.

Jessop had some bowling practice in case he was required at Leeds but he did not come off as a batsman. Due to some sporadic sunshine it was hard to score and 24 wickets fell in a day for 267 runs. Kent started well and looked like getting more than the 141 they made while Dillon, Humphreys, and Woolley were the only ones who deserved any credit.

When Gloucester came in Langdon and Board made 39 before the effects of the roller wore off, but no one could make any headway against Blythe and Woolley. Jessop went in early and made 49 but thereafter there was a procession, and Blythe who bowled at the top of his form conceded 6 runs from his first to sixth wicket. The home side were out for 73 and after the second innings Kent won the game by 52 runs.

The gallant trio of bowlers were then joined by Fielder as Kent defeated Northampton at Gravesend, and at the same time England engaged with Australia for the third test played at Headingley on 1 July.

Due to his apparent indisposition - Blythe was passed up in favour of Rhodes, and the side were strengthened with C.B. Fry and Walter Brearley however the match was still lost by 136 runs.

Kent then went to the Amblecote Ground at Stourbridge to play against Worcester on 5-7 July, and faced a side captained by Henry Foster which also included Ted Arnold another England colleague. The home team did well scoring 360 in their first innings and F.A. Pearson made 161, whereas the bowler took only one wicket for 67 runs.

This was not a promising start and did not indicate a large victory for Kent but the visitors then produced an unlikely total of 555. Such success was down to a most brilliant tenth wicket stand as Woolley made 185 with twenty-four 4's and the impregnable Arthur Fielder scored 112. In fact, the two added 235 runs in just 150 minutes!

Blythe did not feature in the batting and was out for nought, but then stepped up and took seven wickets for 44 runs the others going to Fielder. Worcester were all out for 162 and Kent secured an amazing victory by an innings and 33 runs, their combination of batting and bowling excellence overturning the largest of totals.

GENTLEMEN v PLAYERS

Fielder had already received a chance to prove himself in the representative game of 1906, but Blythe had to wait a long time for such an honour to be bestowed. His chance came that very season at the Oval on 8-10 July as he joined his team-mates Humphreys, Woolley, and Fielder in a Players' side captained by A.F.A. Lilley.

The opposing Gentlemen provided little enigma in terms of their game since the captain was C.B. Fry and the other members included Warner as well as Dillon, Hutchings, and Carr from Kent.

In fact, this was one of the mysteries at the time - namely that so many Kent players could appear in this and other prestigious fixtures yet fewer of them enjoyed putting on the England jersey.

During the first innings the Players scored 203 with Woolley on 55 but Blythe was stumped on 7 after one of Carr's googlies. The Gentlemen then made just 110 runs, and Blythe took five wickets for 48 including his own captain Dillon and the tail-enders.

The second innings saw Tom Hayward go out lightly but Ernie Hayes his Surrey colleague produced the best performance, and the Players reached 189 although Blythe went for nought. However, the Kent bowler then really enjoyed himself as he produced a match-winning performance.

Initially he took the openers - Dillon caught by Woolley on 17 and P.R. Johnson of Somerset bowled for 0. In fact, his deliveries were irresistibly attracted to the wicket and he clean bowled Warner on 20 and Fry on 4, took Sydney Smith (of the West Indies) on 37, Johnny Douglas of Essex caught by Woolley on 11, and D.W. Carr for only 7.

Blythe's figures at the Oval were thus seven wickets for 55 runs and the Gentlemen were out for a total of 218. As a result of his performance the Players won the game by 64 runs, and the bowler (whatever the concerns of the selectors) was returned to the England squad having taken twelve of the best wickets for 103 during the game.

Kent, meanwhile, played four home games up to the end of July and won three of these fixtures with a combination of high scoring batting and profitable bowling. In the games at the Nevill Ground, Blythe took eight wickets for 49 against Derby and scored 38 runs in a draw against Sussex, but made less of an impact in the other two contests.

The fourth test then took place at Old Trafford on 26-28 July and Blythe and Barnes combined to bowl out the Australians for 147 - their respective figures 5-63 and 5-56. However, England could only manage 119 whereas the Kent bowler was bowled on 1 run in fourteen minutes.

MacLaren's side included Warner, Spooner, Tyldesley, J. Sharp, Rhodes, Hutchings, Lilley, and George Hirst but just two of them reached 25 runs. Australia then made 279 but Blythe took only two wickets for 77 and it was Rhodes who did most damage at 5-83. The visitors soon declared and England reached 108 for three but the match was drawn.

Canterbury Week came around again in early August and Kent entered fully into the spirit of things. In the first game they beat Middlesex by an innings and 37 runs, and Blythe had figures of six for 26 in the first innings including Warner caught on 7 runs. He was well supported by Douglas Carr who took eight in total as the Londoners followed on.

The second game of the Week was against Hampshire at the St. Lawrence Ground and the visitors were captained by C.B. Fry. There was glorious weather on the Thursday in front of a record crowd, partly due to the good prospects of the side and through the reputation of the players on display. Fry scored 63 and Charlie Llewellyn made 79 as Hampshire reached 236, but Blythe was quieter taking only one wicket for 77 runs.

Kent were then very consistent in their batting as the first seven reached double figures with Hutchings, Woolley, Mason, and S.H. Day all pursuing the century to make a total of 406. In the second innings Fry made 94 and reached 26,000 career runs, but the rest of the side were less forthright and the visitors were all out for 199.

Blythe took three wickets for 59 runs and Carr did even better with five for 42. Indeed, just 30 runs were needed for a victory and Blythe and Huish were sent in to finish the job off. They promptly made 14 and 16 without loss despite one over bowled down by the effervescent Fry.

The game was won by ten wickets and Blythe, who was clearly held in high esteem by the cricketing public, received nearly £600 for his benefit during the week with some £150 collected at the ground. This money was then added to his fund which was being accumulated (see later).

There was a draw regarding the final test at the Oval on 9-11 August which included Woolley's debut for England. However, the side appeared to be weakened to some extent and despite the presence of Fry, Rhodes, Hayes, Hutchings, and Lilley the bowlers included Barnes and Carr who clearly had limited experience at that level.

The whole matter must have been a disappointment to Blythe since his form was exceptional and his services would have been eagerly rendered. As it was England had lost the series and the Ashes due to the two defeats when he did not play, whereas the match at Old Trafford was the last time that he appeared for his country (on home soil).

A SECOND TITLE

Meanwhile, the next game against Sussex at Hove coincided with the last test and initially Blythe was on standby at the Oval. As it turned out Kent lost Woolley, Hutchings, and Carr to the national cause but Blythe was able to make it down to Brighton just in time for the game. Possibly his thoughts were elsewhere and he made little contribution with just three wickets and no runs while it all ended in a draw.

A similar outcome occurred in the following match at Taunton on 12-14 August. Jack Mason captained the side and scored 111 with fourteen 4's as Kent reached 468 and Blythe finished on 18 not out, but Somerset had only just begun their follow on at the end of the second day.

However, there were some dropped catches and the home side amassed the huge total of 402 leading to a draw. One feature of the second innings was the use of ten bowlers by Kent (only the wicket keeper Huish did not bowl) and six of them took no wickets at all. Indeed, no one could remove A.E. Lewis who made 201 runs with twenty-nine 4's.

With such extemporaneous bowling over some serious batting occurred at the Oval on 16-18 August. Surrey began poorly and but for M.C. Bird's 96 would have had a very low total - the final figure 191 runs. Blythe only took three wickets for 41 whilst Carr took a similar number for 70.

Kent also introduced David Jennings the Mote Park professional to the side, but it was the captain Jack Mason who led the way as he took his team forward to an impressive lead. However, this looked unlikely as the ninth wicket fell with Mason on just 45 runs and the total score on 214.

Blythe then joined his captain at the crease in nonchalant manner and proceeded to adopt an old-fashioned attitude of defiance under the motto "stay in and the runs will come." This enabled Mason to hit out at the ball and eventually he scored twenty-four 4's and 152 not out, whereas Blythe resolutely held on for 29 until he was bowled by W.C. Smith.

This was Mason's third consecutive century and the tenth wicket stand of 141 meant that Kent reached 355. In the second innings Surrey made 182 as Blythe had an analysis of 5-62 and Woolley 4-28 (with 200 in his career). Kent easily won by nine wickets and Blythe registered 1,600 wickets, but it was his prowess with the bat that marked out the game.

A brief respite to the championship took place as Kent challenged the Australians at the St. Lawrence Ground on 19-21 August. The home side did well to make 319 with Woolley and S.H. Day standing out amongst the batsmen, whereas the visitors replied with 522 after very profitable scoring by V.S. Ransford (189) and W.W. Armstrong (107).

There was some heavy rain on the Friday night and Saturday morning and the latter part of the Australian innings was not of a serious nature, while Blythe took no wickets and the game ended in a draw. Dover Week had a similar watery problem and a match with Yorkshire was limited to just two and half hours thus the contest with Hawke, Rhodes, Denton, Hirst, and Haigh was definitely a draw.

Leicester then arrived at the Crabble to see a saturated wicket and there was no play on the Thursday. The prospects did not look good for some honest cricket, however after the visitors took to the crease on the Friday they were dispatched for just 69 runs. It was Blythe and Carr who brought this about taking six wickets for 30 and three for 8 respectively.

Indeed, Kent responded with 193 to leave themselves in a good position whilst the visitors put on 13 runs in the evening, but were all out the next day for 114. Blythe took a further five wickets for 33 and reached 200 for the campaign whereas Kent won by an innings and 10 runs.

The last match of the season took place at Dean Park in Bournemouth on 30 September and the papers noted, "The Kent men were untrammelled with the thoughts of championship, and Hampshire were trying their best to beat the champions." Fielder and Llewellyn were absent due to a match between the M.C.C. and Australia, and Hampshire who included C.B. Fry scored a good total of 265.

The latter had been offered the captaincy of the M.C.C. but declined in favour of Hampshire, an action which made him very popular with the home supporters. Blythe's figures were just two wickets for 59 although this included Fry caught by Humphreys on just 12 runs.

Kent then replied with 323 and Hutchings made a rapid 116 in just eighty minutes scoring some twenty-one 4's; however Hampshire were then all out for 164 due to the bowling of Blythe, Carr, and Woolley. Indeed, Fry was bowled middle stump by Carr in his first over and Blythe likewise dismissed Mead in his first, whereas the Kent fielding remained excellent.

The visitors made the 110 runs they needed in just an hour and won the game by nine wickets, and were undoubted champions of England. There was less excitement than on the previous occasion due to a certain degree of familiarity with the exalted position, and due to the fact that from the start of the season they had been one of the firm favourites.

The local paper noted how they missed the services of Burnup, Blaker, A. Hearne, and Hubble but that Woolley was the most improved player and probably the best all-rounder in England. The side was stronger than the one which had won in 1906 with some fifteen rather than eleven first class players, whilst their fielding was greatly improved.

Lancashire were the hardest side for them to beat mainly due to their fast bowlers, and during the season there were ten "innings victories" some of them by large scores. Kent had won sixteen of their twenty-six games (with two defeats) and Blythe played in all but one. Indeed, his contribution was vital as he notched up his record season with 185 wickets for Kent and 215 in total - his best being 9-42 against Leicester.

Blythe was then selected to play in J. Bamford's XI against Australia at Uttoxeter on 6-8 September. Other players in the side included G. Gunn, MacLaren, A.O. Jones, Lilley, C.P. Buckenham, and Sydney Barnes.

This was to be his last encounter with the likes of Trumper, Noble, and Armstrong and he had a quiet game scoring 17 not out and taking 0-23. In fact, the improvement in the batting of Blythe, Fairservice, and Fielder had been an important element in Kent's success, whilst his swansong with the Australians ended in a draw as only one innings was played.

The season concluded with the showpiece game between Kent and The Rest at the Oval on 13-16 September - the opponents featuring Rhodes, Hobbs, Denton, Hayes, Mead, Warner, Relf, and Buckenham scored 327 with Blythe taking two wickets for 57 runs.

Kent only made 151 in reply and their "improved bowlers" suffered a tail-end collapse - and were forced to follow on to reach 132, but the game was drawn with no play on the third day.

Despite the fact the victory was less notable than on the first occasion, it was still celebrated with a blast on the old burghmote horn and there was a banquet at Canterbury on 23 October. The mayor read out a telegram from the Archbishop and the players received a silver ink stand, whereas several sentiments were expressed that such success might continue and under the captaincy of Ted Dillon there was every chance it would.

BOWLING ANALYSIS

Being Blythe's benefit year there were various assessments of his progress in the press, and one paper displayed a nautical cartoon showing Mr. Blythe (as he hauls in). The caption below it read, "They may not be big uns but my word ain't they biting freely!"

A long article then carried the heading "***Blythe the Bowler*** - *the pride of Kent and the hope of England.*" They wished the game at Canterbury would continue until the Saturday, since this was Blythe's benefit and never did a professional in the country deserve a more "thumping" one.

He looked scarcely older than when he made his debut and at that time *Wisden* noted Kent needed a professional bowler, one as good as James Wootton of 13-14 years earlier - "Blythe may, of course, develop into the man required, but he has not yet done enough to justify us in predicting a great future for him." Ten years later they were forced to eat their words and regarded him as the best slow bowler in the country.

His progress at the club was rapid and in his second year he headed the Kent averages, came third in 1901, and shared with J.R. Mason in 1902. He was first in every year following except 1904 when he trailed Humphreys (on 30 dismissals) and only once failed to take 100 wickets. There was little parallel and in his benefit year he beat all his previous records.

Regarding tests he accompanied MacLaren to Australia in 1901-02 and took 18 wickets at an average of 26.11, and also went to America with Kent and took 23 wickets at 10.65. His first home test was against Australia at Leeds and he took four wickets for 77 runs, then he went to South Africa in 1905-06 taking 113 wickets in all at an average of 12.88.

Blythe was absent from Warner's tour which brought back the Ashes but played South Africa at Lord's in 1907, and was in rare form at Leeds taking 8-59 and 7-40 which enabled England to secure a memorable victory.

He went to Australia once again with A.O. Jones in 1907-08 and although not successful in the tests was top with 48 wickets and an average of 20.12. His bowling at Birmingham in 1909 remained fresh in everyone's minds and he practically won the match with eleven for 102 runs.

Only on rare occasions was his record poor and V.F.S. Crawford of Surrey (then Leicester) hit five 4's and a single off one of his overs at the Oval in 1901, however against Sussex at Tunbridge Wells in 1904 he sent down twelve overs for just a single run scored.

Generally he played to best advantage on a wicket damaged by rain - his break coming back very quickly, and most first class batsmen agreed he was more difficult to play than any other bowler in England.

Blythe did not take his batting too seriously but when in earnest produced a good display. His highest was 82 not out at Nottingham in 1904 (106 for the ninth wicket), whilst as last man at Taunton he made 70 in an hour out of 98. The next year he made 75 against Lancashire at Canterbury as 120 was added again for the ninth - each time with Fairservice.

In 1906 against Sussex at Canterbury he and Mr. C. Marsham put on 111 for the ninth wicket in 35 minutes, five consecutive overs yielding 50 runs. There were also claims by the paper (and Jessop in his epistle) that during his first test in Sydney he astonished the natives by sending five thumping fours past extra cover! - Although the official records dispute this.

He was one of the most successful, popular, and even-tempered bowlers at the club with his familiar hop, skip, and jump only being matched by Alec Hearne and Fred Martin. Indeed, up to the Canterbury game he had taken 172 wickets placing him well ahead of all the other bowlers.

His peculiar halting run consisted of a turn using his left foot as a pivot, a push with his right foot, a light step with the left, and a firm imprint with the right. The latter was pushed rather than placed so the stud marks were plainly visible. After a single hop his actual run began and he then adopted an ordinary approach always pressing more firmly with the right.

Placing the right foot between the creases he would then complete his run by bringing down the left, or sometimes the left was placed forward and the run ended with the right. Indeed, Blythe did not come within sight of the batsman until very late in his run.

Sporting Life judged his technique thus, "He is liable to get good batsmen out on good pitches because he mixes his wits with his length and his finger spin. Watch carefully from behind his arm, and, understanding, you will be given something like an intellectual treat.

The easy action that never varies with the ever varying pace - that should delight you. But still more ought you to be delighted by the judgement with which pace and length alter by the evidence of subtle cunning, observation, patient planning. His bowling looks very simple to the eye. To the spectator the batsman must appear to be part hitting innocent half-volleys and will say with conviction, 'Run out to him, and lift him all over the field!'

It sounds very simple. But between the theory and the successful practice there is one great barrier - the deception of the bowler's flight. For to run out and smite the ball on the full pitch, the batsman must be able to judge before the ball has travelled any appreciable distance in the air the exact spot at which it is going to land.

And that is just where the difficulty comes in with Blythe's delivery since it may drop much shorter than there appears any possibility of its doing. The apparent half-volley in the air is often a good length ball at the pitch.

In addition there is a thoughtful brain governing the easy swinging arm which is happy to give away a boundary in the hope of securing a wicket. Two real undistinguished half-volleys, two brilliant boundary hits, and the batsman is ripe for more - a third ball looking just the same, but really so cunningly different - a little slower, a little shorter, a little wider, and the ball spins away into the hands of cover!"

These were fine accolades and Blythe received eight collections during his benefit year, each being made at the two games of the four County Cricket Weeks. However, his fund remained open until the end of June following hence it eventually generated £1,519 13s 8d. [1]

The committee did not initially give any money directly to the bowler but placed it in the Army & Navy Investment Trust, Bankers Investment Trust, and Grand Trunk Railway of Canada - the latter was partly built by Betts & Son and M.P. Betts was a cricketer for Kent and scorer of the first Cup Final goal. Meanwhile, Blythe received an income of £60 per annum from these three speculative investments.

---

[1] There were several other plusses for Blythe including the hotels that he stayed in viz. Green's Railway, Hastings; "London," Bournemouth; Royal, Cheltenham; Plough, Northants; Clarendon, Derby; the Trafford Hotel; Angel, Chesterfield; King's Arms, Sheffield; and Clarence Gardens, Scarborough.

Some were of considerable historic significance viz. Old Ship, Brighton staged a ball for the Prince Regent in 1819; the Mitre, Gravesend dated from about 1795; the Hotel Restaurant Buol, Oxford was 18th century and opened from 1893-1915; the Grand, Leicester was built in 1898; and Grand Central, Leeds once the Bull and Mouth which used the former name from 1903-21.

CHAPTER 14

South Africa 1909-10

Blythe's county form up until the Great War dictated that he should play in the national side, but he was chosen on only one further occasion and was passed up three other times. Some have suggested this was due to his lack of "fitness" for test cricket, although the fact that he played in such games after his health was brought into question disputes this.

Clearly test players are selected on many criteria and there was competition from other bowlers such as Barnes, Rhodes, Woolley, and Frank Foster. To focus in on his health appears to ignore other factors such as age, place in the team, style of bowling, and vagaries of the selectors - vagaries that have dictated the progress of players throughout the game's history.

Nevertheless, Blythe had a good innings in test cricket and was selected for the test series in South Africa in 1909-10, which was his fourth and last tour abroad. The side sailed on the Union Castle mail steamship the R.M.S. "Saxon" (6,336 tons) under the master J. Tyson with some 500 passengers including the Bishop of Peterborough and Lt. Gen. Sir Samuel G. Calthorpe. The vessel was bound for the Cape and then up the coast to Natal.

Blythe arrived at the Waterloo terminus with his cricketing paraphernalia and joined the train for the journey to the docks at Southampton, the same docks where the "Titanic" would depart just over a year later. Indeed, the provincial station was just a short distance from the customs house.

It was the 6 November and the warmth of Table Mountain beckoned the cricketers as they buttoned up their overcoats against the chilly wind. But the wind was bringing about a substantial change and all of the gentlemen and players travelled "first class cabin" on this occasion.

Leveson-Gower and Frederick Fane were to captain the side whereas the batting line-up included Hobbs, Rhodes, Denton, and Woolley. There were a number of bowlers including Claude Buckenham of Essex and Simpson-Hayward of Worcester whereas Bert Strudwick of Surrey held the wicket. Others in the side were G.J. Thompson, M.C. Bird, and N.C. Tufnell who had also kept wicket for Cambridge.

Amongst the players only Buckenham and Woolley were new to the sea although Bird had never been further than the Canaries. During an earlier trip to Australia, Hobbs was ill all the way out and during the return felt better only after leaving the Great Australian Bight, so it was no surprise that it was he and Woolley who first 'went under.'

Denton, meanwhile, being aware that he was not a good sailor was well prepared but couldn't persuade the others to partake of his pills, whereas after a few days (and not very far out) half the team were down sick.

By the time the ship reached Madeira the weather was so rough that the passengers were advised to stay on board. However, Woolley, Strudwick, Blythe, and Buckenham were undeterred and risked a dangerous trip to the shore to spend a few hours looking around, although all sports and deck games were out of the question at first.

Despite such problems most of the voyage was smooth and shortly after leaving Madeira there was a clear run of fourteen days before Cape Town. In fact, at the beginning of the fortnight there was some very hot weather, and with the sea subsided there was an opportunity for some sport and a fine programme of entertainments.

PRACTICE PITCH

With regard to this the players came prepared and were not hampered in their preparations due to a lack of equipment. The previous trip to South Africa had seen them reduced to playing games of deck hockey and they were determined that no repeat should take place.

In the past, attempts for some 'serious practice' had involved a rope ball, but the "Saxon" provided a good opportunity as the promenade deck was 270 feet long and 13-17 feet wide. The only drawback was the height since the adjacent boat deck was only 7 feet above the floor.

However, the long stretch was promptly transformed into a cricket pitch using regulation nets brought from Lord's to net in the space, while some matting was placed down and drawn very taut by the sailors. Stumps were then fixed into a heavy wooden base and the game was carried out with all the advantage of a fully-equipped practice pitch.

The wicket itself was reasonably true and had a foundation of teak rather than asphalt or concrete as found at the Oval or Lord's. All of the players had practiced on matting before (on such a surface), but this was the first time play had taken place under conditions equivalent to a matting wicket on the land. In fact, the main drawback was a slope from the bowlers end and from leg side to off - plus the restrictions of height.

All kinds of touches improved the training such as the use of Wisden's regulation balls, and there was no danger of the ball going over the side or of hitting the passengers. Simpson-Hayward also used wash-leather gloves under his batting gloves to stop slipping, a device he found helpful in hot countries where he had played some nine times before.

The bowlers only had a short run up and Blythe found the ceiling on a number of occasions, whereas Simpson-Hayward had to discard any use of his "flighty one." Despite any such obstacles some good practice was had by all and more than just ordinary physical exercise. In addition to this, a slip-catching device patented by Ayres Ltd. was used on a daily basis thus some fine work was done.

Scores of passengers gathered around the nets to witness the spectacle and rounds of applause met every profitable ball or catch. Captain Wynyard who accompanied the squad was M.C. or overseer, but Leveson-Gower being under greater pressure adopted a more critical eye.

All of the players benefited in this way except for George Thompson who fell ill with tonsillitis shortly after leaving Madeira. In fact, a number of the team suffered likewise, however Dr. Stevens pulled the "windmill bowler" through with a dose of "Nuvite" and he was soon himself again.

With the sporting practice well in hand there was time for some more general entertainments. These included a top performance by the "Musical Madcaps," a clever troupe of entertainers who were shortly to open down in Cape Town and had plans for an extended tour.

Blythe, as always, was prepared to play his part and was "no duffer with the fiddle" an instrument that he played with his right hand. Indeed, in the winter months he was a member of the Tonbridge Orchestral Union and was also seen in the orchestra at the Oxford Music Hall. [1]

The headline in the paper regarding the trip stated - *"Blythe in the Band."* And with this in mind noted that Ernest Killick (of Sussex) was a good performer on the clarinet and piano, George Gunn (of Nottingham) was a capital pianist, and Claude Buckenham (of Essex) played in private.

Initially there was a concert on Tuesday, 16 November as they reached the tropical regions, which was held on the third class deck starting at 8.30 p.m. The band began the concert with a grand march and later did a selection of tunes entitled "The Arcadians," whilst there were several songs including "There's a Land" and "Killarney," and Mr. Colin Blythe entertained the audience with a moving violin solo of "Ave Maria."

Sentiment from home filled the air as Miss Rae Fraser followed this with a recitation of "Bow Bells" and Mr. W.G. Sutton sang "toorali-oorali-ay." There were then further songs and the band did a characteristic piece "In a Pagoda" and lastly a Japanese romance entitled "Poppies."

---

[1] Charles Morton "the father of music hall" built the Oxford Music Hall at 12-14 Oxford Street, near to Tottenham Court Road, in 1861 and it became a prosperous variety venue. It was altered to a theatre in 1917 and modernised four years later but was demolished for a Lyon's Corner House in 1926.

Suitably mellowed the passengers took part in three days of sports and games the committee including the England captain Mr. H.D.G. Leveson-Gower, whereas Captain E.G. Wynyard (who was only to play in regional matches) was referee for these events. The sports included the usual potato race, egg and spoon, whistling race, and finished with a tug of war, the latter being first against second saloon.

Strudwick was winner of the potato race and the "are you there" contest whilst Simpson-Hayward and Bird also had some successes. However, the professionals generally avoided sport since they did not want to risk any injury, although Rhodes and Hobbs were winners of deck competitions such as quoits, bridge, whist, and other games - several times.

With barely time to catch their breath after such excitement there was a final concert in the first class saloon on Saturday, 20 November at 8.30 p.m. Lady Gough-Calthorpe presented the sports-day prizes with some grace these being purchased on board, and the concert included a number of songs however the highlight was a farce "Their New Paying Guest" by S.C. Caldwell. Mrs. Leveson-Gower played the part of Mrs. Loveday and Miss Fraser her daughter Grace.

Regarding the purpose of the trip the players kept very fit and Captain Wynyard indulged in skipping whereas the others used brisk walking around the decks. Indeed, the fourteen seemed determined in their purpose being one of the most "serious" outfits ever to visit South Africa.

The "Saxon" soon arrived in Cape Town below Table Mountain and the mayor F.W. Smith hosted a luncheon at City Hall on 23 November. After renewing his acquaintance with familiar sights and old friends, Blythe played in some provincial games but was left out of the first three tests.

LOCAL MATCHES

The first contest was against the Western Province Colts at Newlands one of Blythe's more successful grounds on 1-2 December. This provided some practice for the visitors and experience for the opponents whilst Frederick Hopley of the Colts who played for Cambridge made 96. Blythe took three early wickets but did not bat and the game was eventually drawn.

A more serious match was played against the Western Province from 4-6 December, the side including J.M. Commaille and Murray Bisset who were to appear in the national side and also the colt Fred Hopley. The M.C.C. had a good start and Jack Hobbs made 114 at a run a minute as the team reached a total of 351 runs. The home side were then all out for 67 and 151 thus the visitors won by an innings and 33 runs.

A number of bowlers were used in this rather rapid dismissal and Blythe took five wickets in total, however soon afterwards they left Newlands and headed for some much stiffer tests in the interior.

The first match was against Griqualand (West) at the Eclectics Ground in Kimberley on 10-13 December - Blythe didn't play and despite some good scoring by the fifteen the M.C.C. won by 200 runs. The next opponents were an Orange Free State 15 at the Ramblers Ground, Bloemfontein on 15-17 December - the team staying at the Hotel Imperial.

M.C. Bird of Surrey scored 115 runs with nine 4's and six 6's, and Blythe was 15 not out in the first innings for a total of 231. The home side then put on 112 but Blythe showed his form taking seven for 38, whereas the tourists made a further 216 and won again by 200 runs.

There was then a tougher test against The Reef at the East Rand Mines Ground, Boksburg just east of Johannesburg on 21-24 December. On this occasion Hobbs, Rhodes, Fane, Blythe, and Woolley were matched up against players of the calibre of Tancred, Vogler, and Snooke.

Hobbs started well with 39 and Rhodes made 24 but Gordon White and Bert Vogler with his varied repertoire soon bowled them out. Only Blythe made a stand of 35 before he also fell to the South African googly specialist and the final total was 157. Snooke made 72 in reply out of 160 runs and Blythe took three for 37, whilst the M.C.C. reached an identical score for three wickets but the game was drawn - two days being lost to rain.

A variety of questions had been asked about the previous tours abroad regarding team selection, especially in South Africa four years earlier when there were "calls for reinforcements." Up to this point there appeared no reason for any such alarm or apprehensions - but the next game sent out a clear signal that the cavalry might yet be needed!

Faulkner, White, Snooke, Sinclair, Vogler, and Schwarz were just some of the stars in the Transvaal team who played at the Old Wanderers from 27-30 December. Clearly they had shown some reserve regarding the festive period and scored 260 in their first innings, whilst only George Thompson of Northampton had any success at bowling (with 5-85).

The M.C.C. replied with 196 but Transvaal then scored 421 with G.A. Faulkner 148 not out. Hobbs and Rhodes started well and David Denton made 63 in reply but they were all out for 177 and the game was lost by 308 runs, while Blythe took just one wicket during the contest.

However, despite the defeat they enjoyed the social side and were invited to a dinner at the Carlton Hotel and a performance at the Empire Theatre on New Year's Day. Mayor Harry Graumann was host and Leveson-Gower responded whereas the menu was opulent and most appetizing.

SOME TESTS (1-3)

Of the Transvaal players L.A. Stricker and J.W. Zulch both did well and joined A.W. Nourse, J.M. Commaille and other team members in the first test at Johannesburg on 1-5 January. The game was played on a gradually improving wicket thus South Africa made 208 and England 310, the best effort coming from Jack Hobbs on 89.

The South Africans added 345 to set a reasonable target and Buckenham and Simpson-Hayward took the majority of wickets, although some seven bowlers were used. As a five day match the scoring of runs was promoted but some of the England batsmen struggled thus Rhodes went out for 2 and Fane for 0. G.J. Thompson stayed in at 63, Leveson-Gower made 31, and Simpson-Hayward added 14 at the end - but it was just too late.

England were all out for 224 and lost the game by a small margin of 19 runs, the main damage being done by Vogler who had taken seven wickets for 94. Clearly the South Africans (based mainly in the Transvaal) were still a force to be reckoned with on the international stage.

Blythe then returned to the side and played in two games against Natal in the middle of January 1910. The first of these was a three day match which took place at Lord's, Durban and by the second day only the first innings was completed. A.W. Nourse did well for the opponents and Blythe took four wickets in each innings but the contest was drawn.

There was a second game against the side at the Oval, Pietermaritzburg from 14-18 January. Natal had scored 250 in their first innings at Durban but perhaps the effort was too much and they soon regretted their decision to bat. Blythe set about them with some guile taking seven for 20 and they were all out for a very poor total of 50 runs.

The M.C.C. then scored 229 with Fane making 70 and Leveson-Gower a half-century at 56, whereas Natal managed 203 as Blythe suffered a loss of form and took no wickets in his twenty-eight overs. Woolley, Wynyard, and Bird then finished off the game and it was won by nine wickets.

Meanwhile, they enjoyed some sightseeing and visited the Howick Falls twenty miles north of Pietermaritzburg. "The Tall One" was near a town of that name situated amongst some stunning scenery - its large resplendent pool of glistening rocks bedecked with mossy water droplets.

During the sojourn in Durban the team stayed at the Royal Hotel near the harbour which was built of wattle, daub, and thatch in 1845, but by the time of their visit it was considerably expanded. Indeed, they returned to the grand residence for a luncheon with the mayor on 20 January.

The second test then took place at Lord's, Durban on 21-26 January and was the first international there (one of four up to the 1920s). Both sides scored exactly 199 runs, but England could not find their length on the matting wicket and again used seven bowlers - Blythe being absent.

In their second innings South Africa stepped up a gear and G.C. White made 118 as they reached a total of 347. The game was still in the balance on the Tuesday evening (25 January) with Hobbs and Rhodes on 15 for nought. However, the players then enjoyed a banquet at the Marine Hotel with a programme of songs, toasts, and a run-diminishing menu.

Indeed, this included hors d'oeuvres, consomme, sole Florentine, poulet, cotelettes en aspic, roast turkey, salad, gateau-praline, iced pudding, and various aperitifs - a mouth watering feast that would probably find no place on a modern sports dietician's rigorous schedule!

Jack Hobbs then led the charge and made 70 but apart from Thompson and Bird there was little resistance, and despite Leveson-Gower's effort at the end they were all out for 252. As a result the test was lost by 95 runs and the series was clearly slipping away from them.

The next test was not scheduled until March, but with two defeats some serious practice was needed and five provincial games were played during February. Blythe featured in all of these contests and thus had another chance to secure his place in the test side.

In the first instance the M.C.C. travelled south to East London and stayed at the Beach Hotel which was the first to be built on the Esplanade in 1894 (it was demolished in the 1960s and replaced by the Kennaway). The visit began with a banquet at the historic Deal's Hotel in the city on 29 January (see previous trip) with a fine menu and a series of toasts.

A first class game was then played against the Border club at Jan Smuts Ground and Blythe reached 1,650 wickets during the contest. Meanwhile, the scores remained very even - all of them about 150 in each innings and the M.C.C. won the match by four wickets.

The second Cape Province game was inland against a N.E. District 15 at Sandringham, Queenstown on 4-5 February - a type of match that Blythe enjoyed since he took seven for 41 from a total of 81. The M.C.C. replied with 239 and in the second innings the bowler took four for 12 as they succumbed at 95 - the game won by an innings and 63 runs.

The squad then continued to St. George's Park, Port Elizabeth and played the Eastern Province in a 'three day' match on 11-12 February. Blythe took five for 21 as they were all out for 45 whereas the M.C.C. made 263 and won the game by an innings and 139 runs - in the second innings he took two for 11 and they were dismissed again for only 79.

Thereafter, they returned north to play the Transvaal at Johannesburg and enjoyed a banquet at the "New Club" on 19 February. Blythe took six wickets including White and Sinclair, and the M.C.C. won a close but high-scoring contest by some 50 runs (each innings being over 240).

A second game against the Transvaal at Berea Park, Pretoria on 22-24 February was ruined by the weather, the only play taking place on the first day with the home side making 371 runs for three wickets.

Blythe still failed to do enough to merit his inclusion in the test side and did not take part in the test played at Johannesburg from 26 February to 3 March. The high scoring continued and the first innings had two totals of over 300, whereas David Denton made 104 with eighteen 4's before being bowled out by Vogler. South Africa only managed 237 in the second and the M.C.C. won by three wickets but again used six bowlers.

Just prior to departing Southampton, Mr. Leveson-Gower learned that an extra match had been arranged for Kimberley, and the players were all extremely pleased to hear about this (see earlier).

In addition, there were prospects of the trip being extended to Rhodesia, and overtures were made to the Chartered Company in the hope the players might be invited to visit the Victoria Falls. There were a few days spare at the end of the tour, but it is unlikely this occurred since several of the team needed to return to England quite urgently.

"NEWLANDS"

Then, with some of the bowlers failing to make their mark, Blythe was given his chance in the final tests played at Newlands, Cape Town starting on 7 March. Possibly the presence of more moisture in the wicket favoured his game, and fate gave him the opportunity to build on his substantial test record at a venue that was on occasions kind to him.

F.L. Fane was now appointed captain and Leveson-Gower sat out having scored only 6 and 12 runs in the last test. The sides were closely matched for the first contest and England made 203 with Woolley on 69, whereas South Africa made 207 but Blythe took no wickets. In the second innings Woolley again led the way with 64 but they were all out for 178 leaving the home team in the ascendancy.

England failed to put on a winning total and their seven bowlers did little better. Blythe took two for 38 (Nourse and Snooke) but South Africa made the required 175 and won by four wickets - taking the series. Despite such success the jury remained out and they were under scrutiny with regard to the forthcoming Australian tour and the triangular tournament.

It was essential they showed to good effect however the first test was won by too narrow a margin, the victory at Durban revealed a weakness despite a large score, the third was lost and on the Wanderers wicket no less, and the fourth won the series - but only after England had some cruel luck in losing their fast bowler at the most critical stage of the game.

The home supporters were not convinced and the last game did nothing to reassure them. One matter of contention was the use of the googly and the *Cape Times* suggested that the English were attempting to master it, whilst the South African batsmen had spent far too much time on it. In particular they bemoaned the absence of openers Tancred and Shalders who could always put on a high score whatever the conditions.

Then there was the question of the Newlands pitch. For those who were accustomed to the ground it was quite excellent to play on, but was much slower in pace than those found elsewhere during the tour.

In general it was preferable to play on turf wickets, but the need for a substantial adjustment from matting wickets was often quite a handicap. Perhaps to have an ant-heap wicket with turf outfield was the best solution or so said one newspaper correspondent! The outcome was that there was a long time to watch the ball off the pitch at Newlands, and once a man was settled in - it was generally hard to remove him.

The two countries played the last test match there on 11-14 March in a time of great upheaval within the country. King Edward VII had recently passed an Act to form the Union of South Africa from the former four colonies, the Act to take effect on 31 May following.

Alfred Milner, the High Commissioner, had imposed several policies that attempted to shape the country's history for decades to come. After the end of the Boer War he encouraged the emigration of whites from Britain to form a majority, planned to Anglicize and reduce Afrikaans identity, and enforced labour laws and controlled the movement of Africans regarding work in the goldfield regions.

Thus commensurate with the cricket tour and reports of sticky wickets or fast outfields there were cartoons of the country's prospects. De Waal and others opposed Milner most vehemently, comparing his imperialism and racially-toned policies to the actions of the siren of Lorelei (in Germany) - luring the nation into conflict with town pitted against country.

No doubt there was little sign of such upheavals as the players stayed in the comfort of their hotels, however when the teams came out at Newlands it was also a watershed for Blythe. He was about to take part in his final test match although he was unaware of this fact, one for him that was to be (without doubt) very successful.

England won the toss under their captain F.L. Fane who decided to bat on the Friday morning, although being a weekday the number of spectators was considerably reduced.

However, the absentees missed a great display of attacking cricket from the openers with Hobbs making 187 and twenty-three 4's supported by Rhodes who made 77 runs. Indeed, by the end of the day the tourists had reached a considerable score of 407 for the loss of seven wickets.

This score-line produced substantial interest on the Saturday thus 5,000 spectators came out to Newlands, crowded into the stands, sheltered under the oaks, and stood five to six deep around the boundary.

Despite the torrid heat of the day and the dust they arrived by car and carriage, expectant to see how South Africa would bat when faced with such a formidable score. Few thought they would reach the target whereas most believed a good score would be made and in the region of 300 runs - of this there was little doubt, but how wrong they were!

The remaining English wickets were soon gone in seven overs with the score on 417, while Zulch and Commaille opened for the South Africans. There was little sign of the free strokes and sound defence that had been such a feature of the 1906-side, and the over-emphasis on dealing with the googly meant the team were unprepared for the orthodox.

All the more so since on that morning the pitch seemed to have a definite nip (not present the day before) which meant the ball turned sharply when least expected - these being the ideal conditions for Blythe.

The *Cape Times* expounded his merits from bay line to mountain top and said they never under-estimated him despite his youthful appearance. Under such conditions there was no advantage for a fast bowler like Thompson whose arms moved like "the sails of a windmill," but more for a player like Blythe who it was said of - "England cannot hope to win a test without his assistance." Yet, he was the very antithesis of a left-hander.

One expected a stocky square-shouldered fellow to come to the crease but instead there was a bowler who seemed slow and unsure at first glance. However, he was then seen to have an action so easy and so simple.

Unlike other orthodox bowlers such as Briggs, Peel, Rowe, Rhodes, and Middleton or Bill Howell the Australian he was tall and slim, being of a fragile countenance that belied his great abilities.

Indeed, this was just an initial assessment and as he shaped for his run his demeanour, like Holmes, was instantly changed and his genius was revealed. The born cricketer was then present in every movement with a well-judged graceful swing prepared over some six-yards, which all of a sudden came into view from behind the umpire's arm.

Amblecote, Stourbridge

Kent played Worcester on 5-7 July 1909 and a victory seemed unlikely as the home side made 360

However, Woolley (185) and Fielder (112) put on a remarkable tenth wicket stand for a total of 555

Blythe then took 7 for 44 to complete the job and Kent won by an innings and 33 runs

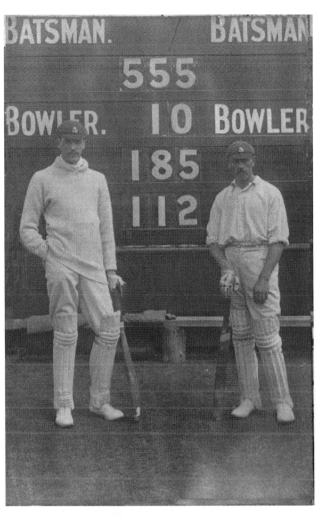

South African Tour

November 1909 - on the deck of the "Saxon" bound for Cape Town

The M.C.C. arrive in Cape Town

This was to be another difficult tour as the series was lost although there were victories in Johannesburg and at Newlands - In the fifth test Blythe took 7 for 46 in eighteen overs to the amazement of the spectators

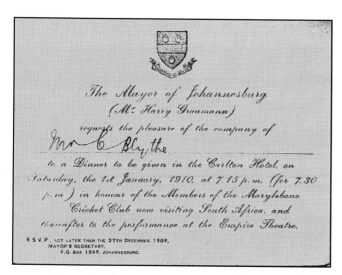

A dinner to celebrate the start of the first test in Johannesburg, 1 January 1910

Howick Falls - "The Tall One"

All of Blythe's tours involved a good degree of sightseeing and he visited these falls just north of Pietermaritzburg

Newlands, Cape Town

A banquet during Blythe's final test match

He took three wickets in the second innings and his last dismissal was his 100th test wicket

Blythe was a slow left-arm orthodox bowler and used a great degree of finger spin (as in the picture)

He could generate as much spin as he liked - producing breaks both ways (at will) and varied this with both pace and flight

Of those who faced him - Jessop said he was the best, Fry noted how he had few superiors on a difficult wicket, and Warner that he was the very model of a left-hander and no finer bowler of his kind had ever appeared

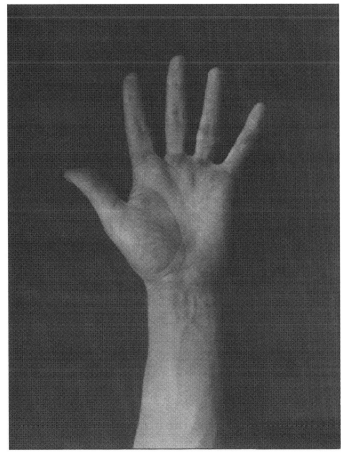

Two "Hat Tricks" in 1910

Blythe continued to show remarkable form - taking a hat trick against Surrey at Rectory Field on 23 June, and another against Derby at Gravesend on 7 July

The "cartoon" depicts five wickets in ten balls v Surrey (with the hat trick)

In the match against Surrey, Blythe took five wickets in ten balls, including the "hat trick."

Belmont, Kent

Some pre-season practice "off the roller" at Lord Harris's estate on 20 April 1911

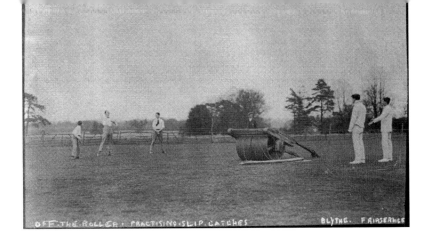

In the Nets

Blythe gives some advice to the next generation

Kent - 1913 Champions

With the help of Blythe they also won in 1906, 1909, and 1910

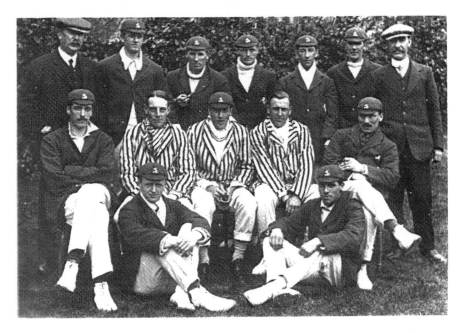

Back: W. Hearne, Blythe, Humphreys, Seymour, Hubble, Fairservice
Front: Woolley, Hatfeild, Dillon, Powell, Huish   Hardinge, Jennings

The Angel Ground, Tonbridge

One of his most successful venues

Blythe lived on the hill behind at St. Mary's Rd. and "Emohruo" ....

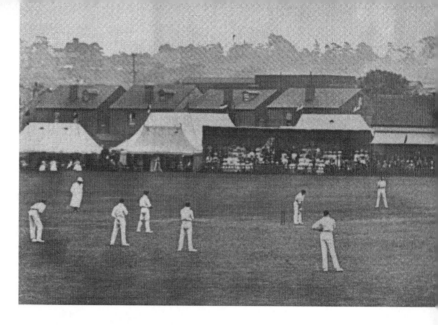

Blythe at the Angel Ground

He bowled Frank Mitchell of Yorks. there with his first ever ball in county cricket, and it was his second home after Canterbury

His style as a slow left-hander was to use "a hop, skip, and jump"

He took 9-30 against Hants in August 1904 - and won a gold medal and was Wisden *"Cricketer of the Year"*

He also took 5-8 against Warwick in June 1913, and with Woolley dismissed them for 16 runs!

26 Troutbeck Road, New Cross

Home of Walter Blythe from 1913 - after his children left home

Chamonix, France

"Social season" January 1914

Blythe was a real celebrity - and was pictured with the international bobsleigh winners, and Count Betrand de Lesseps in his aero-sledge

The "Great" War - Blythe joined the local Kent Fortress Engineers at the outbreak of war, and stands outside the Constitutional Club, Tonbridge before travelling to the main depot at Gillingham in October 1914 - **Right:** Corporal C. Blythe

The Crabble, Dover (a natural amphitheatre) - Blythe played in Kent's first game there against Gloucester in July 1907, but it was an army camp by August 1914

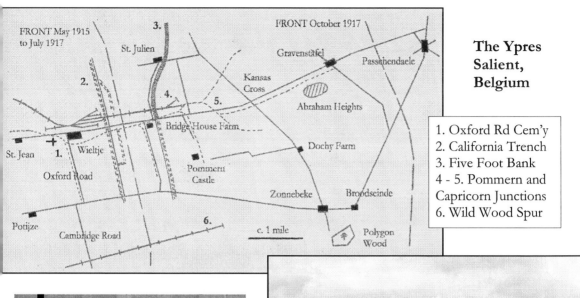

The Ypres Salient, Belgium

1. Oxford Rd Cem'y
2. California Trench
3. Five Foot Bank
4 - 5. Pommern and Capricorn Junctions
6. Wild Wood Spur

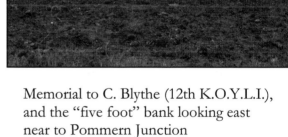

Memorial to C. Blythe (12th K.O.Y.L.I.), and the "five foot" bank looking east near to Pommern Junction

St. Lawrence Ground

The obelisk to Blythe, Hutchings, Jennings, et al was erected at the entrance in 1919 - plans to store it during building work were put on hold

Tonbridge Church - wall of south aisle

Sidney Blythe (1897-1916)
He fought in Gallipoli and
France but died on the Somme

Charlie Blythe - also had
cricketing talent and was in
business with his father and
brother Jack

The Blythes afterwards - at 26 Troutbeck Road
Nellie, Jack, Walter, Connie and (to front) Elizabeth,
and Leonard and Florence De Saulles

Standing in line with the wicket his approach was not apparent until just a yard from the crease, whilst his action was further concealed until his back-stretched arm came above the shoulder. His swing was so deceptive that the uninitiated eye might have expected a right arm delivery.

The paper added, "Blythe, to my mind, would make an ideal poker player for he has such an innocent expression of countenance, and is such a finished artiste in the concealment of all that his hand holds. It is impossible for the batsman to gauge either pace or break."

This they believed was a crucial factor in his success and it was one of some interest to the cricketer himself. Keeping the article he ringed around in pencil the section stating - "Blythe, to my mind, would make an ideal poker player for he has such an innocent expression..." since it clearly amused him that this was how he was considered.

No doubt he was far from naïve on the matter, knowing well that such a deadpan expression and deceptive approach concealed some considerable guile and tenacity when delivering the ball. Further to this it is probable that he also indulged in a 'real' game of poker, since he was rumoured to have initiated a little card school during the sailings.

However, that was not all regarding the imminent demise of the South African batsmen; the wicket was good and the runs were expected but on several occasions Blythe outwitted his opponents by utilizing "the bluff." The side had practiced long and hard at defending the break but were compromised by the most simple-looking ball, which was exactly what it professed to be - a simple straight delivery, and nothing else.

J.W. Zulch put up the best defence for the home side, although he was of the modern school who had trained for every eventuality of the turn of ball on the matting wicket. He remained in throughout the innings and scored the highest total of 43 which gives some idea of the collapse.

Blythe proceeded to take seven wickets for 46 runs on a batsman's wicket (in less than a couple of hours) and five of his eighteen overs were maidens. The on-looking crowd were most despondent and there was little noise except for a "phew" when a ball whizzed just above the wicket, or an "oh" when a catch was missed or a player just reached the crease.

After lunch more spectators arrived to witness the proceedings and some found shelter under the fir trees close to the entrance, but most of them had to brave the glaring heat of the midday sun.

The main feature in Blythe's success was the way in which he concealed both flight and pace, whilst sending down his special ball that swung with the arm from the off to the leg. Indeed, during the innings there were to be several good examples of his great ability.

For instance Murray Bisset played a weak stroke off one of Blythe's balls and was caught by Rhodes, thus he was sent back to the pavilion on just 4 runs. This was a most uncharacteristic dismissal whereas both Snooke and Vogler were clean bowled by Blythe for nought.

Later on in the short innings Reggie Schwarz (who was born at Lee near Blackheath) was dealing well with Blythe's trap on the leg side. At this the bowler moved the fielders to the off side with the suggestion that he was playing for a catch in the slips - but this wasn't his intention at all. He soon sent down the half-volley since he had his eye on the outfield and Schwarz was promptly caught by Denton at the boundary.

South Africa were dismissed for 103 runs in 38.5 overs, but in the follow on Snooke and Faulkner began to score and at the end of the day the team were 102 for three wickets. By that time a cooling breeze had sprung up and the shadow of the trees crept perceptibly closer to the crease.

The *Cape Times* labelled this debacle as "Black Saturday" since it was a lamentable collapse on the part of the home side. However, they added that the spectators saw a masterly bowling performance by Blythe which was described as "a triumph of genius allied to skill."

ONE HUNDRED UP

In the evening there was a complimentary banquet for the two teams at the Mount Nelson Hotel, Cape Town. This included a fine menu of European food and some excellent dancing and music by composers such as Weber, Mendelssohn, Schubert, Wagner, and Bizet.

W.V. Simkins president of the Western Province Cricket Union proposed the King, whereas the Hon. William P. Schreiner K.C. (a former P.M. of Cape Colony) proposed the M.C.C., and Hon. J.T. Molteno speaker of the House of Assembly (and of the first Union parliament) proposed the South Africans. Such were the circles in which Blythe of Deptford moved!

The players all had a much needed rest on the Sunday and play was started again on the Monday. Due to the collapse there was a hardy crowd of just 500 spectators first thing in the morning, and despite some dew the wicket had barely worn at all while the outfield remained hard and fast.

There were several rain-clouds in the sky above, floating past off Table Mountain and their shadows were somewhat disconcerting to the batsmen. During the morning 108 runs were added for the loss of two wickets and due to such success the crowd increased considerably after lunch.

The captain Snooke made 47 but the best effort came from Faulkner who was on 99 when he was caught by Woolley off Thompson. After making two great hook shots he seemed certain to reach the century, but displayed that usual degree of anxiety on nearing the coveted target and as a result weakly touched the ball with the bat's edge.

Blythe was quieter in the second innings and took three wickets for 58 whilst the other wickets fell to Thompson and Woolley. Meanwhile, Bisset also made some good strokes which brought cheers from the crowd, and Schwarz put on a further 44 thus the stigma of an innings defeat was just avoided as the side were all out for 327.

David Denton then scored the 16 runs needed to win and England had their victory by nine wickets. However, the Monday was South Africa's day as they put on a sound display of batting which suggested that something incredible might still happen. Their effort was reminiscent of the teams of old and Faulkner gave one of the best performances for his country.

Regarding the M.C.C. they had proved themselves as "a team" in every sense of the word during the tour. It mattered little whether the side was captained by Leveson-Gower or by Fane, since the players worked for the common interest and the fielders always backed up the bowlers.

They provided some dazzling exhibitions of fielding and the placing of the field (as shown in the final test) had been reduced to a fine art. Again and again they confirmed that old cricketing maxim "the saving of a run is every bit as valuable as the making."

During the tour the side played attractive, vigorous cricket and the way in which they responded to two defeats confirmed their character. To come back and win in Johannesburg and then to have such a large victory in Cape Town was a credit to the M.C.C., and several valuable lessons had been taught to the South Africans.

They had surpassed Warner's team of 1906 who only managed one victory and in general played right to the end of every match with much conviction. In addition they disproved the theory that test matches could not be won without a fast bowler, since C. Buckenham was unable to play in the final outing though an injury rather than through design.

But most of all the last test match at Newlands was Blythe's success. His dismissal of seven players on the second day in front of a large crowd, and in response to earlier criticisms of his ability on such a stage, was a good rebuff to those who might still reproach him.

The *Cape Times* had no doubt that he was vital to England's progress and that he was a great genius with the ball. Significantly, he bowled the last ball down to S.V. Samuelson in the second innings - clean bowling him for 7 and the South Africans were all out. Not only was this the last ball of the innings but it was the last ball of Blythe's test career.

Indeed, given his success in the game this was quite an astonishing fact and one that is hard to understand. Further to this with Samuelson's wicket he reached a total of 100 test wickets, his best being 8-59 and his average 18.63, whereas on four occasions he took ten wickets in a match.

This was certainly a profitable tour for Blythe on an individual basis and the best one he played in regarding team success. The M.C.C. then boarded one of the mail packets back to Southampton near the end of March, and the bowler prepared his talents for the next county season and a defence of the championship by Kent.

CHAPTER 15

Champions Again

Colin Blythe and his team-mates arrived back at Southampton in April 1910 as spring heralded the new cricket season. However, the former was not to know that his test career had ended even though there were several further opportunities for him to shine on the international stage.

Johnny Douglas of Essex captained a side to Australia in 1911-12 which included many quality players viz. Hobbs, Gunn, Mead, and Strudwick as well as Rhodes, Woolley, and Barnes. It was a combination that paid off since the series was won emphatically four to one, although Douglas also lost all five games down under just after the First War.

This was followed by the promised triangular tournament in England in the summer of 1912 the other two participants being Australia and South Africa. In this instance C.B. Fry captained the side and as stated Barnes, Rhodes, Woolley, and Foster were preferred as bowlers.

Blythe's omission remains a mystery given his form in the closing test in Cape Town and his ongoing success at county level. The only explanation for this oddity is some prejudice in the selection procedure going back to the medical report after Edgbaston, although there was also a degree of conflict between Blythe and Fry at the time (see later).

On this occasion the selectors were well vindicated in their choices since England were unbeaten and won four out of six, Australia won only two, and South Africa failed to win. A great result for England.

The M.C.C. then travelled to South Africa again in 1913-14 also under the captainship of Johnny Douglas. With England on a considerable roll the side was similar to that which travelled to Australia two years earlier, and they came home undefeated with four wins and a draw.

With such effective competition, Blythe, who was edging towards the age of thirty-five could not force his way into the side. However, his career was far from over and he was still to produce some of his best cricket with his bowling remaining constant in almost every domestic season.

He then concentrated on life in Tonbridge but the new season began on a sombre note, since Edward VII died on 6 May and in an atmosphere of national grief the regular fixture between Kent and the M.C.C. had to be cancelled. There was a game at Oxford University six days later and despite Blythe taking five it was lost by eight wickets, whilst Kent scored just 70 runs in their second innings.

TWO HAT TRICKS

The season proper began against Middlesex at Lord's on 16-18 May and in a remarkable first innings there were three centuries for Kent. Dillon made 115, Woolley reached 120, and A.P. Day was not out on 111, whereas between them they scored forty-five crowd-cheering boundaries.

On the second day the side declared having reached 500 for eight wickets and Warner and his team tried (but failed) to match them. Indeed, Warner went for nought to Percy Morfee the fast bowler and the other wickets fell very quickly. Blythe eventually took six wickets for just 27 runs and Morfee four for 70 runs as Middlesex succumbed on 105.

There was an improvement in the follow on as the home side made 197 although Warner was yet again bowled by Morfee for nought - the bowler making his debut in first class cricket! This was a remarkable score as Kent won by an innings and 198 runs, all the more so since Middlesex were one of their chief rivals to win the championship.

The next game against Lancashire at Old Trafford was scheduled for 19-21 May but the King's funeral was on the middle day and as a result there was no play. With just two days played for the enjoyment of the spectators the game ended in a draw and did not count towards the championship.

In addition, the players had to adjust to a new system for calculating points in the contest. From that time onwards it was percentage of wins to games played and this was shortly to have an affect on the outcome.

The squad then went on their annual trip to Northampton on 23-24 May and although Blythe was quieter there than usual, his team-mates were not. Fielder took twelve wickets in total and the home side were all out for 69 runs in the second innings as Kent won by 241 runs.

A significant varsity clash also followed at the end of the month. Kent travelled to the F.P. Fenner's Ground at Mortimer Road in Cambridge, and both sides put on over 200 runs in the first innings with Blythe 23 not out. However, the home side which included Neville Tufnell collapsed in the second and were all out for just 45 runs.

Only J.F. Ireland reached double figures making 18 and Blythe did most of the damage taking 'six for 19' - the others to Fielder and Woolley. Kent won by ten wickets and Blythe reached 1,700 for his career while at Oxford there was a matching performance. E.G. Arnold the Worcester right-hander opened at University Parks with '215' including twenty-nine 4's and two 6's although the game was drawn. There was then a cartoon of the two players "*With Honours at the Varsities*" (showing their two scores).

Kent also went on tour and won at the County Ground in Derby, and beat Denton, Haigh, Hirst, and Rhodes of Yorkshire at Dewsbury by eight wickets. Despite losing the next game at Leicester they won both fixtures of Tonbridge Week and were clearly in a strong position.

With this in mind Surrey must have been unsettled to see that their next fixture was against Kent at Rectory Field, Blackheath on 23-25 June. On paper they appeared to be a good side under their captain M.C. Bird ably supported by Hayward, Hobbs, and wicket keeper Strudwick but they soon came up against a bowler who was in impressive form.

Surrey went in to bat first and the England duo Hayward and Hobbs both made around the fifty-mark, but the remainder of the team were dismissed for just 26 runs and they were all out for 133.

Blythe's figures were seven wickets for 55 runs in twenty-seven overs and this included his first hat-trick of wickets. In addition to this he took four wickets in just five balls - and five wickets for the addition of no runs in ten balls. Woolley took the other three, whilst the two Tonbridge bowlers were supported in their efforts by Fielder and Fairservice.

Kent then went in to bat and Dillon the captain led the way making 65 and reached 8,500 runs in his career, however the weather intervened and Kent finished at 134 for three by the end of the second day. A very promising match witnessed no more play and thus ended in a draw.

The newspapers noted afterwards that Blythe had accomplished so many wonderful performances, that it was a great surprise to learn that until last Thursday he had never managed a hat trick. His greatest feats were often saved for an important game and on more than one occasion it was Surrey who had this doubtful honour.

Hayward and Ducat were dismissed with the first/last balls of a maiden over then Strudwick, W.J. Abel (son of Bobby), and W.C. Smith with the second, third, and fourth of the next. The statistics of a hat trick with two other wickets for no runs was truly amazing, thus the paper had a cartoon of Blythe "the juggler" with ten balls and stumps in the air!

Johnny Douglas and Essex then came to Gravesend at the end of June and the orthodox left-handers Blythe and Woolley took all the wickets as Kent won by an innings and 81 runs. Blythe took four and seven wickets and reached 1,750 for his career, whereas Essex made identical totals of 109 in each innings against Kent's total of 299.

There was a large victory by an innings and 142 runs against Sussex at Hastings at the start of July although the wickets were taken by Fielder and Woolley. Hutchings made 144 and Woolley put on 117 as Kent moved up a gear and challenged for a second title in a row.

Indeed, in the next game against Derby at Gravesend played on 7-9 July the bowler Blythe took his second hat trick of the season. Initially he clean bowled the captain Albert Lawton followed by Howcroft and Beet thus the visitors were all out for 170 runs with Blythe taking six for 60.

In reply Kent put on a varied performance and the captain Dillon was out for 3 runs, but Humphreys made 81 and Charles V.L. Hooman who was making his debut for the side scored 64 runs. [1]

Blythe also relished the challenge and added 30 runs at the end playing with the other tail-enders as the wickets fell. In fact, his first run took him to 3,000 runs in his career and his effort helped take Kent to a total of 247. Derby then made 144 in their second innings and Blythe took another five wickets for 63 runs (the others to Woolley), whereas Kent went on to win the game by a comfortable six wickets.

THE 1910 SEASON

Tunbridge Wells Week was a prodigious success from 11-16 July but Blythe missed both games which were won by over 300 runs apiece. In the first Somerset made a record low score against Kent of 50 runs, whilst the side against Lancashire included both Hooman and Henry Preston.

There was then an important contest against Yorkshire at Mote Park in Maidstone on 21-23 July. Kent won the toss and batted although there was a collapse at the end and they finished on 203, whereas the visitors were all out for 120 and Blythe took 5-64 whilst Woolley took 4-50.

The second innings saw a similar pattern as Kent scored just 173 with a further tail-end collapse - seven of the wickets falling to S. Haigh. However, Rhodes then made just 21 runs before being clean bowled by Blythe, and Hirst was caught by Hooman off the same bowler on 10 runs. The result, Yorkshire were all out for 78 and Blythe and Woolley took 6-31 and 4-41 respectively and the game was won by 178 runs.

There was a significant victory over Plum Warner and Middlesex at the St. Lawrence Ground on 1-2 August, when James Seymour scored 193 and the home side won by an innings and 150 runs. Being their main rivals other than Surrey the importance of this 'second' win was quite obvious.

Kent beat Gloucester at home in the other game of Canterbury Week then went to the College Ground, Cheltenham for a return fixture played on 11-12 August. The visitors won the toss and soon put on a record score

---

[1] Charles Victor Lisle Hooman was born at Ditton, Kent in 1887. He played for Oxford from 1907-10, had fifteen matches for Kent, and was an amateur golfer for England. His father Thomas Charles appeared in the first Cup Final.

of 607 declaring with just six wickets gone - Humphreys made 162 runs, Seymour reached 90, and J.R. Mason was not out on 121.

Gloucestershire captained by Gilbert Jessop then replied with 168 and 97 runs in their two innings, most of the wickets falling to the googly specialist Carr whose figures were 5-68 and 6-42 whereas Blythe took five in total. Kent had won by an innings and 242 runs and with just four games to go had already secured their second consecutive championship.

The club's famous bowler was largely responsible for the ongoing success and when not on the field the players may have flicked through the latest *Vanity Fair*. Fielder leaned across to Woolley and announced "Cor blimey, ere's our 'Charlie' imself right on the front page." In fact, an image of the bowler appeared on "8 August" and prints were also made. [2]

Meanwhile, there were two victories during Dover Week and in the second game against Hampshire on 18-19 August Kent won by ten wickets. The fine batting continued as Humphreys made 130, Seymour scored 155, and Blythe took three in each innings and reached a total of 150 wickets for the season. Not surprisingly there was a dip and they lost to Surrey at the Oval and drew with Hampshire in the last game at Bournemouth.

Kent were champions again ahead of Surrey and Middlesex led by their great all-round captain Ted Dillon, having won nineteen out of twenty-five games and lost only three. Their batsmen continued to be prolific and the figures for the season were certainly most impressive i.e. Hutchings 1,461, Humphreys 1,618, and Seymour 1,546.

Regarding the bowling Blythe played in all but two matches and took 163 wickets being mainly backed up by Woolley on 132. Fielder who was ill appeared eighteen times taking 77 and Carr bowled in ten games from July taking 63, whereas Fred Huish the wicket keeper secured 43 catches and 30 stumpings which was another good season.

Some relaxation then followed as Blythe travelled to the North Marine Road Ground in Scarborough. Initially he joined the Players for a game on 5-7 September the side including Hobbs, Rhodes, Tyldesley, Denton, Hirst, A.E. Relf, Woolley, Haigh, W.C. Smith, and Strudwick.

The Gentlemen were captained by Leveson-Gower and featured Warner, Bird, Douglas, Fane, Hutchings, Tufnell and two Fosters. Despite some reasonable scores the game ended in an honourable draw whereas Blythe bowled both Hutchings and Warner in the first innings.

---

[2] *Vanity Fair* was a London magazine from 1868-1914 and most issues had a full page colour lithograph of a celebrity. These were its chief legacy with c. 2,000 in total whereas Lord Harris (1881) and G.L. Jessop (1901) also appeared. The one of Blythe was by "A.L.S." from J.F. Mockford's photo at the Angel Ground.

There was also a reunion for the M.C.C. South African tour players who took on Lord Londesborough's XI on 8-10 September. The opposing side including Warner, Douglas, Tyldesley, Hutchings, and Hirst won by 97 runs although Blythe took five for 25 in the second innings.

The season concluded with Kent against The Rest at the Oval on 12-15 September, whilst Sir Marcus Samuel hosted a meal for the players and the committee at the Savoy on the 13th. In the game Jessop led the opponents to 404 with Warner on 126, Blythe's only wicket being that of Jack Hobbs. Kent achieved half that sum and after a declaration lost by 244 runs, whilst the bowler reached 1,850 wickets during the game.

LOCAL RESIDENTS

Blythe enjoyed considerable success on a personal level and his team-mates on a collective level, thus he left 40 St. Mary's Road and moved to a more substantial property in the spring of 1911.

In fact, there was an extensive cricketing clique living within this district of Tonbridge. William Fairservice and his wife Lucia, a possible relative, lived at 42 St. Mary's Road at the turn of the century and later moved to Barden Road, whereas W.J. Fairservice son of Walter was born at Nunhead in 1881 and was a store-keeper for a sports shop in Camberwell.

Likewise, Harry George Day a cricket ball maker lived with Emily his wife and a son at 20 Springwell Road, which crossed St. Mary's Road near to Blythe's house - and was also groundsman at the Angel Ground.

His occupation was of some interest and Tonbridge was a centre for the manufacture of cricketing paraphernalia. There were at least three cricket ball manufacturers in the vicinity including Thomas Ives & Son who initially operated north of the town, but then had an address 66 Quarry Hill Road with works at Preston Road - near to Blythe. Indeed, the second firm of J. Wisden & Co. were just around the corner at Baltic Road.

Further to this Thomas Francis (late Dark) was a cricket ball manufacturer and bat maker at Watts Cross, Hildenborough near to Stocks Green Road just to the north, his other address being Lord's Cricket Ground. At a latter date Horace H. Hitchcock was also a manufacturer there.

Claud Neville Woolley (registered as Colin) was born in the town in 1886 and Frank Edward a year later. Their father Charles William Woolley was a dyer at 72 High Street then ran the *Medway Cycle Works* at the same address, later residing at Avebury Avenue near both Barden and Preston Roads. Arthur Fielder also moved to Douglas Road just to the south in 1910 so it was little wonder that Blythe remained in the vicinity.

His colleague Fairservice joined the team four years after him but resided at 2 Cicely Villas, Goldsmid Road from 1905-08 and down the street at "Belmont" (see below) from 1910-14. This was situated on a hill just above the Angel Ground and railway leading up to the Pembury Road.

In addition, the latter had a son Colin who was born in 1909 and also became a Kent cricketer, whereas Harry Ives cricket ball manufacturer lived at "Beverley" just a few doors up from Cicely Villas.

No doubt their presence prompted Blythe to move to Goldsmid Road and he occupied a house called "Killarney," which was the second one on the east-side next door to Ives. It was just a short distance from the Pembury Road and he renamed it as "Emohruo."

This was probably an idea he picked up in Australia since the locals often used "Dunroamin" or failing that the aforementioned - indeed this was not a derivative of Aboriginal origin but simply the reverse of "Our Home." Today, there are a number of Edwardian properties remaining at the end of Goldsmid Road and the second of these was probably his.

THE 1911 SEASON

Just before the season started Blythe and Fairservice were invited down to the pretty cricket ground at Belmont for an impromptu practice session. This was situated on Lord Harris's estate near the village of Throwley south of Faversham and ten miles west of Canterbury.

It was a private venue and they spent some leisurely time bowling in the nets and practicing slip-catches off the roller. This was a brief moment of Edwardian innocence that belied the maelstrom yet to come. [3]

By then, the Kent squad were undoubtedly the best team in the country although they lost the opening game of the season to the M.C.C. at Lord's. Blythe still maintained some consistent form and took 5-88 and 5-56 but the opponents finished the match 94 runs ahead.

There was also a defeat by Oxford University at University Parks on 18-20 May. The home side took the game by seven wickets and some wondered if the Kent bubble had burst - but that was not to be the case.

---

[3] The first baron, General George Harris fought for the R.A. in America and India and purchased Belmont an 18th century house designed by Samuel Wyatt in 1801. His grandson George F.R. Harris the 3rd Lord was a Governor of Trinidad and the first president of Kent in 1870. His son George R.C. Harris (1851-1932) was born on the island and played cricket in the Eton v Harrow match at Lord's. He became the 4th Lord in 1872 and took control of Kent having a fine career, and was captain of England in Melbourne as early as 1879.

Indeed, some normal service was resumed when they took on Middlesex at Lord's on 22-24 May. Kent went in to bat and made 300 runs the best performances coming from Hutchings and Woolley, whereas the tail-enders Fairservice, Blythe, and Fielder all made over 20 runs.

Warner was then bowled by Blythe for just 1 run as Middlesex succumbed on 143 and Kent followed this up with 294 - the bowler finishing not out on 21 runs when the visitors declared. During the second innings the home side improved and Warner made a century out of a score of 279, but Kent won the game by 172 runs. Blythe was quieter in the second session and it was down to A.P. Day who took eight for 49.

The next two games saw the bowler renew his acquaintance with sides that were generally less than pleased to see him, except in terms of those who enjoyed watching fine exhibitions of bowling and cricket.

In the first instance the Kent side travelled to Aylestone Road, Leicester on 25-27 May. Initially, there was little amiss as the home team scored 270 and the visitors replied with 197 although the weather held up proceedings. On the third day Leicester came in to bat and despite openers Cecil Wood and Albert Knight they were all out for just 26 runs!

Seven of their batsmen registered nought as a score whereas Blythe took six wickets for 10 runs in just five overs. Woolley also took four wickets for 16 runs and Kent won by nine wickets - their second innings batsmen being Dillon, Humphreys, and Seymour.

This was followed by a visit to the County Ground, Northampton and Kent put on 394 with Humphreys scoring 144 runs. Blythe caused his usual havoc there taking five wickets for 72 and four wickets for 58, and after a follow on Kent won by an innings and 56 runs.

The subsequent games in June saw further progress and Gloucester were defeated at Gravesend by 263 runs, there was a draw with Hampshire at Southampton, and Lancashire were beaten by three wickets at Old Trafford. The latter was a fine victory under the captain Ken Hutchings as Kent won despite some very high scores from their opponents, with James Seymour making 196 including twenty-three 4's.

There were reverses against both Essex and Northampton at the Angel Ground during Tonbridge Week, followed by draws at Bramall Lane and Trent Bridge, and then two good victories at the Crabble in Dover.

In the first game Kent beat Nottingham by 153 runs and in the second innings they dismissed their opponents for just 84 with Blythe and Woolley taking all the wickets. Against Leicester they declared on 530 for six wickets and won by an innings and 179 runs, whereas Blythe took five wickets for 45 and also five for 104 during the game.

Lord Harris founder of the modern Kent side also continued to maintain an interest and made "positively" his last appearance that season at the age of sixty. His first game for the club took place in 1870 and his final analysis was 278 innings, highest score 176, and average of 30.04.

Kent played India at Catford on 3-4 July the side including Dillon, Lord Harris, L. Troughton, A. Snowden, Fielder, Woolley, and Fairservice but Blythe did not play. In the first innings Dillon made 130 and Lord Harris scored 36 for a total of 318, whereas India followed on and Harris bowled ten overs taking one wicket for 34 runs. Indeed, they won the game by nine wickets and Woolley passed 6,500 runs.

SOME CONTROVERSY

Further successes ensued that month with home victories over Somerset, Worcester, and significantly Middlesex - followed by an important game against Surrey at Rectory Field on 27-29 July.

The visitors went in to bat and made 218 but Kent replied with 245 the best effort by James Seymour who scored 118 runs. It was a tight game and Surrey made a further 240 but Kent eventually won by four wickets, while Blythe batted first with Fred Huish in the second innings and made 28 with 3,500 for his career. Woolley also scored 42 in twenty-eight minutes with six 4's and a 2 off eight balls whilst reaching 7,000 runs.

There were then two victories away at Sussex and Worcester which put the Men of Kent in an admirable position and presumably added a degree of pressure to their season. Such pressure became apparent when C.B. Fry and Hampshire arrived at the St. Lawrence Ground on 7-9 August.

In the first innings the visitors batted well and Fry made 123 before he was bowled by Blythe, stumped Huish, whilst with several other good scores the side finished on 339. There was then a challenging performance from Kent with Woolley making 108, although near the end Dillon was the only one who showed any kind of resistance.

Huish added a useful 27 and Blythe was caught on 14 but Dillon was left with only Fielder and Carr to assist him. With the score on 302, Fielder came in and drove the ball back with some force to the bowler Kennedy who easily caught him. However, in making the catch he split the nail of his forefinger on the left hand and was forced to retire.

Hubble, the twelfth man for Kent, then came in to field for Hampshire as a substitute. Not long afterwards, Dillon who was forcing the runs hit a ball to cover point and the substitute dashed in and caught it near the ground, just as everyone looked to see if it would reach the boundary.

It was an exciting end to the innings although Hubble may have blushed at dismissing his own captain, whereas the crowd to their credit were most sporting about the whole affair (at that stage).

After some uneven batting Kent finished slightly behind on 324, whilst the best performance came from Humphreys who succeeded in wearing down the bowling as Woolley put on the runs. The latter showed some splendid confidence in his batting although on two occasions, once at the slips and another time at mid off, he was almost caught out.

With the game in the balance Hampshire came in to bat at the end of the second day, and C.B. Fry held the crease for an hour and a half firstly with Alex Bowell and then with A.C. Johnston. By the end they had 86 runs for the loss of one wicket but they were favoured by fortune as Blythe, Fielder, and Carr continually beat them without hitting the stumps.

There had been considerable issues between Blythe and Fry regarding the matter of test cricket, most of the comments coming from the latter and such concerns resurfaced at the end of the game. Indeed, with the game still in progress the newspapers carried the headlines: "Unhappy incident, C.B. Fry's queer complaint about Blythe - bowling *into* the sun." An issue which they elucidated as follows:

"In the last over Blythe pitched up a couple of full tosses, from each of which Fry scored, but complained that the ball was lost in the sun's rays and that he could not see it. There was apparently some discussion, but Street (who had played for Surrey), the umpire, on being appealed to, ordered the over to be finished. There was a good deal of hooting as the players left the field, and Fry had to run the gauntlet of some adverse criticism from the crowd as he entered the pavilion."

There was clearly a lot to talk about however on the last day Fry was out on 112 and his side reached 319 without the injured Kennedy. Kent had an almost impossible task in the time available, and despite Hutchings score of 103 not out they finished on 223 and the game was drawn.

Blythe took just two wickets in the first innings including Fry and thereby reached 100 wickets for the season and 1,950 for his career. Possibly the controversy encouraged the captain Dillon to use him less on the final day and in fact seven bowlers were then employed.

With the game over and the honours even the press turned to the matter of "Fry's queer complaint" and announced, "Is a bowler justified in sending down full pitches?" They believed this was a novel cricket point to discuss but at the same time a peculiar form of protest, whereas Fry was unfairly and rudely treated by the crowd at the close of play especially as he was the probable England captain for the next tour of Australia.

He remained much in the public eye firstly with regard to his invitation to lead the M.C.C., and secondly because of a letter to the press concerning his inability to give a quick answer to the selection committee. *The Field* had asked for £5,000 to be raised to enable him to make the journey, the money being needed to keep up the work of the 'training ship Mercury' of which Fry was the principal director. [4]

Regarding the game - Fry had objected to Colin Blythe sending down full pitches with the sun behind him causing the controversy. In fact, the former once complained that the light was too good, whilst Blythe made a similar objection to the umpire when bowling to A. Marshal at the Oval.

No law existed against the full toss but there was clearly a timing problem with the sun in the eyes. Whether this was good reason for a protest was clearly a matter of argument, and the proper course was to object to the light although the rules usually referred to poor light:

"The umpires may decide, on appeal, that there is not sufficient light for play. Should the light improve before the time for drawing stumps, they shall, without waiting for instructions, call upon the players to resume the game. In the event of the captains agreeing to the condition of the ground or light, the umpires will, so far, be relieved of their responsibility."

Generally the captains would decide but it was the most extraordinary of circumstances if the game were stopped because the light was too strong. This was the dilemma of the situation. Blythe was not a fast bowler nor was he known for sending down full pitches - however, the protest created a conundrum which might add a further impediment to bowling.

Bobby Abel who like Blythe learnt the game locally in Southwark Park was a cricketer for Surrey and had an outfitters emporium near to the Oval. On his retirement in 1904 he coached there and at Dulwich College, and was promptly consulted on this exigent matter by the *Evening Times*:

"The point raised is undoubtedly a very peculiar one, and I don't think it has ever previously been brought up by a cricketer, but I fail to see how such a protest as Mr. Fry is reported to have made can receive reasonable support. Mr. Fry's objection appears to me to have no sound base. If a bowler is not to accept the advantage of varying circumstances, how is he going to dismiss a batsman?"

---

[4] C.B. Fry took part in athletics at the Queen's Club, played professional football, enjoyed Rugby Union, and was a cricketer for Sussex and Hampshire his average being 50.22 (only Ranjitsinhji did better). With his wife Beatrice he helped to run the "Training Ship Mercury" on the River Hamble for forty years this being an institution which prepared boys for the Royal Navy. Fry was also an unsuccessful Liberal candidate and wrote several sports books.

Abel believed the current wickets favoured the batsman and it was only natural that a bowler should take advantage of any circumstance presented which assisted him, and therefore added:

"Personally, I should have dealt with full pitches for a whole day without even thought of complaint, especially so with a slow bowler as is Blythe. A batsman should make it his business to deal with all manner of attack no matter how it comes."

Abel played on many occasions in the glaring sun and said he just had to put up with it; Blythe could not prevent the sun from glaring whilst a hat or a cap was the most effective remedy! No further laws were wanted to add to the already complex rules - but the issue would no go away.

Indeed, H.C. McDonell who played in the game for Hampshire published a pamphlet "What is Cricket" three years after his retirement in 1924. This considered a number of similar disputes and issues of fair play and clearly given his allegiance came down in favour of C.B. Fry.

A memorandum followed from the Kent Committee refuting the account stating that Blythe did not adopt a deliberate course of action. There was no evidence that Dillon asked the bowler to send down full tosses for the purpose of catching Fry in the slips, and Blythe and his team-mates were not surprisingly upset by all the accusations.

The batsman made his appeal and the umpire asked Blythe to stop such deliveries, resulting in a considerable dispute among the players. A number of versions of the event persisted and the truth became hard to ascertain but clearly much was made of the whole situation.

SEASON'S CLOSE

Returning to the championship fray Kent took on Lancashire at the St. Lawrence Ground but lost by nine wickets, then went to Taunton and beat Somerset by an innings and 225 runs. Possibly due to the furore Blythe was absent from the first game and his replacement Hubble scored 60 and 53, whereas the bowler played little part in the second.

Despite this he came back to form against Gilbert Jessop and Gloucester at Cheltenham on 17-18 August. Kent won the game by an innings and 94 runs, and Blythe took eight wickets for 45 and then six wickets for 39 as the home side were forced to follow on.

Then, after a defeat against Surrey at the Oval there was a dramatic game versus Yorkshire at Canterbury on 24-26 August. The visitors batted first and were all out for 75 runs as Blythe took 5-35 and Woolley 5-39, while Kent finished on an improved 151 at the end of the first day.

Wilfred Rhodes made 37 in a second innings affected by rain however Yorkshire were dismissed on the third day for 79, with Blythe taking six wickets for just 28 runs - the others falling to Carr and Woolley.

It was then a simple matter for Humphreys to score the 3 runs that were needed to win and Kent were the victors by ten wickets. The side also won the final contest against Essex at Leyton by a similar margin although Blythe was quieter on that occasion, and initially it looked as if Kent had won a third championship in a row.

Their figures certainly supported such success and Fielder who enjoyed his benefit took 119 in the season on fast wickets, whilst Blythe recorded 138 despite the conditions and played in all but one game. In terms of batting Humphreys reached 1,773, Seymour 1,737, Woolley 1,676, and Hardinge was on 1,146 although there was a lack of amateur support.

Kent had won seventeen matches and lost four out of twenty-six, but it was Warwickshire who were champions for the first time. The winners had a percentage of 74.00 however under the new system the Kent side were on 73.84 and a hat-trick of wins was narrowly missed. Whether this was a true reflection of events was hard to ascertain, since the two teams did not play one another to resolve who was really pre-eminent (yet).

CHAPTER 16

Later Career

During the closed season Woolley headed off to Australia with the M.C.C. but Blythe and his colleagues remained in England dreaming of what might have been in terms of the championship.

In fact, there were numerous problems in the 1912 season and Dillon only appeared in ten games due to an injury. Several amateurs were unavailable and Woolley missed five games because of the triangular tournament, but he still had figures of 1,373 runs and 103 wickets for Kent.

There were also changes at the coaching level and Captain W. McCanlis finally retired having first played for the side back in 1862. His role was of great significance since he coached most of the young players in the squad viz. Blythe, Seymour, Humphreys, Hardinge, Hubble, and Woolley.

BLYTHE'S BATTLEFIELD

On a personal level Blythe had another very good season producing some of his best performances although in the first game Kent lost to the M.C.C. at Lord's by some 73 runs. However, they then beat Somerset at Gravesend on 16-17 May by a margin of 280 runs.

Kent went in to bat first and made 261 with Humphreys scoring 92 whilst Somerset were all out for 158 and Blythe took seven for 78 - in the second innings the home side reached 251 and the bowler was run out on 14 at the end. The visitors were then dismissed for just 74 runs and he took another six for 31 including Len Braund clean bowled on 3 runs. Woolley took the other four whilst Blythe reached 2,000 wickets.

There was then a sequence of three games at Headingley, Old Trafford, and Trent Bridge but these resulted in a defeat and two draws. In addition Hampshire made a record of 599 against Kent at Southampton on 27-29 May in a game that was drawn - although Blythe did not play.

The "northern tour" then took them back to Aylestone Road, Leicester on 6-7 June and Blythe produced a performance that was soon compared to his formidable enterprises at Northampton in 1907.

Initially, Leicester won the toss and their captain John Shields confidently decided to bat - but regarding previous meetings he should have been more cautious. A succession of players nervously came up to the crease and they were undone mainly by "the reputation of Blythe."

The pitch itself was not one that indicated a complete collapse as it was quite dead to the bowler, and it was skill combined with a genuine fear in the batsmen that led to the amazing outcome. Only Albert Lord who scored a low total of 7 runs in just five minutes and hit the only boundary made any kind of stand against Blythe's attack.

The rest came to the crease with a melancholy demeanour regarding their imminent fate, and either tried to be wildly intrepid or remained completely helpless against the bowling. Indeed, not one batsman made double figures and all were out for 25 runs in just fifty-five minutes.

"*Blythe's Battlefield*" was the headline which recorded that he was solely responsible for Leicester's record lowest score. His ball by ball analysis was quite astounding and read seven wickets for 9 runs in 7.5 overs with three maidens, whilst Woolley added three for 15 runs in 7 overs.

Analysis v Leicester: M M Mw 1w 1w 1w 2ww 3w (1 extra)

Blythe had a great record against Leicester since their first meeting in 1906 and was continually favoured with the good fortune of rain-assisted pitches. This feat clearly ranked with his nine for 16 against Hampshire [sic] and ten for 30 against Northants in 1907, whereas his records against the Midlands side were almost too numerous to mention.

He had taken fifteen wickets for 102 and a further eleven for 63 in the two engagements of 1909, and in particular six wickets for 10 runs (on a poor pitch) in 1911 when Leicester were restricted to a previous low score of 26. However, his most recent seven for 9 was "the storming success of his life" and firmly planted him as the ogre of the Leicester batsmen.

His triumph on the Thursday was mainly due to a swinging delivery rather than the regular break, and an improvement in batting thereafter suggested that the Leicester batsmen succumbed far easier than was necessary. It was simply his reputation that had made them so nervous.

The rest of the match showed Leicester cricket in a better light and when Kent came in to bat they only did marginally better. Five wickets were gone for just 50 runs and only J.C. Hubble made any kind of stand reaching 46, whilst it was J.H. King who matched the Deptford man with an equally remarkable eight wickets for 26 runs.

Hardinge made some good off drives and Woolley rode his luck whereas Hubble produced some dashing cricket and hit six 4's to the boundary. In fact, the total would have been less than the 110 achieved if the captain had not replaced Askill with Brown and Skelding - the latter bowlers were quite expensive opposite King and in seven overs took nought for 38 runs.

Initially, Leicester looked in trouble again in the second innings and there was an indication the game would be over in a day. Wood and Mounteney were both gone with the score on 21, but the dismissal of the latter (who was also a player for Grimsby Town) caused a major problem.

Blythe sent down one of his swinging balls and Mounteney responded very hard; it hit the bowler just above the knee-cap sending him writhing in agony to the ground. The ball glanced off and continued to mid on who made the catch but Blythe could not bowl again that evening.

A.E. Knight and H. Whitehead then consolidated the position scoring 40 runs in just twenty-five minutes, before the latter was dismissed near the boundary by one of many fine catches. This left the score on 66 for three at the end of the first day, and in three and a half hours on the Thursday there had been 23 wickets and just 201 runs!

J.H. King took up the cause on Friday morning with some hard-hitting and using considerable vigilance took the score to 126 with little assistance. However, Blythe, despite a limp, carried on with the same consummate skill and had him caught by Hardinge on 49, which was the best score of the match. Due to the effects of rain and 'drying of the sun' the pitch became quite tricky and he soon brought the venture to a close.

In fact, in his last twelve balls Blythe took four wickets for 7 (including a six by Shields) and the final five batsmen went for 29 runs, which left Leicester on a total of 155. The bowler took six of the seven wickets in the morning for 27 runs, which combined with his two from the night before left an analysis of eight for 36 off 12.1 overs.

Fairservice and Woolley, however, were not at their best and any large arrears might have presented a problem. Humphreys and Hardinge were soon bowled out but Woolley was missed twice and by lunchtime 17 runs were needed. There were urgent requests from the crowd to continue and shortly afterwards the 71 runs required were reached.

The match was won by eight wickets whilst Blythe's previous successes against Leicester paled as he took fifteen wickets for 45 runs. It was a great performance and the papers noted the game came to an abrupt end at 2.10 on the Friday, no play being necessary on the final day.

However, the next game at Northampton saw Kent lose by four wickets (they also lost the return at the Angel Ground), and the only other victories in June were against Sussex by seven wickets and Worcester by an innings and 55 runs. In fact, the bowler entered into a purple patch and his side arrived at Tipton Road, Dudley to play the latter on 27-29 June. Kent batted first and Seymour made 80 and Woolley 117 (including eleven 4's) as the visitors raced forward to reach 300 all out.

Worcester then had time to make just 14 runs before play ended on the first day. During the night there was almost constant rain and as a result the pitch was rendered quite soft at the start of play, whereas their lot was not a happy one as they faced Kent's left-handed duo.

Only Arnold produced a good effort and with Burns added 35 runs but was out to a brilliant right-hand catch by Huish off Blythe. Afterwards the player B.G. Stevens who had once been at King's College, Worcester made some confident stokes and at lunch the score reached 90 for five.

At the restart Blythe was found to be almost unplayable on the difficult pitch taking the last five wickets for just 21 runs added, his figures for the innings - eight wickets for 55 runs off 31.1 overs.

The home side were all out for 123 and after some more rain were forced to follow on. Initially, there was a slight improvement but the pitch soon became treacherous and Woolley removed most as they were all out again for 122, Blythe taking two wickets and also two catches.

THE 1912 SEASON

Such brilliance continued in the next game against Essex at Gravesend on 1-3 July with the headline *"Blythe's Day."* Kent batted first and Seymour hit fifteen 4's as he made 111 the side reaching in total 304. Johnny Douglas then led Essex in to bat and at the end of the first day Fane and Freeman held the crease on 58 runs for the loss of three wickets.

Although on the second day some smart fielding and a wicket to the liking of Blythe upset the visitor's plans. Initially the two openers put up a good defence but Fielder bowled the pro Freeman's leg stump, and Fane an Old Carthusian was joined by C.P. McGahey.

Eventually one hundred was reached but McGahey was bowled out by Fielder soon after prompting a complete collapse. Blythe finished off the innings in sensational fashion taking four wickets for 5 runs in 5.2 overs with two maidens (his figures 4-29), aided by some capital fielding especially from Collins in the slips - Essex were all out for 131.

Dillon was absent and there were some new names such as G.C. Collins, C.S. Hurst, and C.E. Hatfeild in the side. Kent decided to bat again rather than enforce the follow on, and by the end of the second day (when rain had stopped play) they were 215 ahead with one wicket gone.

Only the weather could prevent a victory for the home side and on the third day Kent declared at 174 with three wickets down. The visitors were soon all out for 89 the dismissals going to Woolley (7-25) and Blythe (3-61) whereas the game was won by a margin of 258 runs.

There was another resounding victory at the Oval in the next match, as Surrey were all out for 89 to the bowling of Blythe and Woolley. Despite some improved batting in the second innings Kent won by nine wickets and this set them up for Tunbridge Wells Week - a real war of the roses.

Lancashire came to the Nevill Ground first on 8-10 July and scored 274 with Blythe taking 3-32, whereas Dillon made 134 as Kent reached 420. In the second innings Lancashire including the Tyldesley brothers were all out for 126 and Blythe took 7-40 (another ten wicket match), and there was no need to bat again with 20 runs in hand. However Kent lost to Yorkshire the eventual champions by an innings and 45 runs.

The South Africans then arrived at Mote Park on 18-20 July and Blythe renewed his former acquaintance with the likes of Tancred, Nourse, White, Faulkner, and Snooke. During the match he took four wickets but the proceedings eventually ended in a draw.

Surrey endured their usual problems at Rectory Field on 25-26 July as James Seymour scored 117 and Kent raced ahead to finish on 383 runs. Hayward was then bowled out for nought by Arthur Day although Hobbs and Hayes made some semblance of a stand.

However, Blythe then took four wickets for 10 runs in the middle order (Campbell, Abel, Myers, and Strudwick) and the visitors were all out for just 110. The follow on was enforced and despite 54 runs from Hobbs the second innings saw a score of 197. Blythe took another six wickets for 60 in 21 overs and the game was won by an innings and 76 runs.

Blythe's form was irresistible and unplayable and no doubt Kent could have had another championship but for their injury problems. Nottingham came to the St. Lawrence Ground during Canterbury Week on 8-9 August and the home side put on a target of 236 runs.

Like their neighbours Leicester the visitors struggled to cope with the fine bowling and G. Gunn had a highest score of 18 out of a total of 58 runs! In fact, Blythe had taken five wickets for 28 and Woolley five for 29 both of them sending down sixteen overs apiece.

A.O. Jones the captain of Nottingham was already familiar with Blythe from the test matches and should have known what to do. However, unlike their Midlands counterparts his side were totally bamboozled and some in the crowd rubbed their eyes for fear they had fallen asleep!

This time J.R. Gunn put on a "high" score of 12 but no one else could emulate such "success" or even reach double figures. All of the side were out again on 58 runs with Blythe taking six for 28 and Woolley four for 29 each of them bowling just ten overs. It was a feat to match the one at Leicester and the victory was by an innings and 120 runs.

A draw occurred against Gloucester at the Crabble on 22-24 August but it was only the weather that stopped a probable victory. Jessop and his side made just 67 runs in the first innings and it was Kent's bowlers that again led the way - Blythe with 5-27 and Carr on 5-38.

The reply from Kent saw them reach 106 whereas Gloucester were then all out for 95 with Blythe taking 2-54 and Carr an excellent 8-36, however no play was possible on the third day. A draw also took place in the last game against Middlesex at Lord's with no play over two days and Blythe took four for 58 whereas Woolley reached 10,000 runs.

With triangular matters in mind Australia bowled up to the St. Lawrence Ground, Canterbury on 29-31 August, however the contest was likewise ruined by the weather and also ended in a draw.

Kent had eventually won fourteen games and lost five during the season and finished a creditable third. Indeed, with second place in 1908, victories in 1909/10, runners up by the smallest of margins in 1911, and a third place despite some handicaps in 1912 they were clearly pre-eminent and that was soon to be confirmed (see below).

Not only was their batting excellent but the bowling was of the highest calibre. Blythe played in all but one of the twenty-six games and took 178 wickets with a best of 8-36, whilst achieving his top average of 12.26 and a record number of ten-wicket matches (8). Meanwhile, he was backed up by Woolley as discussed and Carr the googly specialist on 56.

PROPERTY RIGHTS

His win-bonus lodged safely in the depository Blythe then turned to some pecuniary matters of his own. The property "Emohruo" in Goldsmid Road had originally cost about £800 with a mortgage of £400 and a similar sum which was on loan from his father.

In November 1912 he wrote to the Kent Committee asking for permission to have £500 released from his investments to repay his father and to meet unspecified liabilities (mortgage and taxes). Permission for this was finally granted but with a caveat regarding depreciation of securities. Some of the investments had not done as well as expected so they suggested that he left £60 in - and kept the other £33 (from the extra £100).

Blythe was not happy with this arrangement and sent them a letter back on 10 March 1913, stating he would prefer to receive the whole sum rather than re-invest. Soon afterwards they agreed to pay the full £500 which left about £1,000 in investments from his benefit year. Clearly, these sums were most important to his future and later appeared in his will.

Meanwhile, the success of the previous year was a springboard for Kent's fourth championship in eight years which duly followed in the 1913 season. This began at Hove with a nine wicket victory over Sussex although they lost to the M.C.C. at Lord's by six wickets on 15-16 May.

Despite this they immediately bounced back against Oxford at University Parks just three days later. Woolley put on 224 runs in 270 minutes and the visitors reached 480 whereas Blythe took five for 68 and four for 27 in the follow on. The game was thus won by an innings and 101 runs.

There were then sterling victories over Leicester and Somerset whilst the next game kept things in the family way. Northampton went in to bat first at the County Ground on 29 May and the openers were William East and Claud Woolley (see later) the brother of Frank. The latter was bowled by Blythe and caught behind by Huish on just 4 runs.

In addition John Seymour the brother of James came in for Northants at number seven and was bowled by Fielder on 7 runs. The rest, however, did rather better and Sydney Smith of Trinidad (later New Zealand) made 133 and they were all out for 298 runs. Blythe's figures during the innings were three wickets for 47 off twenty-five overs.

Kent soon improved on this and James Seymour made 91 whereas Frank Woolley was out on 33 taking the total to 403. In the second innings the home side did poorly and Claud Woolley went out for 5 runs whilst John Seymour made 27 the total being 141. Humphreys and Hardinge soon made the 39 needed to win and Kent had a victory by ten wickets.

The side then travelled north to Park Avenue and played out a draw with Yorkshire on 2-4 June. Woolley made 81 and Blythe scored 14 out of a total of 251, whereas Yorkshire were dismissed for 217 (Denton 85) and Blythe took four wickets for 64 runs. His fourth wicket saw him reach a total of 2,200 and he scored a further 10 runs in the second innings.

This was followed by a game against Lancashire at Old Trafford on 5-7 June and Kent put on a good total of 354. The home side which included Johnny Tyldesley were forced to follow on as Fairservice took ten wickets in total - Kent winning the game by a ten wicket margin.

There were then further victories over Worcester and Essex followed by a significant match against Warwickshire at the Angel Ground on 19-21 June. This was the first meeting between the sides for fourteen years and in some ways settled the close-run finish of the 1911 season.

The visitors captained by Frank Foster won the toss and made 262 runs on the first day, whereas Blythe took 2-50 and Woolley 5-44 including Percy Jeeves (a name used by P.G. Wodehouse). Kent fell behind and they were all out for 132 on the third morning after rain hampered play.

Blythe made 6 runs in the innings but was caught by Willie Quaife after a right hand delivery from the eponymous Jeeves. However, he returned the compliment as Warwickshire scored their lowest-ever total against Kent. Not one player made above 5, there were five noughts, and they were all out for 16 runs in 10.2 overs! Blythe and Woolley had identical figures of five wickets for 8 runs in five overs with one maiden each.

It was a crushing blow to the pride of the champions of two years earlier, and clearly showed that the narrow margin by which Kent were beaten was not a true reflection of events - the disastrous innings lasted just 43 minutes! Woolley then scored 76 not out as the home side made 147 and won by six wickets which was a great victory on their home turf.

THE 1913 SEASON

Later in June there were defeats against Gloucester and Nottingham but after that things only got better for the Men of Kent. Surrey suffered their "annual defeat" at Rectory Field by six wickets on 3-5 July as Blythe and Woolley took the wickets, whereas the latter made 177 with twenty-eight 4's. They also beat Warwickshire at Edgbaston two days later by an innings and 51 runs with Blythe taking five wickets (in the first).

Tunbridge Wells Week came in the middle of July but was a washout and began with a draw against Worcester with no play on the second day. This was followed with a game against Yorkshire as Blythe (5-30) and Woolley (4-40) bowled the visitors out for exactly 100 runs. Kent replied with 135 and Seymour made 75 but there was no play on the last two days.

There were victories over Lancashire and Middlesex at Maidstone (now with its own cricket week) which started up a good run, although there was a defeat to Surrey at the Oval on 11-13 August by an innings and 40 runs. This time their batting was superior especially Hobbs on 115, and Bill Hitch took a creditable eight wickets for 48 runs in a first innings collapse.

The season ended with a draw against Somerset, a victory over Leicester, and two wins at the Crabble to leave the side well ahead. The last game was against Middlesex at Lord's on 28-30 August and Kent scored 236 with Hardinge on 110. In reply the home side made 131 and Blythe took four wickets for 37 the others falling to A.P. Day and Fielder.

However, in the second innings Kent stumbled and only Humphreys and A.P. Day made any kind of stand being all out on 124 runs. Warner was bowled by Carr for 4 but J.W. Hearne made 96 before he succumbed to Fielder and the game reached its climax. Blythe was not on form that day but Middlesex were all out on 224 and Kent won by just 5 runs.

Edward Dillon had skilfully captained his side to a third championship although he resigned the position soon after due to business commitments. Blythe took part in every game as Kent won twenty of their twenty-eight fixtures and lost on only three occasions.

Indeed, they finished eleven points ahead of their nearest rivals Yorkshire and despite the absence of Hutchings had comprehensive batting figures yet again: Hardinge (2,018), Seymour (1,980), and Humphreys (1,056).

Woolley had scored 1,737 runs but was restricted to 83 wickets due to a thumb injury late on - whereas Fielder took 115 and Blythe had 167 wickets. Huish the wicket keeper was aged forty-two and had played since 1895 but took 32 stumpings and 70 catches, whilst this was the high point for the team as the 'final' season loomed before them.

At the start of September there were some exhibition games and Lionel Robinson held "a house party" at Old Buckenham Hall near Attleborough in Norfolk. The proprietor was head of an Australian mining company and had an interest in horse racing and cricket, whereas the property a grand stately home was situated amongst some fine parkland.

His side were captained by Bosanquet of googly fame and also included George Gunn of Nottingham, Sydney Barnes, C.P. Buckenham of Essex, and Reggie Schwarz the South African. The opponents were a Kent XI captained by J.R. Mason and included Hardinge, Humphreys, Seymour, Troughton, Baker, Weigall, Huish, Carr, Blythe, and Fielder. The contest ended in a draw and Blythe scored 13 runs taking three wickets. [1]

The players then all travelled to Scarborough on the Yorkshire coast and Blythe appeared in his third (and final) Gentlemen v Players at the North Marine Road Ground on 4-6 September. The Gentlemen who featured Fane, M.C. Bird, G.A. Faulkner, Mason, Jessop, J. Douglas, Leveson-Gower, and Carr scored 266 and Blythe took three for 50 runs - including Jessop who made 119 with seventeen 4's and two 6's.

The game remained even and the Players who included Hobbs, Rhodes, Seymour, Humphreys, and Hirst replied with 270 then the Gentlemen made 255. In the last innings the game was very close and J.W. Hitch of Surrey was the tenth man (not out) on 68, but Blythe was caught by Guy Napier off a Jessop ball on 4 runs with the score on 245 - as a result his side lost the closely fought contest by just 6 runs.

---

[1] There was also a game between an L.G. Robinson XI and the Harlequins at Old Buckenham on 28-30 August 1913. The former included Johnny Douglas, L.H.W. Troughton, G.A. Faulkner of South Africa, Archie MacLaren, R.O. Schwarz, and L.G. Robinson in his only senior appearance whereas Harlequins had Bosanquet, Captain E.G. Wynyard, and Leveson-Gower.

Blythe was moving in some top circles and the next game at Scarborough was arranged by William H.F. Denison of Beverley (Lord Londesborough) on 8-10 September. The latter married the daughter of Henry Somerset the 7th Duke of Beaufort and was a patron of both Yorkshire cricket and his own team. Indeed, his father was an M.P. for Canterbury thus cementing a significant connection to the Kent club.

The home side included players from the earlier fixtures such as Hobbs, Rhodes, Faulkner, Jessop, Hitch, and Barnes whereas the Kent eleven were captained by Mr. Mason and included J.C. Hubble, D.W. Jennings, and W.J. Fairservice. However the number of games took its toll and the latter team made few runs, Blythe did not bowl, and they lost by 337 runs.

The season concluded with Kent against The Rest at the Oval on 15-17 September. Hirst and Rhodes joined the champion-side and they made 154 whilst Warner and the opponents reached 266 runs. However, Kent were then all out for just 67 with Barnes taking seven for 20 and the game was lost by an innings and 45 runs.

THE FINAL SEASON

Meanwhile, Blythe enjoyed a winter's holiday to Chamonix possibly with other cricketers in the closed season. An eagle-eyed photographer spotted the celebrity there and took a picture of him ice skating for *The Illustrated Sporting & Dramatic News* dated 31 January 1914.

Indeed, the other pictures were of the international bobsleigh winners and Count Betrand de Lesseps (son of the famous Suez Canal builder) in his air-propelled sledge - which could achieve speeds of 80 k.p.h.!

Kent took to the field in 1914 under new captain Lionel Troughton of Dulwich College, a relative of M.A. Troughton and C.S. Forester. They missed Douglas Carr who only played once whereas Woolley remained on form scoring 2,102 runs with 119 wickets, and despite a dry summer there was no restriction on Blythe and his wicket-taking.

The first contest was against the M.C.C. at Lord's on 9-11 May and was a good start to the season. Neville Tufnell captained the home side but they only made 134 runs as Blythe took four wickets for 55. However, Woolley, Hubble, and Troughton then piled on the runs in the middle order to reach 276, and the M.C.C. succumbed to Blythe (3-40) and Woolley (7-56) as they lost the game by an innings and 19 runs.

Kent put on some more high scores against Somerset at Taunton in their first championship match, Humphreys making 121 not out and won the game by 193 runs. It was a good start but was hard to sustain.

An interesting fixture followed against Oxford at University Parks on 25-27 May, which witnessed the first appearance of A.P. Freeman who with Frank Woolley took all records before them (after the war). Freeman a right arm leg break, googly bowler first played for the Kent Second XI in 1912 and was nurtured along by Blythe in his final season.

During the match Oxford made 337 with Blythe 4-59 and Kent scored 571 the bowler being not out on 17 runs. Freeman then took two for 109 off his 29 overs whereas the university reached 323 for a draw.

After another draw with Leicester they played Sussex at Hove on 1-3 June and the home side made 323 - Kent replying with 286. Of the batsmen Woolley scored 60 however Blythe recorded the highest total of 61 before he was caught by Albert Relf off a delivery from George Cox.

Sussex then made a further 265 but declared on seven wickets and Blythe took four for 97 runs reaching 2,350 for his career. At the end of play the visitors scored 202 for six wickets and the match was also drawn.

The next game at Northampton on 4-6 June was a mirror reflection of the previous visits to the County Ground and Blythe was again in good form. Kent had a poor first innings and were all out for 86 while Northampton made 141 which appeared hopeful for the home team, however the whole situation changed during the second innings.

James Seymour made 110 and Woolley scored 79 thus the side declared on 339 for nine wickets, putting Northampton in to bat on the third day. There was then a rapid collapse as Blythe took his 'usual' seven for 15 runs off 9.4 overs and they were all out for 57 - the other wickets being taken by Woolley, Fielder, and Fairservice. Yet again Blythe had dismissed most of the Northants players and the game was won by 227 runs.

There was then a large defeat by Lancashire at Old Trafford followed by Tonbridge Week in the middle of June (it was to be Blythe's last). The first game versus Hampshire saw Kent lose by 133 runs whilst they challenged Rhodes, Hirst, Denton, and Yorkshire at the Angel Ground on 18-20 June. The visitors were dismissed for 227 and Blythe took four for 42 runs but this gave no indication of the events to come.

Kent then put on a match-winning 493 with Hardinge and Woolley close to a century, while Yorkshire needed over 200 to save the game but were all out for 117. Blythe did not bowl in the second innings and Arthur Day took six wickets for 36 - the margin being an innings and 149 runs.

There were victories over both Leicester and Gloucester and a return was played against Yorkshire at Bramall Lane on 6-7 July. The normally reliable Yorkshire were soon all out for 101 using the same combination of bowlers viz. Woolley, Blythe, Fielder, and Fairservice.

Kent then made 126 and Yorkshire responded with exactly 100 runs off 31 overs. In the first innings Blythe took just two wickets for 22, but in the second his analysis was eight wickets for 55 off 15.2 overs including the trio of Rhodes, Denton, and Hirst (all of them caught).

It was a very good haul and Kent soon scored 77 runs to win the game by five wickets after two days. In addition they beat Somerset and Essex, lost to Nottingham at Tunbridge Wells by a small margin, and had good wins over Gloucester and Middlesex at Mote Park, Maidstone in the July.

At the end of the month they headed up to Trent Bridge and some large scores left them 100 runs ahead on the third day - but with only the home side left to bat the result looked like just a formality.

The Nottingham team included both George and John Gunn who played for England, but there was soon an unlikely reverse. The first two batsmen scored some 33 runs between them but it was all downhill thereafter and a complete collapse saw the side all out for just 53.

Yet again the match revealed a great understanding between Blythe and Woolley as they took five for 20 and five for 32 respectively, each in ten overs - thus Kent had an unexpected victory by some 47 runs.

They then returned to Rectory Field to play Surrey on 30 July and on the first day scored an innings total of 349. Over the next three days there was a display of batting excellence as Hayward, Hobbs, and Donald Knight all made centuries with forty-three 4's between them.

Blythe took just two wickets (for 85) including Hayward who was caught by Woolley, whilst Hayward and Hobbs the openers both finished on 122 runs apiece and Surrey scored 509 in total. Kent finished the third day on 260 for seven wickets and the game was drawn, whereas Blythe reached the milestone of 2,450 career wickets (near to a significant total).

DARK HORIZONS

However, the whole matter of playing cricket and winning and losing was overshadowed by some extremely serious developments.

The Archduke Franz Ferdinand, heir to the Austro-Hungarian Empire, was shot by a Bosnian Serb in Sarajevo on 28 June and Hungary declared war on Serbia on 28 July. Indeed, while Kent entertained Surrey at Rectory Field their neighbours Germany also declared war on Russia.

Canterbury Week commenced on 3 August with two teams to play at the St. Lawrence Ground. It was to be a cricket festival with the usual popular performances by the Old Stagers, however many started to believe that it should all be cancelled forthwith.

In fact, as Kent and Sussex took to the field on the first day there were further developments. Germany declared war on France and initially held a line in disputed lands near to the border, but this was tactical and they also invaded neutral Belgium forcing Britain to enter the war.

Under such a cloud the visitors batted first and they were all out for a substantial score of 384 on the second morning, with Blythe taking six for 107 - Kent replied with a total of 291 the latter being stumped on 22. Meanwhile, during the game the bowler made repeated trips to the press box to ascertain the latest news regarding the conflict.

On the final day Sussex declared on 78 for eight with Blythe taking 4-39 and Woolley 4-37. However, despite a good effort by Seymour with 48 the last six batsmen added only 32 and they lost by 34 runs.

Northampton, the next opponents at the St. Lawrence Ground, appeared a better prospect and Kent started with 301 runs. The visitors were then all out for 70 as Blythe took five for 24 and Woolley five for 23.

In the follow on the visitors managed an improved total of 179 but were well-beaten again by a good margin of an innings and 52 runs. In the second instance Blythe took three for 56 and Woolley had figures five for 65, thus there was the usual outcome against these Midlands opponents.

Meanwhile, the conflict had spread with clashes in Togoland (near Ghana) and South West Africa (Namibia), whereas the British Army advanced into Belgium to support the French. As a result the Oval was requisitioned and the game against Surrey was moved to Lord's on 10-11 August.

Kent batted first making 140 with half centuries from Woolley and S.H. Day, but Tom Hayward recorded 91 and with Hobbs his opening partner and 'Cambridge' colleague they added 107 - the total being 234.

A number of bowlers were used including Fielder, Woolley, and A.P. Day whilst A.P. Freeman made his first championship appearance (one of six that season). However, it was Blythe who received all the accolades as he took nine for 97 runs off 25.5 overs, and only Woolley's dismissal of Abel stumped by Huish on nought denied him all ten wickets.

Despite the bowler's efforts Kent were unable to build on this and were all out again for 140 runs - Surrey soon made the 47 they needed and won by eight wickets. However, the championship was secondary as Kent went to Edgbaston to play Warwick on 13-14 August, and won by nine wickets in two days with Freeman taking seven for 25 in the first.

Kent then played twice at Canterbury since the Crabble was transformed into an army camp. Initially they drew with Lancashire and then took on Worcester - Woolley reached 160 not out with twenty-five 4's, S.H. Day made 109, and Blythe added a useful 23 for a total of 461.

Worcester replied with 245 and the bowler took four for 63 but the best was yet to come. There was another remarkable collapse as he took seven for 20 in seven overs (the others to Woolley) and the side were all out on just 62 runs - Blythe also reached 150 wickets whereas the match was won by an innings and 154 runs.

The day after the game the British fought their first battle at Mons and Charleroi on 23 August, but in the ensuing weeks both they and the French retreated as the Germans advanced. Despite this the season continued and Kent also defeated Warwick at Gravesend by 99 runs.

Blythe's last professional match was played against Middlesex at Lord's on 27-28 August. The home side scored 205 and he took five for 77 the other wickets falling to Woolley and Freeman, whilst Kent replied with 116 including Hardinge on 58 and Blythe bowled out on 5 runs.

Middlesex then added a further 276 and he took two for 48 but Kent despite Humphreys, Hardinge, Seymour, and Woolley scored only 67 runs. Blythe was 'not out' at the end of the game and his fourth wicket secured the coveted total of 2,500 wickets during his career, which was a satisfying end to proceedings just in the nick of time.

The bowler did not play in the last game against Hampshire at Dean Park and clearly minds were elsewhere as the game was lost by an innings and 83 runs. Their rivals Surrey won the championship and Kent came third again after winning sixteen of their 28 games (with seven defeats).

Blythe ended his career as he began and in his last season made his fourth highest score of 61, took eleven catches, and secured 170 wickets with an average of 15.19. He had taken more than 150 wickets in every season but one from his marriage in 1907 up until 1914.

Throughout his career he maintained such form without deviation and if anything his bowling and fielding had improved during the latter seasons, although his best batting had taken place in 1904. There was no reason that his career should have ended at this point and he would no doubt have continued if circumstances had not intervened.

CHAPTER 17

The Great War

With the start of war in Europe the cricket season came to an end, although there was still soccer during 1914-15 and the Khaki Cup Final took place at Old Trafford at the latter date, but with some muted applause.

There was a great atmosphere of patriotism at the start of the war which had been in no way dented by problems experienced by the British Army in the Crimea and more recently during the Boer War. The fact that outdated methods and training had led to great losses in what were forerunners of the new conflict, did nothing to diminish unrivalled enthusiasm and gung-ho tendencies in Kitchener's recruiting rallies.

The Blythe family and the cricketing fraternity were no different in this respect and as the last few balls were bowled down the crease, plans were well underway. Blythe had trained with his father as a civil engineer thus he decided to put his skills to use within that Army division.

KENT FORTRESS

The Royal Engineers had long been established as a permanent fixture at Chatham and the School of Military Engineering began there in 1812. The officers were trained to a high level of mental and physical fitness and were leaders in design, whereas they joined with men of the Sappers and Miners to form one Corps in 1856. Several of the officers played cricket for Kent and their soccer team won the F.A. Cup in 1875.

In addition to the regular army there were a number of territorial units or volunteers in the county and the Kent Fortress Engineers were formed at the Drill Hall, Chatham in 1908. Their colonel was Sir David Salomons of Broomhill, Tonbridge who was a nephew of the first Jewish M.P. [1]

This section of the R.E. had their main unit or works in Gillingham but there were others at Tonbridge (1), Ashford (2), and Southborough (3) and two more were established at the latter site (6-7) in 1915 - there were also works 4-6 which were involved with electric lighting.

---

[1] David Lionel Salomons (1851-1925) was the son of Philip Salomons of Brighton and Emma Montefiore. The family were founders of the modern Jewish Church in Britain and David was brought up by his uncle the first Sir David Salomons M.P. He married Laura Stern of the Goldsmid family and was an author, barrister, and a local councillor - Goldsmid Road was named after the family.

Some difficulty exists in tracing the history and makeup of these units for the simple reason that they were territorial. Indeed, the records of the unit are sparse to say the least and those sources that are available are often contradictory regarding their information. However, it appears that the units were also divided into front line 1/- and home troops 2/-.

With hostilities well under way there were recruiting drives throughout the country and clearly the cricketers as a group talked amongst themselves on the issue of joining up, hence Blythe and his famous colleagues Hardinge, Fairservice, and Hutchings joined the army almost immediately.

Blythe had an initial months training as a reserve in Tonbridge but was sent away to the main depot at "Woodlands," Gillingham in October 1914. Much was made of the event in the newspapers and a local sports journalist put considerable 'spin' on the occasion, joking about the size of Blythe's rucksack as he arrived for his sojourn in the army.

Several other cricketers joined the Fortress Engineers with him and they all congregated at the "Constitutional Club" in Tonbridge prior to boarding the train for the Medway towns. Blythe apparently quipped that despite the size of his baggage there was still more to come (including his violin) as he waited for his comrades to arrive.

This was clearly a convivial gathering with much amusement that belied the serious nature of the project in hand, and the others in the party were David W. Jennings who played for Kent since 1909 and his brother Thomas who later appeared for both Surrey and Devon. Not long afterwards Claud Woolley the Northampton player and the brother of Frank arrived - as did Henry J.B. Preston a Kent regular since 1907.

A large degree of badinage took place between the five recruits and one issue was who would be first to secure a promotion. Apparently Blythe kept the party in good spirits and claimed he would be *first* since the recruiting sergeant had entrusted him with all of their papers!

A fair crowd gathered at the station to see them off no doubt including their families and as the train pulled out there was generous applause. The recruiting sergeant turned on his heels and walked off saying, "good luck to them, five of the best they are," whilst the reporter *The Pilgrim* spun a caricature of events - apparently being quite liberal with the truth.

At this time the Kent Committee exerted a degree of pressure and those who had not signed up by Xmas had their pay docked shortly after. Blythe then did some recruiting, helping to recruit 25 men and in terms of pay received 24s a week and 15s separation. He did not particularly enjoy army life but was soon promoted to corporal and to sergeant, then joined 2/7 Company one of the newly formed home units.

There was, however, a far more serious side to events and each field company was attached to a division of the main army. The Kent Fortress Engineers thus sent troops to Gallipoli in 1915 and 1/3 Field Company was led by Lieutenant David R. Salomons only son of the commanding officer. The troops came mainly from Tonbridge and after moving to Gillingham were one of the best bridge-building sections in the Engineers.

On 11 October 1915 they departed Devonport - one of the last units sent to Gallipoli, and two weeks later reached Mudros Bay, Turkey where they transferred to H.M.S. "Hythe." There were stormy conditions and after a bad collision the vessel sank with considerable loss of life especially those from the Tonbridge area. Lieutenant Salomons was one, and was last seen on the bridge having given away his life-jacket to another man.

These were sobering events that transformed the opinion of many who had joined up in such high spirits only a short period earlier. Indeed, the initial conflict on the Western Front had involved the traditional use of armies, but by early October this had degenerated into trench warfare with the British encamped from Ypres, Belgium down to the Somme and the French protecting Paris near to Verdun.

Meanwhile, as news filtered back about the loss of the "Hythe," life went on at Gillingham. Blythe was stationed there for over two and a half years and soon took part in some sport - but injured his ankle in late 1915 and was unable to join the new soccer team. However, he then played cricket with C. Woolley, Fairservice, and the Jennings brothers in May 1916 beating an R.E. side by an innings (with figures 3-33 and 4-3).

In June they beat a South African team at Gravesend and he took 7-36 and by the August they were playing regular matches including at the Oval and Lord's. They also played against the Chatham garrison when he had figures 14-85 and Linden Park from Tunbridge Wells whose side included Huish, Seymour, Weigall, and Fielder - the latter game was lost whilst Blythe took three wickets and was bowled by Fielder for nought.

During the first two years of army service his wife remained at Goldsmid Road in Tonbridge, whilst there has been a certain degree of question over his fitness. It has been suggested that he "stayed at home" due to health problems, but the picture of him "enlisting" shows a man looking quite fit and in fact he was thirty-five years old at the time.

In any case the Fortress Engineers played a vital role and were part of the "Southern Army Home Force." One of their main duties was to secure the coastal defences should there be an invasion or attack from the sea or air, as well as a role in training and bridge building. Apart from that the unit gave a home to those who became unfit or sick as a result of the war.

SIDNEY BLYTHE

The cricketer Colin Blythe was the eldest of six brothers and three of them fought in the First War to some considerable cost. Alexander Blythe (1892) had died of consumption in 1912, thus there was some consternation and concern when Sidney the youngest signed up at the outset.

The latter was born at 26 Wotton Road, Deptford on 21 March 1897 and was educated at Greenwich Central School on the north side of Blackheath Hill - near Deptford Bridge and his parents' home at 374 New Cross Road. After leaving school he worked as a salesman in the 'historic' Borough Market just beside London Bridge and Southwark Cathedral.

He enlisted at Deptford on 5 September 1914 but the army records state he was "eighteen" and it seems likely he lied about his age. Initially, he was with the Duke of Cornwall's Light Infantry (15474), but then transferred to the 2nd Battalion of the Hampshire Regiment and was sent to Gallipoli and served with the Mediterranean Expeditionary Force in the Dardanelles. In fact, this was to be a most difficult time for him.

A number of regiments including the Hampshires boarded the "Royal Edward" troopship at Avonmouth on 28 July 1915, and the next day she was sighted near the Lizard. Following other such troopships she stopped off at Malta and then departed from Alexandria on 12 August.

Her next destination was Mudros Harbour a natural haven near the island of Lemnos in the northeast Aegean and a short distance from the final stop at the Dardanelles. However, at the same time a German submarine UB14 was patrolling the area, and initially came across the hospital ship "Soudan" on 13 August but allowed her to pass by.

Soon afterwards the submarine spotted the unescorted "Royal Edward" which was sailing near to Kos just north of Crete. A torpedo was released from a distance of about a mile and hit the unsuspecting troopship in the stern. Indeed, this was a fatal attack and the vessel sank within six minutes and of the 1,500 crew and troops only 500 survived.

Sidney and his comrades spent four and a half hours in the cold Aegean waters finally being rescued by the "Soudan," two French destroyers, and several local trawlers. The disaster was made all the worse since many of the soldiers had just finished a boat drill when the attack took place, and were stowing equipment below as events unfolded.

The Gallipoli campaign and naval attack in the Dardanelles had been going on for several weeks, hence Sidney and surviving members of his regiment were then sent to Suvla Bay. The latter offensive took place in August and witnessed one of the largest battles at the end of the month, but with little achieved and only sporadic fighting all British troops were withdrawn in late December (for his part he received the "15 Star" medal).

Attention then turned to France and the Somme in particular the area to the south of Arras and east of the city of Albert. Indeed, there was little rest for the beleaguered troops from the horrors and hopelessness of war, and the 2nd Battalion were then dispatched to the Somme in March 1916 with many others for the major July offensive.

The 1st Battalion of the regiment had been stationed in France from the outbreak of war, and Sidney (No. 11746) transferred across to them before the primary attack or perhaps during the ensuing advance, whereas the stories of heroism and conflict were strangely intertwined.

Orders were sent out to all of the battalions on 23 June including the 1st Hampshire and the 12th K.O.Y.L.I. (see later) who were in fact stationed within half a mile of one another. The "secret instructions" said there would be an initial bombing of enemy lines then an advance right along the front in the Somme valley, but the plan was fatally flawed as the German troops hid in their bunkers waiting for the helpless allies to advance.

This was a most unlikely venue for such diabolical warfare with ancient villages, church spires, rolling farmland, wooded copses, streams, and grand vistas more suited to brush and canvas than to the bomb and gun.

The orders stated "the attack will be made in a series of bounds" and each group was to be identified by a shoulder strap of green, red, brown, or blue. Some saps (right-angle trenches) were to be built forty yards out while each man was to carry waterproofs, grenades, sand-bags, flairs, 170 rounds, wire-cutters, two gas helmets, water containers, steel helmet, socks, towel, soap, hairbrush, knife, fork, toothbrush, and a ration bag.

But this was no holiday outing since sixty pounds of equipment had to be carried five to seven miles to the front before the assault even began! It was pure folly on the part of the senior officers who had completely misjudged the likely resistance from the "bombed-out" German lines, and the British troops were weighed down to their utmost peril.

The 1st Hampshire part of the 11th Brigade, 4th Division which included the Newfoundland Regiment waited for the final advance near to Beaumont Hamel - a rustic village reached down a narrow country track.

Apart from the Newfoundlands all fourteen of the divisions were in fact British and were positioned along a twenty-mile front. This reached from the northern flank at Serre where the 12th K.O.Y.L.I. were situated right down to Maricourt just east of Albert, but with a diversionary attack in the area of Gommecourt towards Arras in the north.

The troops assembled at 5-50 a.m. on 1 July as the sun rose across the trenches and the fierce bombardment began. At 7-40 whistles issued forth right along the front to announce the advance and the divisions emerged from the relative safety of their saps and trenches.

The 1st Hampshire had orders to take Redan Ridge an exposed and high location, and were led into battle by C.L.W. Palk but lost 320 out of 500 men - three small walled-cemeteries are found in the location. Sidney may have been present during the attack or remained with the 2nd Battalion to the south, but then joined the former as they advanced to the east as the Somme conflict continued for another five months.

After the attack the 1st Battalion retired to Maillet and then further back to Bertrancourt, but had moved on again to Beaumont Hamel by 10 July. A week later they were entrained at Doullens to the north and travelled up to the "Ypres" sector where they stayed for almost two months.

They then returned south and initially marched to Cardonette north of Amiens whereas they arrived at Corbie on 25 September. Soon after they continued up the valley to the south of Albert and reached Meaulte on 4 October, reaching the front at Guillemont on 17 October. As a result they took up a position in "Frosty Trench" near to Lesboeufs.

The Guards had captured the latter in September 1916 after some fierce fighting, whilst there was an attack on the enemy lines on 23 October with the assistance of the 2nd Royal Dublin Fusiliers. The main objective was the "Boritska Trench" situated approximately 1,000 yards to the east - which is now covered by fields with the A1 motorway in the distance.

Initially, A and C Companies went forward at 2-30 under heavy fire from farm buildings, shell holes, and trenches held by the enemy. The right flank entered the German trench but they were forced to retire to Lesbouefs and by this time there were 202 casualties. At the same time the artillery shelled Le Transloy to the northeast which was still in German hands.

Sidney took part in the assault on Boritska Trench and his commanding officer stated, "He went over the top with the others and got back safely and after that he went out again to help a wounded corporal. He bandaged him up and had just finished the job when he was shot and died at once. His was one of the best of so many brave deeds done on that day and no man could do better than give his life for another."

The Somme Battle finished in November 1916 and was one of the worst of the whole conflict, whereas on the first day a half of the 120,000 who fought were casualties and 19,000 died - with 60% of the officers. The total for the whole conflict over five months was 420,000 casualties with 125,000 dead although the French to the south lost even more.

Many of those who died had no known grave and others were buried in nearby cemeteries identified only by their battalion and regiment. Near to the village of Lesboeufs is the large Guards Cemetery and within its walls are several graves to the 1st Hampshire dated 20-25 October - some have no name and it is possible that Sidney was buried there or nearby.

After the war a large memorial was designed by Sir Edwin Lutyens high on the hill at Thiepval with the names of 73,000 men who died in the Somme; all of them have no known grave and the name of Sidney Blythe appears on it. Meanwhile, his parents provided details to Marquis De Ruvigny who attempted (but failed) to catalogue all the soldiers who had fought.

THE YPRES SALIENT

One of the major theatres of the First War was centred within the vicinity of Ypres in Belgium. After the great retreat there was a stalemate at Marne near to Paris in mid-September, whilst to the north the Germans continued to move west until October 1914; however the conflict then deteriorated into trench warfare and the battle-lines were drawn out.

Regarding Ypres the initial front was about four miles east of the city and consisted of a large curve near Passchendaele which continued southwest along a natural wooded-ridge or "The Bluff." Early command centres in the vicinity such as Castle Hooge (rebuilt as a hotel) were rapidly destroyed by shell fire and the troops retired into bunkers and trenches.

The Germans had gained considerable ground by the May and were then positioned in a line from Ysef Canal in the north to Wieltje and Hooge and finally onwards along the ridge. Ypres was in fact a city under siege, a star sitting defiantly in the crescent of the German trenches, whereas its fine churches, mediaeval buildings, historic cloth hall, and moat were eventually bombed into almost complete destruction.

The main front and its related trench systems ebbed and flowed with the tide of battle, thus trench maps show how major landscape features and man-made constructions were both altered and rearranged.

However, once the Allies were driven from the ridges in May 1915 there was little change over the next two years, and the civilian population was then evacuated from what remained of the city.

In 1917 the Allies again took the offensive and tried to break through the German lines and extend the salient eastwards, leading to some of the worst fighting of the war comparable to the Somme. Initially the front remained close to Wieltje with no mans land to the east, and the supply routes just behind were called Oxford and Cambridge Roads.

During the advance one of the most significant needs was to maintain good access routes (especially railways), and for that purpose each regiment had a pioneer battalion. Thus, the 12th King's Own Yorkshire Light Infantry arrived at Ypres as part of the Fifth Army in July 1917. [2]

Originally there was no main rail-link to the front but a line was built past the north of Ypres to a depot at St. Jean, and then to extensive sidings next to the pastoral village of Wieltje (now just off the N313). In addition the battalion began to build light railways and trench tramways in the district, but it was a dangerous occupation close to "the zone of conflict" thus ten ordinary ranks were killed and wounded on 2 August.

The army soon progressed past the California and Cambrai trenches and there was a battle at Pommern Castle a mile east of Wieltje that same day. The latter an important defensive position was built solely of sandbags and concrete, whilst it faced Iberian Farm with Low and Frost Farms to the south. Initially the battalion maintained the main line and sidings but then constructed loop lines into the spurs as the troops advanced.

At the start of September they operated on the Bedlington loop and the Cambridge spur, but suffered casualties due to shelling and bombing by enemy aircraft. Further work was done on the main line and from St. Jean to Potijze, whereas Major C.B. Charlesworth became commander and the advance reached Gravenstafel - about three miles to the east.

In early October they were assigned to Wild Wood Spur to the south and on the 3rd several men were wounded on the Forest Hall line. Indeed, 156 new troops arrived from their base as reinforcements and later that month "Passchendaele" began - one of the worst conflicts of the war.

---

[2] The King's Own Yorkshire Light Infantry based in York had two battalions but this was increased to twelve in the war. The 12th Battalion was established by local miners as a pioneer battalion in November 1914 under Lieutenant Colonel E.L. Chambers. After some initial training at Fovant near Salisbury they embarked for Egypt in December 1915 and were part of the 31st Division.

However, they sailed to Marseilles in March 1916 and 1,000 men travelled up to Amiens, the final destination Bus les Artois on the front line. They were attached to the R.E. and dug ponds and wells, maintained roads, and established trenches at night in the area of Courcelles, Colincamps, and Maillet.

On 1 July they formed part of the force to capture Serre a village on an exposed ridge above Luke Copse and were to dig five saps into no mans land. During the assault they lost 197 men but far more were lost by the 'Pals Battalions' part of the same brigade, and today there are moving memorials and remains of the trenches at the site. They did further work at Bus les Artois, Colincamps, and Thiepval and went to Vimy Ridge in March 1917 but left for Poperinge in June.

COLIN BLYTHE

After Colin Blythe was transferred to Gillingham his wife left "Emohruo" and removed to 100 St. James's Road in Tunbridge Wells, a small terraced property at the base of the hill near the town. This was close to where she grew up and the couple gave this as their address from 1916-17.

Blythe, meanwhile, was sent for several months training at the R.E. camp at Marlow, Bucks in the summer of 1917 - a temporary site under canvas with practice trenches. He played several games of cricket there and also went up to Lord's taking 7-26 in June, whilst his last game was at the latter venue for the Army and Navy (or England XI) on 18 August.

The side took on an Australian and South African team which was quite fitting given his previous overseas test career. In addition, it was arranged by his mentor Plum Warner and was to raise money for Lady Lansdowne's officers' fund - the other players Tyldesley, Hendren, Fender, Hardinge, and D. Jennings. The sides scored 106 and 242 apiece whilst Blythe was out for nought and took 1-54 in fourteen overs. [3]

Yet, despite keeping his hand in with these practice games he decided to give up professional cricket due to his prolonged absence (and the fact he was then aged 38 years). With this in mind he had an interview at Eton College just a short distance from Marlow, and thus accepted a post on the cricketing staff which was to commence after the war.

By that time he asked to be transferred to an active unit and probably the news of his brother's death was a catalyst for the decision. Contrary to other claims the Army clearly believed him fit enough for the front line.

As a result he made a will and left everything to his wife excepting some items for his father viz. two violins, his silver cricket mementoes, pictures, bowls, clocks, watches, books, and any personal belongings he fancied.

Lastly he noted that Kent C.C.C. were trustees of £1,200 which were now invested in the Membakut Rubber Co. (400 shares) and Court Line Shipping Co. (200 shares), whereas he also had an insurance policy of £500 - out of these he wanted £300 paid to his father this being an amount he owed him. The will was then signed in the presence of Gertrude Blythe and her mother Deborah "Brown" on 24 August 1917.

---

[3] There was also a game between an England XI and the Dominions at the Oval on 5 August 1918. The side featured a host of stars including Hobbs, G. Gunn, Woolley, Hardinge, Warner, Douglas, and L. Tennyson and the scores were 166 and 194 in a game that was drawn.

He was then drafted from the Fortress Engineers to the 12th Battalion King's Own Yorkshire Light Infantry (No. 49296) on 25 September and by the October arrived in Ypres (or "Wipers"). The reinforcements included Claud Woolley and other Tonbridge men who transferred with him.

They may have crossed the "Menin Gate" site and mediaeval moat to the devastated country beyond, or, perhaps, joined the battalion on the very railway they had built travelling past ammunition, supplies, troops, and wounded beneath the glowing, graphite smelling skies.

From that point on Blythe learnt exactly what war was about and how his brother had died in the most frightening of circumstances. The remains of trenches and cemeteries of the fallen were all around, the desolate reminder of what had taken place over three years, and only the stolid railways tried to impose order on the putrefying mud and destruction.

On 4 October fifty troops were seconded out to Wild Wood Spur, 550 remained on the Forest Hall line, and Blythe and "B Company" went for training in light railway construction at Watou near Poperinge. A few days later the battalion were billeted in various camps and worked on the Wieltje (Forest Hall) and Bedlington lines, and did an extension to the Gravenstafel line as the lengthy assault on Passchendaele commenced.

The main railhead reached a trench/five foot bank at Bridge House Farm, whilst supplies continued on a light railway network beyond Pommern and Capricorn Junctions. "B Company" returned to the front on the 27th inst. and work commenced on the Pommern Castle line however fourteen of the battalion were killed and wounded there on 29 October.

Three days later work resumed on all four lines with Blythe probably at Forest Hall or Pommern Castle, although the former name is obscure and does not appear on any trench maps. Lieut. Noble was wounded there on 7 November, and the next day a German shell landed killing the cricketer and three others whilst six were also injured.

News of the tragedy soon reached home as Claud Woolley was amongst the wounded and several local men were present. The other casualties being privates O.T. Salt of Tunbridge Wells, Harry Dye of Wortley Leeds, and Edward Bennett of Chatham who were all buried in Oxford Road Cemetery at Wieltje - another man Ernest Smith died a few days later.

The plot where Colin Blythe was buried (I L.2) was begun in August 1917 and another the next month, whilst these were joined up with other graves brought in from surrounding areas - the cemetery and main railway fell into German hands in the spring offensive but were later retaken. Meanwhile, the Allies captured the ruins of Passchendaele a few miles to the east, thus the K.O.Y.L.I. left the vicinity on 17 November.

However, there was a huge cost in terms of the dead and wounded and this was one of the worst battles of the whole war (3rd Battle of Ypres) with 140,000 men lost for only five miles gained.

Oxford Road Cemetery is now in a quiet location on a side road close to Wieltje with its quaint slumbering farm-houses, although a controversial bypass cuts through the Ypres Salient just to the east. Controversial in that this was the site of some of the worst fighting along the front from 1915-17 and thus a grave for many of the unknown soldiers.

The road going eastwards from the village is bisected by the bypass and continues just beyond, but nothing remains of the main or light railways at Pommern and Forest Hall which Blythe worked upon to such great cost. However, there is evidence of the war with concrete structures and a trench turned irrigation channel (once a major German defensive site) just north of Bridge House Farm and cemetery. But most remains are long gone buried beneath the Flanders mud and its ploughed furrows.

The Oxford Road Cemetery is one of the smaller ones and has the usual cross of remembrance, war stone, and neatly kept graves some of them to the unknown soldier. Just opposite is a memorial to the 50th Northumbrian Division whilst the inscription to the cricketer reads as follows, and includes the K.O.Y.L.I. emblem of a bugle around an English rose:

"49296 Serjeant C. Blythe King's Own Yorkshire L.I. 8 November 1917 Age 38 - In loving memory of my dear husband the Kent and England cricketer." One rather moving touch not present at the other graves is the occasional presence of a worn cricket ball situated just at the base - several cricket enthusiasts visit the memorial to Blythe and place a ball there which is eventually removed by the C.W.G.C. once it rots away.

WALTER BLYTHE j.

The second of the Blythe brothers had a very different life and there is no indication that he was involved in any sport like his elder sibling.

He was born at 39 Gosterwood Street in Deptford on 23 May 1886 and baptized at nearby St. Luke's, residing there with his family in 1891. The next year they moved to 26 Wotton Road and he was probably educated at Clyde Street School just behind the house, whereas he was described as a general labourer aged 14 at the latter address in 1901.

It is unclear what he did in the early part of the 20th century but it seems likely he had a different personality to Colin Blythe and enjoyed a rougher existence. Apart from his casual line of work he had an anchor tattooed on his right forearm and a heart, anchor, and initials "W.B." on the left.

New Zealand was a forward looking country at the time and gave women the vote in 1893 then became an independent dominion in 1907. Without doubt considerable opportunities were available thus Walter left his family and immigrated just before the war in 1913.

He did not settle in one of the major urban areas (such as they were at the time), but travelled to the sparsely populated South Island and resided at Blenheim part of the northern Marlborough Province. He then worked as a fitter and had an address Bradford House, Wynen Street in Blenheim but not long after his arrival the war broke out.

New Zealand backed up the home country in the conflict from the start and Dr. Russell Adams examined him at Blenheim for service with the N.Z. Expeditionary Force in December 1915. However, at that stage he was rejected due to having flat feet and like his brother was then engaged with the First Reserves.

Moving north, he then worked as a fitter at the Dominion Paper Co. in Wellington a paper that was started on Dominion Day, 26 September 1907. Presumably he worked on either the presses or delivery vehicles, and gave an address 132 Austin Street which was high on the hill just below Mount Victoria. In fact, it looked down on Basin Reserve the most historic cricket ground in New Zealand (established in 1868).

Like his elder brother he was no doubt deeply affected by the loss of Sidney thus he attested for service with the N.Z. Expeditionary Force at Wellington on 16 June 1917. With severe losses in Europe more men were needed and although they commented about his flat feet they also noted that "they did not trouble him."

He was described as having an apparent age of 34 years being 5'10" high and 10.5 stone in weight with a 36" chest, blue eyes, and dark brown hair. His sight-hearing were normal and he had no illnesses whilst it was noted with some significance that he "never" had a fit. The only other matter was his teeth which although passable were in need of some attention.

Indeed, being fully fit he signed an oath of allegiance to the King stating he would follow "any orders," whilst he gave his father Walter Blythe at 26 Troutbeck Road, New Cross and Mrs. Sutherly a friend who also resided at 132 Austin Street (his landlady) as next of kin.

With such pleasantries out the way Walter, or Wally as he was commonly known, was made a private (No. 61505) in "B Company" part of the 30th Regiment on 26 July 1917. After receiving some initial training he joined Troopship No. 94 at Wellington on 13 October and arrived in Liverpool on 8 December. During the voyage he was punished for being deficient in the proper clothing - namely his Army denim trousers!

On his arrival he was sent south to the Sling Camp which was a major army camp near Bulford on Salisbury Plain. It was originally an annexe to another camp but the wooden huts were taken over by the New Zealanders in 1916 and it became the 4th Infantry Reserve Battalion - its aim to train new reinforcements and rehabilitate casualties. [4]

There were four sections Auckland, Wellington, Canterbury, and Otago and Blythe was in the Wellington Regiment. At this time the Russians had capitulated in the East thus the Germans planned a major offensive on the Western Front in the spring of 1918.

As a result he was transferred to 9th Company, 1st Battalion Wellington Regiment of the N.Z. Division, while just before embarkation for the front he forfeited a days pay for being absent without leave. No doubt he went out for some respite or perhaps even visited his family whereas he left for the conflict in France on 14 February.

The New Zealand Army fought in most of the theatres of war and had reached Polygon Wood near Ypres in the winter of 1917-18. With another German advance imminent they repaired and improved the trenches while the N.Z. Division (Anzacs) became the XXII Corps.

The Division was relieved on 24 February and it was at this time that Walter Blythe joined them, first arriving at Abele near Poperinge on the border between Belgium and France. They then went south to the Somme to help stem a breakthrough towards Amiens - their aim to fill a gap in the forces in the Ancre Valley near to Albert.

There was confused and intense fighting in areas such as Colincamps and Maillet but the New Zealanders gained the upper hand and eventually a stable front was formed. Three quieter months then ensued as the German pressure transferred elsewhere, although the line was actually in the same place as during the offensive from two years earlier. Thereafter, they were engaged near Puisieux and reached Grevillers and Bapauame.

Generally, the New Zealand troops were well looked after, there being a well organised network of supply stations backed up by hospitals and good medical staff, extensive training back in England, and a payment system for dependants back home. However, it was during this repeated stalemate that Walter Blythe became a casualty of war.

---

[4] After the war the Sling Camp housed 4,000 men who eagerly awaited repatriation to New Zealand, but there was a large outbreak of influenza and much unrest at the delay with resistance to the military regime. As a result route marches and spit and polish were ordered but there were riots and raids on the officers' mess. The ringleaders were ironically shipped back home, whilst those left behind cut a giant kiwi figure in the Downs which remains there today.

He was admitted to the New Zealand Field Ambulance on 28 June after contracting trench fever (a regular occurrence), although he may also have suffered from the effects of gas. Indeed, he reached the 16th General Hospital (U.S.A.) at Le Treport north of Dieppe on 2 July.

At the end of the month he embarked for England on A.T. "Esseouibo," and thus arrived at the salubrious "No. 1 New Zealand General Hospital" at Brockenhurst in the New Forest on 2 August 1918.

The infirmary was situated south of the village on Tile Barn Hill at the junction of Church Lane and the main road to Lymington. It was initially established as Lady Hardinge's Hospital for the Indian Army in 1915 and due to the large number of huts was known as "Tin Town," whilst it was in a highly rural setting taking the form of a large E.

However, it was occupied by the New Zealand Army from 1916 and then admitted large numbers of casualties from the Somme, whereas to the north of the village Forest Park and Balmer Lawn Hotels accommodated solely officers from the N.Z. Corps. [5]

After Blythe arrived there it was established that he had tuberculosis and he soon received orders to be evacuated home. Generally, it is believed he went back to New Zealand (alone) primarily for his health.

On 28 August he joined a vessel in Southampton and this took him down to the Mediterranean, thus he joined the "Maheno" at Marseilles which left for the Antipodes on 7 September. Like his brothers he was awarded the British War and Victory Medals after serving 1 year and 165 days, whilst on his return he decided to go back to Blenheim.

At this time he was still part of the Army and failed to report to Blenheim Hospital on 24 October, and for a period of five days, thus the relevant pay was deducted. Meanwhile, he was finally discharged as medically unfit for duty "due to illness contracted whilst on active service" on 6 January 1919 - although (of course) the war was already over by then.

Initially he worked as a fitter and resided at Auckland Street in Blenheim then moved to 159 Vivian Street, a main thoroughfare just to the south of Wellington harbour, in 1922. Clearly he remained unwell as a result of his time in the trenches and through illness thus he made an essential visit back to England - consequently, he stayed with his father, mother, and family at 26 Troutbeck Road, New Cross in 1925.

---

[5] No. 1 New Zealand General Hospital was used from 1916-19 and 21,000 troops of the Expeditionary Force were treated, whilst there is a C.W.G.C. cemetery at nearby St. Nicholas's. The former was demolished after the war and became an outward bound centre but there is a plaque just beside the gates (2005).

He then departed on the "Remuera" a N.Z. Shipping Co. vessel under the master J.J. Cameron from Southampton on 23 October. The ship was 7,113 tons and had 607 passengers whereas she was bound for Auckland in New Zealand. By this time he described himself simply as a labourer (or wharf labourer) and clearly worked in Wellington docks.

Blythe continued to live at 159 Vivian Street but died of tuberculosis at Wellington Hospital on 4 July 1927. He had been in the country fourteen years but was unmarried and was described as "a returned soldier," thus he was buried in the servicemen's section of the large Karori Cemetery in the hills just to the west of Wellington.

This states that he was a private in the Wellington Regiment and has an emblem of a fern above the writing "N.Z.E.F." - the minister was the Rev. Horace Christy an Anglican and the total cost of the service was £8 15s. He died a long way from his original home and friends but like his two brothers has a memorial commemorating his army role, whereas the impact on the cricketer's family was both severe and long lasting.

If I should die, think only this of me
That there is some corner of a foreign field
that is forever England   *Rupert C. Brooke* (1887-1915)

They shall not grow old, as we that are left grow old
Age shall not weary them, nor the years condemn
At the going down of the sun and in the morning
We will remember them   *Laurence Binyon* (1869-1943)

Within the call of Britain's bugle - sonny go to war
And in the muck and bullets fear was firmly rapped
To loved ones far away a sole white dove did soar
Trenchant bloody shells, not home for you old chap!   *J. Smart*

CHAPTER 18

Postscript

Walter Blythe and his family moved to 374 New Cross Road in early 1904 but there were several changes after the marriage of his son three year later. Indeed, this was not just with regard to a number of matrimonial unions but also in relation to the family's "mode of earning a living."

In the first instance the eldest sister Jessie Blythe married Francis Woollard at the large St. John's Church on Lewisham Way (towards Brockley) on 19 September 1908. The groom emanated from Fulham at the time whilst the witnesses were the two fathers, one of them being Amos Woollard who was described as a steward and therein lays a most significant story.

The Woollard family came from the small village of Barking, Suffolk and Amos (born 1846) secured work in the village as the servant of a widow. Meanwhile, Henry Hoare a member of the famous banking family was born at Staplehurst, Kent in 1838 and was related to Lord Kinnaird (of soccer fame) - he was also a grandson of Charles Marsham, 2nd Earl of Romney which secured a link to cricketing in Kent.

Indeed, Henry Hoare was married to Beatrice Ann Paley whose family had property in Suffolk, and in this way Amos became under-butler with twelve servants at Staplehurst Place in Kent. He was promoted to senior butler in the household and married Frances Fotherby at Piccadilly in 1875 thus his son Francis was born at Staplehurst in 1878.

At one time Amos was working as butler for the Hoares at their original home in Mitcham, whereas his wife Frances and three children were down in Kent; but eventually transferred to another branch of the family and worked at 22 Bryanston Square and 25 Lancaster Gate - a most senior role. By 1901, his wife lived at Garstons Road, Basingstoke near to one of the Hoare family homes within the town, and his son Francis was an electrical engineer at 31 Cadogan Street in Chelsea.

Henry Hoare Esq. (son of the above) was at the championship dinner in Maidstone and had links to the Marshams, thus there is some coincidence (in terms of cricket) that Jessie then married Frank Woollard.

The father Amos died at Kelvedon Road, Fulham in 1911 and Francis an engineer of 330 Hither Green Lane was one of the executors. There was a close family connection between the couple and Colin Blythe and his wife, and a common interest in cricket, perhaps cemented by such illustrious links albeit as the butler of a prominent Victorian household.

Additionally, the brother Charles Blythe (1889) also had an involvement in the game. He developed a degree of talent as a slow left arm bowler like his more famous sibling, and made his debut for the Kent Colts in 1908 taking seventeen wickets at a rate of 8.64 runs.

The following year he had an offer from Essex and perhaps should have joined Frederick Fane and Walter Mead, since as "C. Blythe junior" he was always going to be up against it. However, he opted for Kent and entered the Nursery receiving pay of 35s a week, but left at the end of the season with his last game against the Band of Brothers (with 1-35).

Possibly he had another eye on the horses and as a "clerk" married Ruby Dorothy Stewart at Camberwell Registry Office on 17 October 1910. By this time there is evidence that he operated as a type of bookmaker with his father at racecourses, whilst he moved to a property 334 Hither Green Lane just two doors away from the Woollards.

There were also two other marriages: Florence to Leonard De Saulles and Alice (Lal) to Reginald Lane in 1911-12, consequently Walter Blythe and his wife removed to a new and smaller property at 26 Troutbeck Road, New Cross in 1913. This was a modern Edwardian semi-detached house however his circumstances (as an engineer) were clearly improving.

With the war looming there was one further wedding and May Blythe married Herbert Smart of an old local family at St. Alphege's, Greenwich on 11 April 1914. The husband was an accountant and they went to live at St. Margaret's Road in Brockley and from there played a further role. [1]

SOME TRIBUTES

As stated, Gertrude Blythe was living at 100 St. James's Road, Tunbridge Wells in 1916-17 - below some more substantial residences by the church, although the C.W.G.C. gave a contact address of 1 Vale Royal.

News of Colin Blythe's death arrived before any official communication as did a number of reports in the press, which was clearly a distressing and harrowing situation for his wife who must have still hoped upon hope that there was some kind of mistake.

---

[1] Thomas Smart was born at Tweedmouth in 1789 and worked as a shipwright in Deptford and at Woolwich from c. 1810 - his second wife Elizabeth Purkis came from the New Forest family who helped take the body of William II to Winchester (ref. the Rufus Stone). His son William Smart built a cooper's business in Bridge Street, Greenwich and grandson George Cloke Smart was the local blacksmith at Lamb Lane but being quite successful later lived at Hyde Vale a Georgian terrace. Herbert Smart (his son) was born at Bridge Street (Creek Road) in 1884.

Nevertheless, *Sporting Life* of London ran a full length obituary to the cricketer on Friday, November 16 just a week after his death: "The cricket world has suffered a great, an almost irreparable loss, by the death in action of Colin Blythe the famous Kent and England slow bowler, one of the best left hand bowlers this country has produced. A German shell is believed to have killed Blythe and four others, and the news reached Tonbridge [sic] yesterday from a comrade in France, who has written to the widow of one of the men. Though Mrs. Blythe has not received an official notification there seems no reason to doubt the sad news."

They then went on to discuss his career and stated that his rise to fame was speedy and he never looked back - although he had a wonderful career it never spoiled the man. He remained simple and unassuming in manner, and would have a tendency to play down his abilities on the few occasions he was persuaded to talk of them.

Some would say that Rhodes was the greatest slow bowler and others that it was Blythe. There were five of the highest class in the last forty years the other three being Peate, Peel, and Briggs but it was hard to decide which of them was the best. Blythe was certainly up there and Ranjitsinhji said that he preferred to face Rhodes, but any such partiality with regard to batsmen was based on their own particular merits.

Blythe was certainly not the least gifted and probably had more resources, whilst one of his greatest assets next to his equable temperament was his easy action - there was no unnecessary strain and he could bowl for hours. He was a willing worker who never complained and against South Africa at Leeds in 1907 he bowled himself to a standstill, but took seven wickets for 40 runs in the second innings and clearly won the game. This followed a first innings of eight for 59 and it was the only test match that was brought to a definite conclusion that season.

The young, slimly built youth attended the Tonbridge Nursery and was mediocre in his first season with fourteen wickets for 310 runs. But in later years he established himself as the best Kent bowler since Jimmy Wootton of the eighties. Like other left hand bowlers he soon came to the fore and his success in 1900 fell short of Wootton but with regard to new advances both in run-getting and the wickets.

He cultivated spin and length with "the ball that goes with the arm" being greatly dreaded, and could break both ways with a variety both puzzling and disconcerting to the batsman. The dry season of 1901 went against him but by 1903 he was the most difficult bowler to face in England and he finished just behind Mead of Essex. During the season he took ten wickets on seven occasions and Surrey were often marked out for special treatment.

Kent won the championship in 1906 but Yorkshire would have held the honour except for a defeat against Gloucester by one run. Blythe remained top amongst the Kent bowlers even though he missed some games that year with a damaged hand.

Water on the knee stopped him briefly in 1908 but he returned with the same desire and nimble spin, and was the mainstay of the Kent attack until 1914. He was adept at lulling the batsman into a sense of security one that would lead him to take a few liberties, however he would just put on more spin and win through in the end. Indeed, in 1909 his team were champions again and Blythe took 178 wickets for 14.07 runs.

He secured a hundred wickets a season for Kent from 1902 except for the year his hand was injured [sic] and was prominent in 1910/13. In his last three seasons he headed the bowling averages for the country retaining both length and spin as before. He went abroad with the M.C.C. four times and played three tests against Australia at home - taking eleven wickets for less than 10 runs apiece at Birmingham in 1909.

Lord Harris also noted: "He had a sterling character and was an influence amongst his class besides being a fine judge of the game. His retirement from the inter state matches was not due to a lack of courage but the result of a physical defect following on any severe mental strain. He never failed in a crisis and joined the Engineers at the start of the war, whilst his capacity for command meant he was soon promoted.

Charlie Blythe was one of a galaxy of great left hand bowlers at Kent and was surpassed by none. During the war he had decided to retire from first class cricket, and accepted a post on the staff of the cricketing ground at Eton College. In his own career he took infinite pains over everything he did, and no doubt would have used both patience and intelligent tuition in imparting his skills to the students. The plan was that once the war finished he would take up his duties at the college."

However, Harris imbued his tribute with social distinctions pertinent to that era and touched on a controversy that was better debated elsewhere. In the first instance the comment about class became outdated with the shells and whiz-bangs of the trenches, and was also a hypocrisy that contradicted the Victorians cherished beliefs about the Bible.

Secondly, Harris revisited the health issue noting his 'retirement' from the inter state matches was due to a stress-related problem. Such a comment was probably out of place since it was quite contentious, being allied to a personal issue not to be so firmly linked with his achievements. Its public nature affirmed a decision by the selectors that they wanted to uphold and in today's climate was politically incorrect.

Another report stated that he was a born cricketer and even the critical C.B. Fry summed up his abilities: "On good wickets when the chances were in favour of the batsman, Blythe like all slow bowlers would come under pressure, but he would not lose his length or try to avoid punishment by shortening it. Some of his best performances thus came when his analysis was not very flattering. However, he had few superiors on a difficult wicket and would then take wickets very cheaply."

It was a fact that no matter how well the batsman did he would never lose his head or his length, and would respect the ability of the player. At the same time he pursued a course of sending down tempting deliveries to an opponent who would then take risks, sure in the knowledge that they would eventually make the inevitable mistake.

There was a "thrill" amongst the crowd to see his shuffling run and when a surface was prepared by sun and rain which made an average bowler look good, Blythe was almost impossible to face. His delivery was of nonchalant air with a great degree of finger spin, then a swerve towards the wicket, and a break back on making contact with the ground.

On many occasions the ball looked almost certain to miss leg stump but whipped back and took the bails - the batsman returned to the pavilion and when asked, stated, simply amazed, "I knew nothing about it!"

What of the Warwickshire batsmen who were dismissed in 62 balls as both Blythe and Woolley took five wickets for 8 runs apiece in 1913, and the great performances against Australia and South Africa at home and abroad? These were just some of his greatest achievements as a player and for his county he took 2,223 wickets at an average of 16.57 runs.

Meanwhile, the sombre mood was broken by a more humorous report. The headline read, *"Cricket has lost her fourth international player,"* one of the best ranking with Peate, Briggs, Rhodes, Peel, and possibly J.J. Ferris of Australia who was faster than Blythe, and also Hallows of Lancashire - but they also noted a rather interesting anecdote.

John Shilton of Warwickshire was once asked a pertinent question by a keen cricket enthusiast, "Who is the best slow left-hander in England?" The professional coyly replied, "Well it's not for me to say, but there's Shilton and...." but the rest of his response was drowned out with some highly raucous laughter. The answer to this exigent question will never be known however Shilton was *never* in the class of Blythe.

Blythe had a very deceptive flight and could make the ball swerve in from the off on an almost still day, and could put as much spin on the ball as he liked. He pitched so often on the wicket that the batsman was compelled to make a stroke and his game was never dull in temperament.

Of no 'recent' bowler could the term *unplayable* be so truly applied as on occasions to Blythe. At times it was impossible to make runs off him - those that accrued 'just happened somehow' and he always slowed down the run getting. In addition, some further letters were received at home:

20 November: The Infantry Record Office, York - "It is my painful duty to inform you that a report has been received from the War Office notifying the death of No. 49296 Sergeant Colin Blythe in France killed in action on 8 November. I enclose a message of sympathy from the King and Queen and pass on the regrets of the Army Council at the soldier's death, whilst details of his burial will be sent in due course."

23 November: The War Office, Alexandra House, Kingsway - To Mrs. Blythe, West Croft, Grove Hill Road, Tunbridge Wells - "In reply to an enquiry made on your behalf by Lord Harris concerning 49296 Sergeant C. Blythe 12th Battalion, King's Own Yorkshire Light Infantry, I am directed to inform you that it is regretted that he has been officially reported killed in action on 8th November. The Army Council wish to express their sympathy and the company sergeant major can possibly furnish more details from his comrades, your obedient servant R.C. Fowler."

23 November: H.G. Day of 47 Mabledon Road, Tonbridge - "It's with a sad heart I write to you to tell you how sorry we were to hear about poor Charlie. I assure you, you have our greatest sympathy in your loss. Mrs. Day and myself feel it very much having known Col so long. It is almost like losing one of our own. There is one thing he died a noble death for his country and us all. Hope you are bearing up, perhaps it is all for the best, goodbye for the present, yours sincerely." [2]

23 November: (Newspaper) - "*Kent's greatest bowler is killed in action.* He was an Englishman and a gentleman, and one of a new generation of professional cricketers who sprang up to mark a new era in the game. They made the dividing line between the amateur and the professional very thin, by their demeanour and their ability to mix in any company. Charlie Blythe was one of the pioneers. He bowled his heart out and was generous to all of his opponents."

---

[2] Henry George Day was born at Penshurst in 1859 and married Emily Carberry in 1893. He resided with his wife and son Harry at 20 Springwell Road, Tonbridge from 1901-04 and was a cricket ball maker and groundsman at the Angel Ground. He appears to be unrelated to the Day family of Marden (see below).

15 December: Lord Harris, 8 Old Jewry, London - "Madam, It is with the most sincere personal grief that I trouble you in your bereavement, to convey to you on behalf of the Kent County Cricket Club and its members, and I feel sure I may add all lovers of cricket in Kent our profound and respectful sympathy with you in your loss. I am sure there are many besides myself who feel they have lost a personal friend, whose high character has won their respect and esteem - I am, yours faithfully, Harris."

THE DAY FAMILY

Mrs. Blythe then resided at "West Croft," Grove Hill Road just above the station and proved her husband's will on 6 March 1918. Shortly after his arrival at the front he produced a second "document" dated 6 October in which he left everything to his wife, and the registry gave probate on both his original will and this short addendum (as A & B) whereas his effects came to just £2,818 13s 8d.

The next year she gave another address 27 Mountfield Road, which was just off Grove Hill Road, and applied for a passport to visit the grave at Ypres. She then travelled down to Dover and across to Boulogne in the August, as did her mother-in-law Elizabeth Blythe and daughter Jessie in common with a large number of grieving relatives at the time.

Two memorials were also erected to the memory of the cricketer, one at the parish church in Tonbridge High Street and a second at the entrance to the St. Lawrence Ground. The first a fine black and white marble tablet with columns, a soldier and flag, and the Kent horse was placed there by his sorrowing widower and his many friends in Kent:

"He played for England at home and in Australia and South Africa. He was the mainstay of the Kent XI from 1899 to 1914. In September 1914 he volunteered and was enrolled in the Kent Fortress Engineers and in a short time promoted to be sergeant. In 1917 he was transferred to the K.O.Y.L.I. and fell in action at Ypres 8 November 1917 aged 38. As cricketer soldier patriot he played the game." [3]

In the second instance the club erected a large memorial to Colin Blythe and other cricketers at the entrance to their Canterbury ground. This was unveiled by Lord George Hamilton in 1919 in the presence of his widow, and gave a few details then stated, "He was unsurpassed among the famous bowlers of the period and beloved by his fellow cricketers."

---

[3] The memorial is in the south aisle now in a separate room, and above is one to 'Frank E. Woolley born in Tonbridge 1887 Kent & England cricketer died 1978.' The two players have roads named after them just off the Hadlow Road.

The obelisk also noted some of his comrades of the Kent Eleven who fell in the service of their country viz. Lieutenant Ken Hutchings who died at Ginchy, France in 1916, and Corporal D.W. Jennings of the Kent Fortress Engineers who died of shell shock at Tunbridge Wells in 1918. [4]

In fact, Gertrude Blythe remained in cricketing circles after the war ended and received a tribute 'token of esteem' (with green & yellow ribbon) from the 1921 Australian-team led by W.W. Armstrong - one of Blythe's former opponents. During the tour they took on an England side captained by Johnny Douglas with L. Tennyson, Hardinge, and Woolley.

Regarding cricket itself Wilfred Rhodes had a return to form and played for England again (in the absence of many others) during 1920-30. He was aged some 53 years at the latter date, and indeed, had Blythe survived he may also have received a similar recall.

George Hirst partner of the former was a spent force as a bowler after the war (but continued to bat) and played some further games aged 47 in 1919. During that time he accepted the post of coach at Eton College - the job Blythe was to have had, and over eighteen years provided students with a firm grounding in the game. His playing career had ended apart from some appearances during the holidays, although he coached at Yorkshire and had success with the likes of Verity and Macaulay.

Gertrude, meanwhile, made a new acquaintance through such sporting circles. The Day family were tenant farmers at Marden in Kent and also for a time at Hartfield in Sussex in the 19th century, but they were occupying 241 acres at Plain Farm in Marden by 1871.

A son Sibery Day then married Julia Lavinia Mercer in 1875 and took up residence at Gate House Farm in the village, employing eleven labourers and four boys on land covering 275 acres. By 1901 his wife was living there as a widow with several children who included Mercer (23) and Sibery (10), while there was a strong cricketing connection in the locality - in fact cricket was played at Blue House Farm where Mercer later resided.

The younger Sibery Day married Madeline Weston in 1914 and had two daughters Zena and Edna, however there was an accident initiated at his residence Brook Farm in 1920. An early bi-plane landed with engine trouble on its way to Croydon Airport and left its passengers behind, but Madeline unwisely accepted the offer of a free ride. It crashed soon afterwards and she died as a result the following year.

---

[4] This stood from the time of its unveiling on an open patch of land just by the gates and turnstiles, whilst nearby was a second memorial to Fuller Pilch who was an early Kent player and groundsman. It was to be removed and stored prior to the building of a modern hotel, but these plans were put on hold.

Sibery Day a farmer residing at Robertsbridge, Sussex then married Janet Gertrude Blythe of Regency Square, Brighton at St. Margaret's, Brighton on 27 June 1923. The new bride by all accounts did not get on with her step-daughters, and regarding her previous life with the cricketer a number of mementoes were passed around the family.

The papers of Colin Blythe initially went to Francis Woollard and his wife Jessie at South View Road, Bromley probably because she was the oldest sibling and perhaps through an interest in cricket and the connection to the Hoares. As a result they remained with the family locally and eventually passed to S.B. Smart through his great love of the game. [5]

In addition, the silver cuff-links given to the cricketer at the Hotel Cecil &c. passed to his father and then to the family of his son Charles, whilst a shrapnel-damaged wallet remained with Gertrude and went to her nephew Frank Day who was president of a Kent cricket club - he later presented this to the county club for their museum.

Sibery Day died at Paris Farm in East Malling in 1941 whereas his widow J. Gertrude Day died at Tunbridge Wells in 1977 - there was a brief notice in *The Telegraph* stating she was the widow of the cricketer.

THE BLYTHE FAMILY

After the war the cricketer's family were depleted and sister Florence (and her young son) died of tuberculosis by 1922; however Walter Blythe senior entered into bookmaking in a big way with his surviving sons Charlie and Jack (John Henry). In fact, there was already a degree of success and it is believed he part-owned a racehorse, whilst his youngest daughters Connie and Nellie are said to have gone to a finishing school in France.

Betting was basically illegal apart from at racecourses and at Tattersalls but was prevalent with bookmakers or turf accountants - most business being done by phone. In 1926 it was legalised through a betting tax and licences for bookmakers, but soon afterwards the tax and a telephone charge were abolished and a "totalizer" introduced. Business was then done through an office, but it was much later that betting shops were permitted.

John Henry Blythe an "accountant" of 26 Troutbeck Road was married to Gladys Winifred Candfield at Greenwich Registry Office on 10 July 1926, whilst Nellie married Arthur Gordon Hills of Bromley in 1930 who in later years was also a follower of cricket.

---

[5] John Francis Spellar is the grandson of Frank Woollard and was a Labour M.P. for Northfield in 1982-83 and for Warley (West) since 1992.

Their father Walter Blythe made his last will on 27 September 1930 and appointed son Charles of 334 Hither Green Lane and F. Woollard of 38 South View Road executors. He left a small legacy to his sisters Emily and Polly (Mary), then asked for £5 per week to be paid to his wife from the business of commission agents carried on by himself and his sons.

In addition he asked that his motor car, which was a large black sedan with running boards and convertible roof, be available to both his wife and the business as before - whilst the residue was for his wife during her lifetime and then for his five surviving daughters.

The only unattached daughter Mabel Constance Blythe was soon married to Alfred Richard J. Swift the next year, and to give some indication of her father's changed status this gentleman was his driver. Indeed, he had come a long way from his days in Evelyn Street and his time working as an engineer in the Woolwich Arsenal, which provided many of the stereotypes for the cricketer's background.

However, Walter Blythe was ill at this stage and suffered badly with dropsy like his father, and was no doubt affected with grief at the loss of four sons and his daughter. As a result he took his own life and died at Greenwich Hospital on Vanbrugh Hill (the old workhouse) on 29 April 1932.

There was a brief notice in the *Kentish Mercury* stating that he was cremated at West Norwood, and that he asked for no mourning or flowers at his special request. Despite this he was clearly better thought of and a memorial was erected in Brockley (Deptford) Cemetery with the names Alex, Sidney, Colin, Wally, and Walter inscribed with their dates. Today, this remains, but is lost within the undergrowth of the cemetery.

The son Jack Blythe was also a cricketer in the family tradition and for many years played for Catford Wanderers on Beckenham Hill, whilst with his brother Charlie he continued to run the business.

Walter Blythe & Sons turf commission agents were at 156a Lewisham Way (Road) right near where the family first lived in the 1940s-50s. They had six telephone lines at this address under the name Tideway, whilst Charles died in 1950 and Jack retired to Upper Beeding and died there in 1977 - a notice in *The Telegraph* likewise stated "brother of the cricketer."

Meanwhile, the next generation took a different route to their forebears and did not take part in the gambling and its associated pastimes. Charles William (or Bill) Blythe was born in 1911 and through a pride in his uncle's achievements was a lover of cricket all his life.

Initially he played for a church team (with connections to Alleyn's) and for Lewes Priory where he ran a printing business, whilst he then moved to Sheffield and was a player and umpire for a local amateur club.

With regard to this he played at Harrogate, Headingley, Uttoxeter, and Old Trafford all grounds familiar to Blythe whereas his particular talent was as a bowler. He was a keen rugby player and after moving to Tunbridge Wells was also a member of the Kent and Sussex cricket clubs.

His cousin Stanley Blythe Smart was born at Brockley in 1915 and likewise was enamoured with his uncle's success all his life. As a boy he went and practiced cricket at the nearby Hilly Fields no doubt hoping to emulate him and was educated at Alleyn's School, Dulwich from 1928-33 - as was his brother Colin Blythe Smart from 1932-36. In fact, the former stayed on at school an extra year not to study but to play cricket!

After leaving he was a member of the Alleyn's Old Boys cricket club for many years, and in this respect played against Micky Stewart (father of Alec) the Surrey and England player when he was at the school. Smart was a good batsman and on occasion made a century whilst he went on regular tours with the club to Corfe Castle and Dorset. He had played cricket with his cousin when younger and in latter years they attended Kent games at the Nevill Ground together.

The *Kent Messenger* then reported on a reunion at the St. Lawrence Ground on 18 June 1956. A luncheon took place on the second day of the Australia game and the guests of Major Gen. C.W. Norman (pres) and the committee were J.R. Mason, C.J. Burnup, A.P. Day, W. Fairservice, F.E. Woolley, and J. Hubble. There was a commemorative photograph just before lunch whilst those unable to attend were Fred Huish and Wally Hardinge.

They reviewed "the golden age" of Kent cricket but in particular the third game at the ground against Worcester in 1906, when on the second night a storm blew down all the tents and the sightscreens! A record crowd saw them win by seven wickets but most thoughts were with Gloucester against Yorkshire in Bristol since the match was settled by one run. As it was Kent were champions whilst the average age of the team was 28 years.

Colin Blythe was clearly hard to emulate and was the essential element in this successful squad. He was remembered for both his incredible talent and artistry with the cricket ball but mostly for his affable nature that endeared him to his colleagues, the press, and the public.

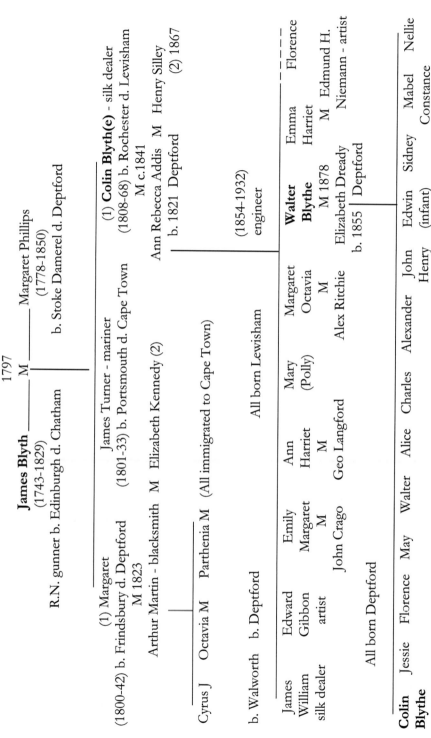

James Blyth
(1743-1829)
R.N. gunner b. Edinburgh d. Chatham

1797 M

Margaret Phillips
(1778-1850)
b. Stoke Damerel d. Deptford

(1) Margaret
(1800-42) b. Frindsbury d. Deptford
M 1823
Arthur Martin - blacksmith M Elizabeth Kennedy (2)

James Turner - mariner
(1801-33) b. Portsmouth d. Cape Town

(1) Colin Blyth(e) - silk dealer
(1808-68) b. Rochester d. Lewisham
M c.1841
Ann Rebecca Addis M Henry Silley
b. 1821 Deptford (2) 1867

Cyrus J Octavia M Parthenia M (All immigrated to Cape Town)

(1854-1932)
engineer

b. Walworth b. Deptford

All born Lewisham

James
William
silk dealer

Edward
Gibbon
artist

Emily
Margaret
M
John Crago

Ann
Harriet
M
Geo Langford

Mary
(Polly)

Margaret
Octavia
M
Alex Ritchie

Walter
Blythe
M 1878
Elizabeth Dready
b. 1855 Deptford

Emma Florence

Harriet
M Edmund H.
Niemann - artist

All born Deptford

Colin Jessie Florence May Walter Alice Charles Alexander John Edwin Sidney Mabel Nellie
Blythe Henry (infant) Constance
(1879-1917) cricketer Kent and England

Appendix I

| First Class Totals | | | catches = 206 | | | | | |

Batting	Match	Inn	NO	Runs	HS	Ave	100	50
C. Blythe	439	587	137	4443	82*	9.87	0	5
D.W. Carr	58	68	18	447	48	8.94	0	0
W. Fairservice	302	419	96	4939	61*	15.29	0	9
A. Fielder	287	380	175	2320	112*	11.31	1	2
A. Hearne	488	833	78	16346	194	21.65	15	71
F. Martin	317	492	118	4545	90	12.15	0	8
J.R. Mason	339	557	36	17337	183	33.27	34	86
F. Woolley	978	1530	84	58959	305*	40.77	145	295
S.F. Barnes	133	173	50	1573	93	12.78	0	2
C.B. Fry	394	658	43	30886	258*	50.22	94	124
G. Hirst	826	1217	152	36356	341	34.13	60	202
W. Rhodes	1110	1534	237	39969	267*	30.81	58	197

Bowling	Balls	Mdns	Runs	Wkts	Best	Ave	5wi	10wm
C. Blythe	103546	4796	42094	2503	10-30	16.81	218	71
D.W. Carr	10706	318	5585	334	8-36	16.72	31	8
W. Fairservice	44913	1999	19419	859	7-44	22.60	39	7
A. Fielder	52074	1740	26852	1277	10-90	21.02	97	28
A. Hearne	61085	4671	23120	1160	8-15	19.93	52	9
F. Martin	67747	5564	22901	1317	8-45	17.38	95	23
J.R. Mason	41945	2238	18993	848	8-29	22.39	35	9
F. Woolley	94824	4151	41058	2066	8-22	19.87	132	28
S.F. Barnes	31430	1600	12289	719	9-103	17.09	68	18
C.B. Fry	9036	494	4872	166	6-78	29.34	9	2
G. Hirst	123387	6015	51371	2742	9-23	18.73	184	40
W. Rhodes	185742	9518	70322	4204	9-24	16.72	287	68

Appendix II

Batting by Season (in England)

Year	Match	Inn	NO	Runs	HS	Ave	50	Ct
1899	4	4	2	0	0*	0.00	0	2
1900	22	29	12	125	15*	7.35	0	11
1901	22	32	8	168	20	7.00	0	8
1902	25	36	7	249	31	8.58	0	12
1903	22	30	10	254	28	12.70	0	14
1904	24	37	11	400	82*	15.38	2	9
1905	27	39	11	288	75	10.28	1	13
1906	18	25	3	246	53	11.18	1	9
1907	27	39	9	264	33	8.80	0	11
1908	28	32	6	241	27*	9.26	0	8
1909	32	38	6	263	38	8.21	0	12
1910	28	38	7	400	37	12.90	0	15
1911	27	35	6	319	47	11.00	0	16
1912	28	32	7	196	26	7.84	0	17
1913	34	46	6	282	37	7.05	0	17
1914	29	38	6	382	61	11.93	1	11

Batting Overseas (first class)

Year	Match	Inn	NO	Runs	HS	Ave	50	Ct
1901-02 Aus	8	14	6	62	20	7.75	0	3
1903 U S	2	2	1	5	5*	5.00	0	1
1905-06 S A	11	15	4	94	27	8.54	0	8
1907-08 Aus	11	14	1	145	27*	11.15	0	6
1909-10 S A	10	12	8	60	14*	15.00	0	3

Home: St. Lawrence 632, Nevill Gr. 376, Angel Gr. 264, Trent Bridge 233, Taunton 222, Lord's 216, Oval 176, Maidstone 163, Catford 160, Hove 149

Overseas: Sydney 118, Newlands 56, Johannesburg 48   (2,813 runs)

Bowling by Season (in England)

Year	Balls	Mdns	Runs	Wkts	Best	Ave	5wi	10wm
1899	757	61	310	14	3-15	22.14	0	0
1900	5053	232	2106	114	6-40	18.47	11	2
1901	5273	261	2151	93	7-64	23.12	4	1
1902	5082	243	1965	127	8-42	15.47	12	3
1903	5554	292	1953	142	9-67	13.75	13	7
1904	6146	274	2705	138	9-30	19.60	9	2
1905	7122	327	3142	149	8-72	21.08	12	5
1906	5321	243	2209	111	7-63	19.90	10	4
1907	6817	291	2822	183	10-30	15.42	17	6
1908	8202	386	3326	197	8-83	16.88	20	6
1909	7643	343	3128	215	9-42	14.54	23	7
1910	6261	274	2497	175	7-53	14.26	18	4
1911	6238	254	2675	138	8-45	19.38	10	5
1912	5517	241	2183	178	8-36	12.26	16	8
1913	6722	290	2729	167	7-21	16.34	15	3
1914	6052	280	2583	170	9-97	15.19	16	5

Bowling Overseas (first class)

Year	Balls	Mdns	Runs	Wkts	Best	Ave	5wi	10wm
1901-02 Aus	1901	103	711	34	5-45	20.91	1	0
1903 U S	336	16	135	10	5-30	13.50	1	0
1905-06 S A	2894	168	1046	57	6-68	18.35	4	1
1907-08 Aus	2360	97	935	41	6-48	22.80	3	1
1909-10 S A	2295	120	783	50	7-20	15.66	3	1

S/Rate (balls per wicket) 41.36 45.46 First Class and Test
Economy (runs per over) 2.43 2.45

Kent Batting 506 inn 111 no 3964 runs 10.03 ave
Bowling 36859 r 2210 wkt 16.67 ave 195 5wi

Appendix III

Test Matches	(19)			Bowling	Result
A.C. MacLaren (Australia)			**1901-02**		-
13 December	1		Sydney	3-26, 4-30	w I 124 r
1 January	2		Melbourne	4-64, 1-85	l 229 r
17 January	3		Adelaide	1-54, 0-66	l 4 wkts
14 February	4		Sydney	1-57, 1-23	l 7 wkts
28 February	5		Melbourne	1-29, 2-36	l 32 r
Australia in England			**1905**		w2 d2
3 July	3		Headingley	1-36, 3-41	draw
M.C.C. (South Africa)			**1905-06**		-
2 January	1		Wanderers	3-33, 1-50	l 1 wkt
6 March	2		"	1-66, 0-7	l 9 wkts
10 March	3		"	2-72, 1-96	l 243 r
24 March	4		Newlands	6-68, 5-50	w 4 wkts
30 March	5		"	2-106	l I 16 r
South Africa in England			**1907**		-
1 July	1		Lord's	2-18, 2-56	draw
29 July	2		Headingley	8-59, 7-40	w 53 r
19 August	3		The Oval	5-61, 2-36	draw
M.C.C. (Australia)			**1907-08**		w1 l3
13 December	1		Sydney	0-33, 1-55	l 2 wkts
Australia in England			**1909**		d1 l2
27 May	1		Edgbaston	6-44, 5-58	w 10 wkts
26 July	4		Old Trafford	5-63, 2-77	draw
M.C.C. (South Africa)			**1909-10**		w1 l2
7 March	4		Newlands	0-26, 2-38	l 4 wkts
11 March	5		"	7-46, 3-58	w 9 wkts

Test Record

Batting

	Match	Inn	NO	Runs	HS	Ave	100	50
Total	19	31	12	183	27	9.63	0	0
Australia	9	14	4	75	20	7.50	0	0
South Africa	10	17	8	108	27	12.00	0	0

Bowling

	Balls	Mdns	Runs	Wkts	Best	Ave	5wi	10wm
Total	4546	231	1863	100	8-59	18.63	9	4
Australia	2085	99	877	41	6-44	21.39	3	1
South Africa	2461	132	986	59	8-59	16.71	6	3

Catches	Australia 2	South Africa 4

On Each Ground

Ground	Balls	Mdns	Runs	Wkts	Best	Ave	5wi	10wm
Newlands	1073	66	392	25	7-46	15.68	3	2
Old Wanderers	785	40	324	8	3-33	40.50	0	0
Sydney C.G.	618	36	224	10	4-30	22.40	0	0
Headingley	423	21	176	19	8-59	9.26	2	1
Melbourne	414	14	214	8	4-64	26.75	0	0
Adelaide Oval	312	19	120	1	1-54	120.00	0	0
Edgbaston	282	9	102	11	6-44	9.27	2	1
Old Trafford	267	10	140	7	5-63	20.00	1	0
The Oval	198	8	97	7	5-61	13.85	1	0
Lord's C.G.	174	8	74	4	2-18	18.50	0	0

Appendix IV

Batting by Team					(Best scores below)			

Team	Match	Inn	NO	Runs	HS	Ave	50	Ct
Derbyshire	7	8	0	91	30	11.37	0	9
Essex	28	39	4	291	26	8.31	0	22
Gloucester	30	39	10	268	33	9.24	0	16
Hampshire	26	30	2	281	34	10.03	0	6
Lancashire	27	45	12	405	75	12.27	1	13
Leicester	17	20	2	136	37	7.55	0	9
The M.C.C.	13	23	4	121	18*	6.36	0	4
Middlesex	27	33	9	168	25	7.00	0	6
Northants	16	22	2	144	26	7.20	0	9
Nottingham	19	30	8	309	82*	14.04	1	7
Somerset	26	31	11	324	70	16.20	1	13
Surrey	30	39	9	215	29	7.16	0	18
Sussex	29	35	7	447	61	15.96	2	12
Warwick	5	5	1	18	9	4.50	0	3
Worcester	29	34	6	249	36*	8.89	0	12
Yorkshire	29	39	13	269	42*	10.34	0	10

1902	Nevill Ground	Hampshire	31
1904	Southampton	Hampshire	34
"	Trent Bridge	Nottingham	82*
"	Nevill Ground	Yorkshire	42*
"	Taunton	Somerset	70
1905	St. Lawrence	Lancashire	75
1906	St. Lawrence	Sussex	53
1907	Catford Br.	South Africa	33
1909	Nevill Ground	Sussex	38
1910	Aylestone Rd.	Leicester	37
"	New Road	Worcester	36*
"	St. Lawrence	Gloucester	33
1911	Nevill Ground	Sussex	47
1913	Trent Bridge	Nottingham	37
1914	Hove	Sussex	61

Bowling	Balls	Mdns	Runs	Wkts	Best	Ave	5wi	10wm
Derbyshire	1684	78	647	58	8-49	11.15	5	2
Essex	7794	338	3055	150	9-67	20.36	11	4
Gloucester	6600	290	2870	188	8-45	15.26	18	5
Hampshire	6354	278	2760	166	9-30	16.62	15	7
Lancashire	6414	276	2836	149	7-40	19.03	15	3
Leicester	4010	182	1583	140	9-42	11.30	18	8
The M.C.C.	2827	105	1238	66	6-29	18.75	5	1
Middlesex	6174	304	2340	142	7-26	16.47	11	3
Northants	4205	192	1574	129	10-30	12.20	12	3
Nottingham	4133	195	1660	85	6-28	19.52	5	1
Somerset	5669	243	2604	158	8-42	16.48	10	4
Surrey	6390	304	2777	185	9-97	15.01	20	6
Sussex	7464	379	2772	117	6-45	23.69	8	1
Warwick	956	60	313	20	5-8	15.65	2	0
Worcester	8084	393	3025	196	8-55	15.43	18	8
Yorkshire	6263	328	2502	154	8-55	16.24	13	6

1900	St. Lawrence	Lancashire	6-40	5-32	11-72
1903	The Oval	Surrey	7-41	5-26	12-67
"	St. Lawrence	Yorkshire	6-35	7-26	13-61
1904	Southampton	Hampshire	7-49	6-42	13-91
"	Angel Ground	Hampshire	9-30	6-46	15-76
1905	Foxgrove Rd.	Surrey	6-80	6-30	12-110
1907	County Ground	Northants	10-30	7-18	17-48
"	Rectory Field	Surrey	7-56	5-34	12-90
1908	Gravesend	Northants	7-57	6-54	13-111
1909	Aylestone Rd.	Leicester	9-42	7-60	16-102
"	County Ground	Northants	5-31	9-44	14-75
"	The Oval	Gentlemen	5-48	7-55	12-103
"	The Crabble	Leicester	6-30	5-33	11-63
1910	Mote Park	Yorkshire	5-64	6-31	11-95
1911	Aylestone Rd	Leicester	4-100	6-10	10-110
"	Cheltenham	Gloucester	8-45	6-39	14-84
"	St. Lawrence	Yorkshire	5-35	6-28	11-63
1912	Gravesend	Somerset	7-78	6-31	13-109
"	Aylestone Rd.	Leicester	7-9	8-36	15-45
"	St. Lawrence	Nottingham	5-28	6-28	11-56
1914	St. Lawrence	Worcester	4-63	7-20	11-83

Appendix V

Bowling by Ground   (over 2,000 balls)

Ground	Balls	Mdns	Runs	Wkts	Best	Ave	5wi	10wm
St. Lawrence	10269	461	4204	281	9-67	14.96	30	13
Angel Gr.	8193	376	3356	164	9-30	20.46	15	3
Lord's	6555	286	2694	151	9-97	17.84	11	2
Nevill Gr.	6371	337	2445	139	8-49	17.58	12	2
Catford Br.	4906	257	1996	124	7-63	16.09	11	4
The Oval	4560	173	2085	106	7-41	19.66	10	4
Mote Park	4078	169	1728	128	8-42	13.50	14	5
Leyton	3633	166	1372	57	8-72	24.07	2	0
Old Trafford	3487	151	1544	84	7-57	18.38	9	1
Gravesend	3382	159	1450	118	7-41	12.28	11	6
Taunton	3121	146	1282	66	7-45	19.42	3	0
Hove	3116	165	1101	47	6-63	23.42	2	0
Rectory Field	3103	156	1292	82	7-55	15.75	8	2
The Crabble	2669	110	1155	77	7-62	15.00	6	3
Worcester	2536	106	1034	53	7-72	19.50	4	2
Northants	1976	93	694	73	10-30	9.50	7	2
Trent Bridge	1899	77	812	28	5-20	29.00	2	0
Leicester	1466	71	572	57	9-42	10.03	6	3
Foxgrove Rd.	1170	43	559	33	6-30	16.93	3	1
Headingley	945	53	349	29	8-59	12.03	3	1
Bramall Lane	682	34	263	17	8-55	15.47	1	1
Edgbaston	619	34	181	19	6-44	9.52	3	1
Old Wanderers	1853	94	727	22	4-92	33.04	0	0
Newlands	1454	95	511	34	7-46	15.02	3	2
Sydney C.G.	1167	56	444	20	5-93	22.20	1	0
Melbourne	1118	53	439	23	4-41	19.08	0	0
Adelaide Oval	1049	46	404	12	5-45	33.66	1	0
Brisbane	303	9	151	12	6-48	12.58	2	1

Bibliography

The family papers of Colin Blythe - newspapers (local and national), match reports, dinner invitations, photographs private and official, war correspondence, and sundry items

Warner, Sir P., The Book of Cricket, J.M. Dent & Sons (1911) and Sporting Handbooks Ltd. reprinted (1945)

Moore, D. and Underwood D., The History of Kent Cricket Club Published by Christopher Helm Ltd. (1988)

Scoble, C., Colin Blythe lament for a legend, Sports Books Ltd. (2005) The Kent Committee records - pay withheld from tour, illness and test matches, benefit year amounts, value of house, matches played in the war, C. Blythe junior, the Day family

Cricket Archive and Cricinfo (w) - reference matches (test and county), statistics, and players' biographies

General Research

The Family Record Centre, Myddelton Street (former)
First Avenue House, High Holborn ref. wills
The Metropolitan Archives, Northampton Road, Clerkenwell - regarding the Duke Street School and St. Luke's baptisms
Guildhall Library and Map Room, Aldermanbury, London

The National Archives, Kew ref. Army and Navy records
ADM 6 gunners passing certificate, warrants, ADM 22 widows pensions, ADM 34/36 pay and ships musters, ADM 51 ships log, WO 95 war diaries, and First War medal records

Lewisham Record Office, High Street, Lewisham
Greenwich Record Office, (Old) Woolwich Arsenal
Devon Record Office - marriage Stoke Damerel
The Edinburgh Room, Central Library - parish records
I.G.I., Free B.M.D., G.R.O. online, census, Scotland's people (w)
Street Directories (various)

Other Research

Bruno Pappalardo, National Archives ref. naval records
Ship records including Age of Nelson (w)
The Proceedings of the Old Bailey 1674-1913 (w)
M. September, South African Archives, Cape Town
Ken Hawley Trust, Sheffield University ref. Addis family (w)

Bill Groom, Tonbridge Castle (Museum)
Bill Gowin re local history including the Bull Hotel
also from The Book of Tonbridge by Frank Chapman
Davyd Power, St. Peter and St. Paul's Tonbridge (memorial)

Kent Fortress Engineers (w) and R.E. Museum, Chatham
P. Bailey Cr. Archive, I.W.M., and KOYLI Museum - ref. Forest Hall
Stedelijke Museum & Documentatie Centrum, Ypres re trench maps
Pam and Ken Lynge - Thiepval Project ref. De Ruvigny's war records
also Westlake, R., British Battalions on the Somme

Professor John G.A. Pocock, Baltimore, USA
Edward Gosnell, Hartfield Road, Cowden ref. Day family
Mrs. S. Wadsworth, Ashtead reference Blythe family
Neil A. French, Alleyn's School Archives

Photos

Most images come from the Colin Blythe family papers in particular his picture collection, newspapers, and mementoes
All original photographs and the Map of Ypres are by J.B. Smart
Picture of Evelyn and Prince Streets by permission of Lewisham RO
Blythe bowling, in his blazers, in his army uniform, the Angel Ground, and the 1913 team by permission of David Robertson, Kent CCC
Photo of Gertrude Blythe by courtesy of E. Gosnell
Photo of Charlie Blythe (junior) courtesy Mrs. S. Wadsworth
The map by date is "out of copyright" whilst other pictures due to age or description as such are within the public domain

Index

Blythe Smart Publications